7/30

GREAT RIVER

GREAT RIVER

An Environmental History of the Upper Mississippi, 1890–1950

Philip V. Scarpino

University of Missouri Press
Columbia, 1985

Library of Congress Cataloging in Publication Data

Scarpino, Philip V.
   Great river
   Bibliography: p.
   Includes index.
   1. Watershed management—Environmental aspects—
Mississippi River Watershed—History.   2. Watershed
management—Social aspects—Mississippi River Watershed—
History.   3. Environmental impact analysis—Mississippi
River Watershed—History. I. Title.
TC425.M6S36   1985   333.91′62′0977   85–1012
ISBN 0-8262-0474-0

Many of the photographs used in this book were reprinted
through the courtesy of the Keokuk, Iowa, Public Library,
the Izaak Walton League of America, and Cornealia Motley.

For my parents
Mary P. Scarpino, Vincent F. Scarpino

Acknowledgments

No one writes a book alone. I want to thank the Department of Interior's Office of Water Research and Technology and the University of Missouri's Department of History for their generous financial assistance. My adviser, Susan L. Flader, first suggested the upper Mississippi River as a topic of study. My work has benefited considerably from her friendship, criticism, and high standards. David P. Thelen and Richard H. K. Vietor have each given much appreciated advice. Christopher C. Gibbs and Kenneth Winkle read several chapters and made suggestions that improved the final product. John Glen, Robert Hunt, Kenneth Mernitz, Susan Mernitz, Jean Roberts, and Steven Watts also read portions of the manuscript and offered helpful comments. Everette Swinney, a colleague at Southwest Texas State University, combined patience, humor, and skill in teaching me how to use an Apple IIe as a word-processor.

Several individuals and organizations aided me in the important task of locating and assembling source materials. The Izaak Walton League of America kindly gave me access to historical records located at the organization's headquarters in Arlington, Virginia. The league's volunteer librarian, Mary Fuchs, proved ever willing to lend a hand. Rene M. Jaussaud, an archivist in the National Archives' Legislative and Natural Resources Branch, provided conscientious, efficient, and professional assistance. Martin Reuss, a historian in the office of the U.S. Army Chief of Engineers, took time from a busy schedule to introduce me to the records of the Army Corps of Engineers. The staffs of Ellis Library, the State Historical Society of Missouri, and the Western Historical Manuscript Collection, all located at the University of Missouri, helped me on innumerable occasions. I particularly want to thank Anne Edwards, Patsy Hahn, and Pat Clemens. Russel Clemens allowed me to use his research notes on the St. Louis Peoples' League, and

Joseph Pratt permitted me to read an unpublished manuscript on the federal Oil Pollution Act of 1924. Finally, Wesley Platner and Mary McConathy Platner graciously shared their memories of M. M. Ellis.

My family has given me considerable encouragement during the years that this project has been in progress. My parents, Vincent F. and Mary P. Scarpino, gave me emotional support and financial subsidies that kept the wolf a few feet from the door. My wife, Betty, gave birth to our son, Samuel, before this book had completed its own gestation. Samuel has tried his best to help me keep my priorities in order. My debt to my wife, Betty, can never be repaid. She took time from her own promising career as a woodworker to enter every word and every revision of my dissertation on a computer terminal. She offered valuable criticism, lovingly shared the life of a graduate student, and kept the faith even when my own began to falter.

P.V.S.
San Marcos, Texas
June 1985

Contents

Acknowledgments, vii

Introduction, 1

1. The Keokuk, Iowa, Hydroelectric Project, 12
Synchronizing the River with the
Needs of an Industrial Society

2. The Keokuk, Iowa, Hydroelectric Project, 50
The Unanticipated Consequences
of River Development

3. Shells, Sewage, and Silt, 80
The Bureau of Fisheries and the
Pearl-Button Industry, 1890–1930

4. Conservation Crusade, 114
The Izaak Walton League of America

5. Pollution of the Upper Mississippi River, 151

Conclusion, 187

Bibliography, 195

Index, 213

The past is in truth the live,
active force that sustains our today.

—Jose Ortega Y Gasset, *History as a System*

Introduction

> But it is certain that man has reacted upon organized and inorganic nature, and thereby modified, if not determined, the material structure of his earthly home. —George Perkins Marsh, 1864[1]

> The destructive agency of man becomes more and more energetic and unsparing as he advances in civilization, until the impoverishment, with which his exhaustion of the natural resources of the soil is threatening him, at last awakens him to the necessity of preserving what is left, if not of restoring what has been wantonly wasted. —George Perkins Marsh[2]

The upper Mississippi River flows for nearly seven hundred miles from the head of navigation at Minneapolis and St. Paul to the mouth of the Missouri at St. Louis. This study examines the evolving relationship between the river and the people who lived along its shores, focusing on the period from 1890 to 1950. The analysis proceeds from the assumption that in modern urban, industrial societies, such as the United States, people have increasingly transformed the natural environment into a human artifact. Such is certainly the case with the upper Mississippi. Between the late nineteenth century and the mid-twentieth century, both the river and its valley underwent major alterations that affected both the face of the land and the underlying fabric of the original ecosystems.

It should almost go without saying that man-induced changes in the environment are not necessarily either "bad" or wrong. Many may be judged good because they have enhanced human health and welfare. Others may be defined as correct because, in the words of Aldo Leopold, they have preserved "the integrity, stability, and beauty of the biotic community."[3] Every summer, tourists and townspeople visit an attractive bluff-top park located in

1. George Perkins Marsh, *The Earth as Modified by Human Action: A New Edition of Man and Nature*, p. 8.
2. Ibid., pp. 38–39.
3. Aldo Leopold, *A Sand County Almanac: And Sketches Here and There*, pp. 224–25.

1

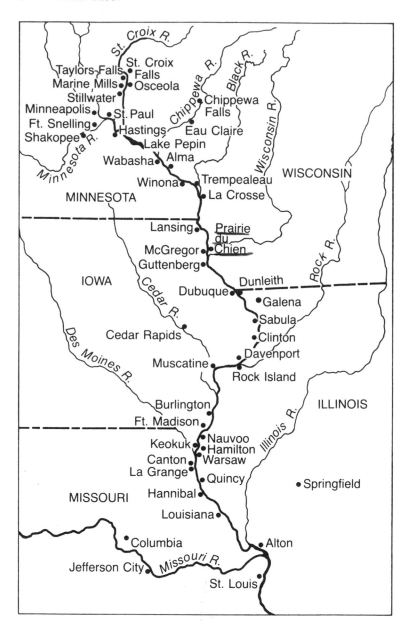

Louisiana, Missouri. From this vantage point, they enjoy a stunning view of the river that in large part has been formed since the 1930s by the Army Corps of Engineers. The fact that this vista has been shaped by the hand of man diminishes neither its beauty nor the pleasure that most people derive from looking at it.

Probing the diverse and often conflicting attitudes toward the upper Mississippi suggests three questions that focus on the dynamic interaction between people and the river: How did various groups try to understand and explain their developing relationship with the river? Why did they attempt to alter or control the river? How did they respond to the often unanticipated consequences of man-induced environmental change? Even though these questions are framed with reference to the upper Mississippi, their answers provide insights into the changing attitudes and actions of Americans toward the larger national environment.

The records of early-nineteenth-century explorers provide a good starting point for an environmental history of the upper Mississippi River. When the United States purchased Louisiana in 1803, it became the owner of the Mississippi from its source to its mouth. After negotiation of the sale, the French foreign minister quipped, "You have made a noble bargain for yourselves and I suppose you will make the most of it." President Thomas Jefferson acted quickly to do just that. In 1805, two years after he dispatched Lewis and Clark on their more famous journey, Jefferson ordered Lieutenant Zebulon Pike up the Mississippi from St. Louis in search of the river's source. Twelve years later, in 1817, Maj. Stephen Long led a survey and mapping party from Prairie du Chien to the Falls of St. Anthony (the future site of Minneapolis) and back downriver to St. Louis. The journals of Zebulon Pike and Stephen Long offer useful and fascinating glimpses of the preindustrial river between St. Louis and the Falls of St. Anthony.[4]

4. Elliott Coues, ed., *The Expeditions of Zebulon Montgomery Pike, to the Headwaters of the Mississippi River . . .*, vol. 1; Stephen H. Long, *Voyage in a Six-Oared Skiff to the Falls of Saint Anthony in 1817.* Pike did not discover the true source of the Mississippi. That honor belongs to Henry Schoolcraft, who followed the river to its source in Lake Itasca in 1832. See also J. C. Beltrami, *A Pilgrimage in Europe and America, Leading to the Discovery of the Sources of the Mississippi and Bloody River . . .*, vol. 2; Martha Bray Coleman, ed., *The Journals of Joseph N. Nicollet: A Scientist on the Mississippi Headwaters . . .*; J. N. Nicollet, *Report Intended to Illustrate a Map of the Hydrographical Basin of the Upper Mississippi River*, House Doc. no. 52; Bertha L. Heilbron, ed., *Making a Motion Picture in 1848: Henry Lewis' Journal of a Canoe Voyage from the Falls of St. Anthony to St. Louis*; Willard Glazier, *Down the Great River. . . .* Glazier made his journey in 1881.

Lieutenant Pike found that the Father of Waters could be unpredictable and unfriendly to navigators. His party left St. Louis on 9 August 1805 in a keelboat loaded with several months' worth of provisions. Four days above St. Louis the travelers were detained by sandbars and had to haul their boat over several of them. On 16 August, the keelboat caught on a log and stuck there until the voyagers managed to saw the log off below the waterline. Downstream from the Des Moines rapids, on 19 August, Pike's craft struck a snag and had to be beached, unloaded, and repaired. Above the rapids the expedition encountered stiff headwinds. Pike noted that they passed numerous islands and that the river was wide and full of sandbars. On 11 September, he reported, "The river has never been clear of islands since I left Prairie Des Chein. I absolutely believe it to be here two miles wide." Five days later, in a sudden, violent squall on Lake Pepin, Pike's boat "plowed the swells, sometimes almost bow under."[5]

Pike followed the river through a wilderness of tremendous beauty, with abundant fish and wildlife. In his journal, he recorded sightings of elk, buffalo, and bears. Near the present city of St. Paul, he saw three bears swimming across the river, "but at too great a distance for us to have killed them." On their return journey in April 1806, Pike's command put in at some islands located a few days above St. Louis to hunt passenger pigeons. Walking through these forested rookeries, Pike was delighted by the sight of a vast congregation of birds whose "noise in the woods was like the continued roaring of the wind."[6]

Major Long had less to report on the subject of wildlife, but he did comment on the appearance and quality of the river water. He had read Pike's journal and remembered that his predecessor had described the Mississippi for quite a distance below the St. Croix as reddish in color in shallow water "but black as ink in deep." (Hastings, Minnesota, now occupies the shore opposite the mouth of the St. Croix.) Long pointed out that the reddish appearance was caused by the color of the sand on the riverbottom, while the dark was "no more than what is common in deep water moderately limpid." He went on to write with some excitement that above the St. Croix the river was extremely clear. The water was "entirely

5. Coues, ed., *The Expeditions*, pp. 4–5, 7, 12, 18, 49, 61. Pike traded his keelboat for smaller craft at Prairie du Chien.

6. Ibid., pp. 76, 212.

colorless and free from everything that would render it impure, either to the sight or taste."[7]

Major Long had high hopes for the future of the upper Mississippi River valley. He identified areas that he believed suitable for grazing and for the cultivation of grain, fiber, and vegetables. Near Rock Island, he found the soil to be excellent and well adapted to the growing of "corn, grain, pulse, potatoes, flax, melons, etc." In the same vicinity, he saw hardwood forests that could supply timber for construction and for many other purposes. Long drew a sharp contrast between resource development, progress, and civilization and what he believed to be the backwardness and savagery of the region's Indian inhabitants. Below Dubuque, he was charmed by the beautiful scenery but appalled that the river's beauties had existed for ages "with none to admire, but unfeeling savages, instead of having delighted thousands that were capable of enjoying them." Ironically, this point of view retained its vitality until well into the next century.[8]

In 1823, six years after Long's expedition, the *Virginia* became the first steamboat to ascend the river as far as the site of St. Paul. During the next two decades, steamboat traffic on the upper river grew very slowly. The primary stimulus for expanded service came from the Galena lead district (northwestern Illinois and southwestern Wisconsin). By 1828, the annual number of arrivals at Galena, Illinois, had reached ninety-nine, and in the 1840s arrivals averaged more than three hundred per year. Not until after 1840 did steamboat travel above Galena reach significant levels. Average annual arrivals at St. Paul showed a slight increase from forty-five in 1844–1845 to sixty-five in 1846–1850. Between 1850 and 1860, Iowa, Wisconsin, and Minnesota experienced a population boom, as migrants swarmed into these formerly lightly settled areas. Steamboat arrivals at St. Paul increased apace, reaching 1,068 in 1858. Thereafter, traffic on the upper river began a slow decline that gained momentum following the Civil War.[9]

7. Long, *Voyage*, pp. 28, 30. Pike described the color of the river's water on pp. 77–78 of Coues, ed., *The Expeditions*.

8. Long, *Voyage*, pp. 67, 69–70.

9. For information on steamboating, see the classic study by Louis C. Hunter, *Steamboats on the Western Rivers: An Economic and Technological History*. Hunter discusses steamboat traffic on the upper river on pp. 43–44. For a more recent quantitative history of steamboating, see Erik F. Haites et al., *Western River Transportation: The Era of Early Internal Development, 1810–1860*. Population increases in Iowa, Wisconsin, and Minnesota between 1850 and 1860 are as follows:

In common with other preindustrial users of the river, steam-boatmen functioned within limits established by the physical characteristics of the river. Steamboats had to follow the river, even though it usually did not represent the most direct route between various cities and towns. Steamboat operators had to adjust their schedules to fit the cycle of the seasons. Winter freezes, summer droughts, and spring and fall floods could delay or halt river traffic. Between 1849 and 1866, ice prevented navigation at St. Paul an average of 143 days each year. Within the limits set by the course of the river and the pattern of the seasons, navigators had to heed the depth of the water and the speed of the current.[10] Before the Civil War, government expenditures to improve the upper Mississippi were small and sporadic, so that the river continued to present many of the same obstacles that had frustrated Zebulon Pike in 1805. Islands, sandbars, rapids, accumulations of drift-wood, and snags all took their toll on steamboats plying the upper Mississippi.

Steamboat operators on the Mississippi employed pilots in order to function as effectively as possible within the limits imposed by the river. In his elegant portrayal of river pilots in *Life on the Mississippi*, Mark Twain insisted that successful pilots combined a superior memory with exactness, judgment, courage, and independence. A pilot had to memorize every detail of his section of the river, and he had to keep abreast of changes in the channel. A pilot had to learn the shape of the river, the face of the water, and the important features of the shoreline. He had to be able to work day or night in any weather. Pilots matched their memory and skill against a fickle river in order to guide their vessels safely through a gauntlet of navigational hazards. Yet, despite the skill of many of these men, accidents, groundings, and delays regularly plagued steamboat travel.

In the last third of the nineteenth century, the steamboating industry fell victim to significant social and economic changes in the upper Mississippi valley. The area developed at a rate that would have amazed Zebulon Pike and Stephen Long. Railroads tied the

Iowa, 192,214 to 674,913; Wisconsin, 305,391 to 775,881; Minnesota, 6,077 to 172,023. See *The Statistical History of the United States from Colonial Times to the Present* (Stanford, Conn.: Fairfield Publishers, n.d.), p. 13.

10. Hunter notes the average annual suspension due to ice at St. Paul and several other cities on p. 221 of *Steamboats*. He discusses obstacles to navigation in Chapter 5.

region together and linked it to a national market. Small towns became industrial cities within which a growing number of factories processed the products of the valley's farms and forests. By 1880, Minneapolis and St. Paul had a combined population of 88,360, an increase of more than 200 percent in twenty years. In 1880, Minneapolis became the most important flour-producing city in the nation, a distinction that it retained for the next fifty years.[11] As the region became more urbanized and industrialized, the uncontrolled, unreliable river no longer offered an acceptable means of transportation. Steamboats rapidly lost business to railroads, which were not hindered by the limitations of the river. Commercial and navigational interests did not give up on the Mississippi. Rather, they turned their attention to forcing the Father of Waters to submit to industrial discipline.

By the late nineteenth century, the modernizing process taking place in the valley had begun to have a noticeable impact on the river and its tributaries. As early as the 1890s, careful observers commented on changes in the environment of the upper Mississippi drainage. In 1892, the *Bulletin of the United States Fish Commission* published an article that painstakingly catalogued the species of fish indigenous to Iowa's waterways. The author chose to preface his otherwise prosaic study with observations on habitat change that had adversely affected Iowa's fishery. He noted that the plowing of the prairies and the draining of wetlands for agriculture had altered the species composition of fish and the volume of flow in the state's rivers and streams. Writing in the same bulletin in 1898, another fisheries scientist argued that plowing, grazing, drainage, and logging had made a similar impact on aquatic habitat in northern Illinois.

In the half century after 1890, man-induced changes radically altered the environment of the upper Mississippi River. Beginning in the late nineteenth century, channel improvements helped to stabilize the river for navigation. Extensive drainage of land for agriculture eliminated overflow habitat crucial to fish and wildlife. In 1913, a Boston-based company completed a hydroelectric project

11. Minneapolis grew from 2,564 inhabitants in 1860 to 46,887 in 1880, while St. Paul increased from 10,401 in 1860 to 41,473 in 1880. See U.S. Department of Interior, *Eighth Census of the U.S., 1860, Population*, pp. 257, 259; U.S. Department of Interior, *Tenth Census of the U.S., 1880, Statistics of Population*, pp. 670–71. Information on flour production in Minneapolis may be found in Raymond H. Merritt, *Creativity, Conflict & Controversy: A History of the St. Paul District U.S. Army Corps of Engineers*, pp. 129–33.

near Keokuk, Iowa, that backed the river up nearly sixty-five miles. By the end of the 1930s, twenty-six locks and dams had transformed the upper Mississippi from a free-flowing river to a series of slack-water pools. In this same period, rapidly growing cities from Minneapolis and St. Paul to St. Louis built public sewer systems that discharged a mounting volume of wastes into the water. Extensive plowing for agriculture speeded runoff that carried an ever-increasing amount of silt into the river. Construction of locks and dams in a river already heavily loaded with silt and sewage aggravated the pollution problem and touched off a heated debate over river use and development.

A number of changes in the modernizing nation at large helped to shape the relationship between the people and the river. Dislocations and tensions associated with the development of a national market were particularly evident in the period shortly before and after the completion of Keokuk dam. The bureaucratization of the federal government paralleled the process of centralization in the private sector. The resulting shift in decisionmaking authority, from the local and state level to the national level, produced jurisdictional conflicts that manifested themselves on the upper river. Notable among these were disputes over public versus private ownership of water power sites and the proper locus for the regulation of pollution.

Growth of an interest-group-oriented political system in the upper Mississippi River valley reflected a national trend toward the fragmentation of society. Between 1890 and 1950, an increasing number of specialized interests made demands on the river. These groups organized themselves into constituencies to promote particular aspects of river use and development. Commercial clubs and chambers of commerce from St. Louis to Minneapolis joined the Upper Mississippi River Improvement Association and the U.S. Army Corps of Engineers in pressuring Congress to deepen the channel in the river. The National Association of Button Manufacturers united with the U.S. Bureau of Fisheries to secure funds for the artificial propagation of freshwater mussels. After its founding in 1922, the Izaak Walton League of America lobbied at the local, state, and national levels for the preservation of opportunities for outdoor recreation.

This study begins with an analysis of the Keokuk, Iowa, hydroelectric project. The Keokuk dam affords a unique opportunity to consider a number of river-related themes over time, in microcosm, and in the larger context of developments along the upper Mississippi and in the nation at large. The chronological scope is broad, from the early nineteenth century, when people first began to dream of harnessing the Des Moines rapids, to at least the 1930s, as the consequences of the undertaking became apparent.

The examination of the Keokuk project is divided into two chapters. Chapter 1 analyzes the historical background of the dam and the local situation at the time of construction. It further looks at the larger context that gave the project life, including the decline of the white-pine industry and the growth of the electric power industry. Chapter 2 considers three responses to the unanticipated consequences of the project: the crisis of unrealized expectations in the dam's service area, incorporation of this discontent into the national conservation debate over water resource legislation, and the growing concerns of scientists in the U.S. Bureau of Fisheries over the impact of dam-related changes on the river's aquatic habitat.

The response of professionals in the Bureau of Fisheries to deterioration of the river environment is further analyzed in Chapter 3, which focuses on how the pearl-button industry was affected by changes in the aquatic habitat of mussels. Fisheries scientists studied the impact on fish and mussels of such developments as the Keokuk dam and Lake Cooper, siltation and urban pollution, navigational improvements, and wetlands drainage. They discovered that the health of freshwater mussel populations provided a good index of water quality. By the 1930s, their studies had helped to bring about a major shift in the bureau's river management policy, from the propagation of useful species to maintaining the biological productivity of water.

Chapter 4 discusses the establishment and rapid expansion of a new constituency for the amenities of the river, the Izaak Walton League of America. As the United States became an urban nation, many people began to view nature less as an enemy or a collection of exploitable resources and more as a playground and a sanctuary. The Izaak Walton League provided institutional expression for this increasingly popular attitude toward the out-of-doors. In 1923 and 1924, the league waged a successful, nationwide campaign to have Congress establish the Upper Mississippi River Wildlife and Fish Refuge and thereby save nearly three hundred miles of wetlands from drainage. On several subsequent occasions, Waltonians rallied to defend "their" refuge from threats posed by navigational improvements and pollution.

The construction of locks and dams brought the problem of water pollution home by backing up urban sewage and industrial effluents in a series of pools. The final chapter examines the divergent policy responses of Minneapolis/St. Paul and St. Louis to river pollution. The completion of the Twin Cities lock and dam, in 1917, and the Hastings lock and dam, in 1930, had a significant influence on a decision by Minneapolis and St. Paul to construct sewage treatment facilities. From St. Louis, however, the Mississippi River still flowed unobstructed to the Gulf of Mexico. In the absence of effective state or federal pollution-control legislation, St. Louis officials elected to dispose of the city's garbage by flushing it through the sanitary sewer system and into the river. The discussion is placed in the context of the decades-long controversy over enactment of federal legislation governing water pollution.

Alterations in the environment of the upper river imperfectly reflected the attitudes of the people who made them. During the late nineteenth and early twentieth centuries, residents of the upper Mississippi valley shared a faith in the abundance of natural resources and in the capacity of flowing water to purify itself. They generally expected the river to serve as a sink for their wastes and still meet the various clean-water demands of society. Commercially exploitable resources were the only aspects of the river to have an active constituency. Although people used and enjoyed the Mississippi in a wide variety of ways, most assigned their highest priority to those qualities of the river that could be developed in order to enhance material progress. Frequently their actions produced not only the intended outcome but also significant unanticipated consequences. In response to these unanticipated consequences, various groups rethought and ultimately redefined their relationship with the river.

By the mid 1920s, a steady degradation of the river environment helped bring about significant changes in attitudes toward the river. Concern mounted, especially among residents of the Twin Cities, as pollution posed a growing threat to human health and welfare. Progressive deterioration of aquatic habitat angered outdoor recreationists and frustrated scientists in the U.S. Bureau of Fisheries who had to confront the failure of their programs for mussel and fish propagation. By the mid 1920s, scientists from the Bureau of

Fisheries and many residents of the upper river valley had begun to focus their attention on the consequences of activities that a decade earlier would have automatically been defined as progress. Within this frame of reference, the Keokuk hydroelectric project provides a starting point against which to measure subsequent changes in the relationship between people and the river.

1 The Keokuk, Iowa, Hydroelectric Project

Synchronizing the River with the Needs of an Industrial Society

The mighty Mississippi River has been hitched to the machinery and devices of civilization. —*Cassier's Monthly*, 1913[1]

> In the wake of the cornplanter, a cotton mill; in the trough of the steamboat, an implement factory; in the trail of the war-painted Indian, a cereal mill; in the long furrow of the grain farmer, men and women tending the shuttle of the world's weaver! The upper Mississippi valley is on the verge of an industrial awakening . . . the power which shifts the scenes and resets the stage: the mighty rushing waters of a mile-wide river harnessed to obey the commands of man.
> —*World To-Day*, 1911[2]

During a four-day period in August 1913, tens of thousands of people packed themselves into Keokuk, Iowa, a Mississippi River city with a population of about sixteen thousand located just north of the Missouri-Iowa border. They arrived by steamboat, railroad, interurban trolley, horse and wagon, and automobile, eager to help dedicate one of the boldest engineering feats attempted in the United States up to that time, the Keokuk hydroelectric project. A huge, monolithic, concrete structure, the dam, powerhouse, navigation lock, and drydock blocked the Mississippi at a point between Keokuk and Hamilton, Illinois, where bluffs constricted the river valley to a width of just over six thousand feet. Christened Lake Cooper in honor of the project's chief engineer, the resulting impoundment backed the Mississippi up approximately sixty-five

---

1. "Power-House for Entire Mississippi," p. 154.
2. F. G. Moorhead, "The Industrial Awakening of the Upper Mississippi," p. 472.

miles, nearly to Burlington, Iowa. It dramatically altered the character of the formerly free-flowing river.[3]

Many of the people who crowded into Keokuk in the heat and humidity of a midwestern summer knew that, by flooding the Des Moines rapids, the dam fulfilled two long-standing regional expectations: it improved navigation and it harnessed the energy of the river. For almost a century rivermen and shippers had cursed the rapids as a dangerous and costly impediment to low-water navigation. The reservoir behind the dam permanently drowned this hazard, which extended twelve miles upriver from Keokuk. Since the early nineteenth century, people living in the vicinity had envisioned putting the rapids to work as a source of industrial power. Keokuk dam had the capacity to generate as much as 310,000 electrical horsepower, or about 7 percent of the developed waterpower in the entire nation.[4]

On dedication day, the overwhelming regional support for the project reflected a predominant emphasis on control of the river and exploitation of its commercially useful qualities. Visitors to Keokuk came to marvel at the structure with which American engineers had beaten and harnessed the Mississippi. The heretofore unconquered Mississippi had been forced to flow through turbines and compelled to labor in the service of man. The river had literally been synchronized with the needs of a developing industrial civilization. Keokuk dam also fit into a larger pattern of historical change that included the end of the white pine industry, increasing

3. "$27,000,000 Dam at Keokuk to be Dedicated Tuesday," *St. Louis Post-Dispatch*, 24 August 1913, part 2, p. 2 (hereafter cited as *St. Louis P-D*); "Keokuk Dam Is Dedicated with Gay Ceremony," *St. Louis P-D*, 26 August 1913, p. 2; "Great Crowds at Dam Celebration," *Canton* (Mo.) *News*, 29 August 1913 (hereafter cited as *Canton News*); "Largest Water Power Plant in the World Will Be Dedicated To-Day," *Hannibal* (Mo.) *Morning Journal*, 26 August 1913, p. 1 (hereafter cited as *HMJ*); "Three States Celebrate Dedication of Cooper Dam at Keokuk," *HMJ*, 27 August 1913, p. 1; "Keokuk Host to 30,000," *Keokuk* (Ia.) *Daily Gate City*, 27 August 1913, p. 1 (hereafter cited as *DGC*). The Keokuk dam dedication lasted from 25 August until 28 August 1913.

4. U.S. Department of Commerce and Labor, Bureau of Corporations, *Report of the Commissioner of Corporations on Water-Power Development in the United States*, pp. xv, 4–6. The bureau estimated the total developed waterpower in the country to be about 6 million horsepower. Excluding developments of less than 1,000 horsepower, Keokuk dam generated about 7 percent of that total. Three hundred ten thousand electrical horsepower equals about 231,500 kilowatts. Because of the need to maintain a safety margin against fluctuations in the river level, the Mississippi River Power Company offered only about 200,000 horsepower for sale.

urbanization, and the development of electricity as a mass production, mass distribution industry.

Genesis of a Dream

The dream of harnessing the energy of the Des Moines rapids for industrial power had its genesis in the early nineteenth century. In August 1835, Robert E. Lee, a thirty-year-old lieutenant in the Army Corps of Engineers, arrived by steamboat at St. Louis, Missouri. Frustrated and bored with a desk job in Washington, D.C., as an assistant to the chief of engineers, Lee had applied for a transfer. His orders placed him in charge of expending congressional appropriations for improvement of the Mississippi above the mouth of the Ohio and for construction of engineering works to protect the St. Louis waterfront from an encroaching island. He proceeded to survey the Mississippi at the Rock River (Rock Island) rapids, at the Des Moines rapids, and in the vicinity of St. Louis's harbor. He also collected, as best he could, information about the Missouri River. Dated 6 December 1837, Lieutenant Lee's first report presented the findings of his surveys and made recommendations for navigational improvements.[5]

Lee's analysis began with a brief summary of the major hindrances to navigation on the upper river. Lee informed the chief of engineers, "The only serious obstacles to the navigation of the Mississippi from the mouth of the Ohio to the falls of the St. Anthony, a distance of about 1,200 miles, are the Des Moines and Rock river rapids." His survey report portrayed the Des Moines rapids, site of the future Keokuk dam, as slightly more than eleven miles from head to foot with a fall of just over twenty-four feet. At the rapids, the Mississippi flowed swiftly over an irregular limestone bed. In several places, the limestone formed submerged rock reefs that stretched from shore to shore. This configuration created a series of pools separated by reefs through which the river had eroded narrow, winding channels. Low-water passage over these chains was dangerous because of the shoal water, the speed of the current, and the uncertainty of the channels.[6]

5. Douglas Southall Freeman, *R. E. Lee: A Biography*, 1:128; U.S. Congress, House, *Rapids of the Mississippi River*, pp. 3–4; U.S. Congress, Senate, *Report from the Secretary of War, in Compliance with a Resolution of the Senate of the 25th Instant, in Relation to the Rock River and Des Moines Rapids of the Mississippi River.*

6. *Report from the Secretary of War . . . in relation to the Rock river and Des Moines rapids*, pp. 2–3.

In making his recommendations for improvement of the Des Moines rapids, Lee rejected an earlier proposal that had called for construction of an artificial channel along the western shore. He instead suggested improving one of the existing natural channels, arguing, "By improving the most difficult passes first, immediate benefit will be obtained. The meeting of boats will not be attended with the same danger as if they were confined to a continuous channel, as advantage may be taken of the pools before alluded to, where the navigation is comparatively good."[7]

Lee's contribution to improving the navigability of the rapids earned him an important, but not unique, place in the early history of river improvement. Historical records reveal no public pronouncements by Lee on the waterpower potential of the rapids.[8] Yet, over the course of the nineteenth century, a legend developed in which he recognized the rapids as a source of waterpower, realized the time for development had not arrived, and predicted future waterpower-based prosperity for the area in immediate proximity to the rapids. Because people believed this myth, Lee played a special role in the events leading up to the construction of Keokuk dam. Beginning in the late nineteenth century and continuing into the twentieth, numerous writers invoked the famous general's name in relating the history of the decades-long dream to develop the rapids. It mattered not a bit that by the 1890s electricity had replaced direct-drive waterpower in development schemes. The Lee myth reinforced a regional belief that prosperity would follow the discovery of a way to put the rapids to work. The myth bestowed Lee's endorsement on the plans that actually came to fruition in 1913 and strengthened the notion that the highest use of the rapids was for power and navigation.[9]

7. Ibid., p. 3.
8. Lee's reports on the Des Moines Rapids may be found in ibid; Executive Documents, *Message from the President of the United States to the Two Houses of Congress, at the Commencement of the Third Session of the Twenty-fifth Congress*, pp. 233–35; Executive Documents, *Message from the President of the United States to the Two Houses of Congress, at the Commencement of the First Session of the Twenty-sixty Congress*, pp. 197–99. See also Freeman, *R. E. Lee*, pp. 137–39, 140–58, 170–83.
9. References to Lee may be found in "Work Is a Product of the People," *DGC*, 30 August 1912, sec. 4, pp. 5–6; "Big Celebration at Keokuk This Month," *Canton News*, 15 August 1913; "The Greatest Thing in All Iowa History," p. 42; "The Water Wheels at Keokuk," p. 534; Harry Kirkland, "The Great Mississippi Dam," p. 337; *Iowa: A Guide to the Hawkeye State*, compiled and written by the Federal Writers' Project of the Works Progress Administration for the State of Iowa, pp. 279–80.

For more than eighty years prior to 1913, many people attempted to harness the Des Moines rapids for industrial power. Their persistent hopes, attempts, and failures, validated by the Lee myth, form the historical tradition of Keokuk dam. Evidence of early, widespread expectation that the Des Moines rapids would one day provide industrial power is contained in a February 1831 memorial from the Missouri General Assembly to Congress. Missouri's lawmakers asked for an extension of the state's northern border from its intersection with the Des Moines River east to the Mississippi. Located in the fork of the Des Moines and Mississippi rivers, this small wedge of territory eventually became the southeasternmost corner of Iowa. Although the memorial conceded that in terms of size the parcel of land had little value to the state or nation, it maintained, "There are many considerations which give to it importance and value." [10]

In fact, the document advanced just three considerations that made the area important. Exclusion of this bit of land destroyed the "compactness" of Missouri. The land was currently used only by mixed-blood and Indian people who could not establish a government and who could not form a separate state or nation. These two reasons clearly paled before the third. The desired area encompassed the entire western shore of the Des Moines rapids and thus embraced

> a spot, which, in future times, will be of immense importance to the commerce and intercourse of the whole western valley. Your memorialists anticipate the day when the obstructions to navigation will be overcome by a canal around those rapids; when the inexhaustible power of that mighty stream [will be applied] to almost every variety of manufacturing machinery, and when a commercial city, will spring up in that wilderness, to serve as the great entrepot of the Upper and Lower Mississippi. [11]

The Missouri legislators who approved this memorial believed that a prosperous manufacturing and port city would "spring up" in that bit of otherwise worthless wilderness. They coveted this sliver of land because of its future economic value, based upon the latent commercial qualities of the Des Moines rapids. This docu-

---

10. U.S. Congress, Senate, *Memorial of the General Assembly of Missouri*, p. 4; also cited in "The Half-Breed Tract," p. 160, and Donald L. Enders, "The Des Moines Rapids: A History of Its Adverse Effects on Mississippi River Traffic and Its Use as a Source of Water Power to 1860," pp. 86–87.

11. *Memorial of the General Assembly of Missouri*, p. 4.

ment is important for what it reveals about the attitudes of Missouri's elected representatives and because it may be the earliest existing record of these sentiments. As such, the memorial provides evidence that in 1831 this vision was neither new nor confined to the area immediately around the rapids. It also places the Missouri General Assembly at the head of a long line of people whose written records attest to the fact that they, too, eagerly anticipated extraction of power from the Des Moines rapids.

Between 1840 and the Civil War, several individuals and the Mormon Church tried to tame the Des Moines rapids. Two examples should illustrate the range of ambition encompassed by the various schemes. During the winter of 1838–1839, approximately fifteen thousand Mormons fled from Missouri to Illinois. They resettled in and around the new city of Nauvoo. Located near the head of the Des Moines rapids, Nauvoo provided the "Saints" with a temporary haven and with access to waterpower. In his February 1841 inaugural address, Mayor-elect John C. Bennett unveiled the Church's first official plan to domesticate the rapids. Bennett proposed that a wing dam be built into the river upstream from Nauvoo. A combination navigation and power canal could then be excavated along a two-mile route running from behind the dam, through the city, and back into the river. Bennett predicted that this project would supply "ample water power for propelling any amount of machinery. . .so essentially necessary to the building up of a great commercial city." Bennett's plan, and a much grander one advanced in 1844–1845, failed for a number of reasons, including lack of capital and nearly insurmountable technical problems.[12]

In the same twenty-year period, several private capitalists also attempted to harness the rapids to industrial water wheels. A plan far bolder than Bennett's was tendered by the Navigation and Hydraulic Company of the Mississippi Rapids. In January 1849, Iowa's governor, Ansel Briggs, signed an act that granted the Navigation and Hydraulic Company the privilege of acquiring a canal right-of-way around the Des Moines rapids. Twelve months later, the chief engineer of the company, Samuel R. Curtis, submitted his report on the project.[13]

Curtis recommended construction of a canal along the Iowa

12. Bennett's address is quoted in "Mississippi River Dam," p. 64; see also pp. 65–69; Enders, "The Des Moines Rapids," pp. 97, 101–31.

13. Samuel R. Curtis, *Engineer's Report No. 1, to the Directors of the Navigation and Hydraulic Company of the Mississippi Rapids; December 1, 1849.*

shore beginning at the head of the rapids and terminating at Keokuk. He further suggested that the canal could be used for both
navigation and power. Curtis contended that enough power could
be developed at the Keokuk end of the canal "to propel a thousand
run of French Burrs" and operate "all the machinery that human
invention can locate within reach of its influence."[14] He then went
on to describe a vision of industrial prosperity that retained its al-
lure until well into the twentieth century:

> Such a water power, situated in the centre of the Union, on the
> greatest water highway. . .where the largest Boats can directly com-
> municate with the Ocean; where the cotton of the South, the wheat
> of the North, and the wool of the Centre, can be accumulated at the
> least possible expense. . . . Such an immense power, thus situated,
> must attract the attention and the enterprize of our most eminent
> manufacturers, and establish at this place the greatest combination of
> manufacturing skill and energy.[15]

The project advanced in Samuel Curtis's report proved far beyond
the technical and financial means of the Navigation and Hydraulic
Company, and construction never began. In March 1867, Congress authorized a lateral canal along the Iowa shore. As a result,
the federal government guaranteed financial support for a project
that put sole emphasis on navigational improvement.[16]

The attempts by the Mormons and by the Navigation and Hydraulic Company to develop the energy of the Des Moines rapids
reveal that the Mormons, in common with their "gentile" neighbors, embraced a traditional nineteenth-century view of the relationship between people and the river. While men like John Bennett may have placed the financial strength of their struggling
community above private profit, they still acted on the belief that
exploitation of the rapids' commercial potential would foster industrial growth and prosperity. Social benefits would then be a natural
derivative of economic progress. This point of view is implicit in
the attempts of the private capitalists, and it became an article of
faith among those in the late nineteenth and early twentieth cen-

14. Ibid., p. 13. Also cited in Enders, "The Des Moines Rapids," pp. 140–47;
and Ben Hur Wilson, "The Des Moines Rapids Canal," pp. 119–21.
15. Curtis, *Engineer's Report No. 1*, p. 13.
16. Newspaper clippings from the *DGC* that discuss the construction of the government canal may be found in the Bickel Collection, binder on "Bridges &
Rivers," Keokuk Public Library, 210 N. 5th St., Keokuk, Iowa, 52632.

tury who inherited the dream to harness the rapids for industrial power.

After the Civil War, many people continued to talk of making the rapids fulfill their promise of industrial prosperity. Several groups expressed an interest in building a wing dam or a power canal on the Illinois side of the river.[17] Interest, however, never matured into action, largely because white pine offered a more profitable alternative for industrial development. For three decades after the Civil War, the upper Mississippi valley basked in the prosperity of an economic boom based on white pine. The highly competitive lumber industry attracted the risk capital and the energy of the region's entrepreneurs.

Before noteworthy logging began in the 1850s, pine lands covered the northern half of Wisconsin. Four major tributary systems of the upper Mississippi, the St. Croix, the Chippewa, the Black, and the Wisconsin, flowed through the pinery roughly from northeast to southwest. This network of streams provided access to the timber and a means of transporting logs out of the forest. The Chippewa River valley drained nearly one-third of Wisconsin's coniferous zone and, by virtue of its area and the size of its pine stand, became the state's most significant lumbering district. White pine was the preeminent commercial species because of its abundance, its superiority as construction material, and its buoyancy (in an age when timber was floated to mill and market).[18]

In the second half of the nineteenth century, successive waves of settlers surged onto the Great Plains, bringing with them a wood-based ethos that had evolved in the forested eastern United States.[19] Their presence on the nearly treeless plains stimulated an unprecedented demand for cheap lumber. Thus, as the line of settlement advanced beyond the Mississippi, the logging frontier cut its way through the pineries of northern Michigan, Wisconsin, and Minnesota. Harvested amid an orgy of waste, white pine from the Chippewa valley and other northern forests was used to build

17. "Historical Review of the Great Keokuk Water Power Legislation and Construction," *DGC*, 26 August 1913, p. 7.

18. Charles E. Twining, *Downriver: Orrin H. Ingram and the Empire Lumber Company*, pp. 29–30, 105. For further information on the white pine industry, see Robert F. Fries, *Empire in Pine: The Story of Lumbering in Wisconsin, 1830–1900*; Ralph W. Hidy et al., *Timber and Men: The Weyerhaeuser Story*.

19. Brooke Hindle analyzes this wood-based ethos in his edited volume, *America's Wooden Age: Aspects of Its Early Technology*.

the homes, barns, outbuildings, and fences of farmers from the Canadian border to Texas.

By the 1870s, rafts of white pine supported a large and growing lumber industry in river ports from Minnesota to Missouri (see Table 1). At Chippewa River mill towns like Eau Claire, workers assembled logs and green timber into rafts and sent them down the Mississippi. In 1878, 498 log rafts and 159 lumber rafts floated under the drawbridge at Dubuque, Iowa. Massive and ponderous, these rafts could cover up to ten acres of water and contain millions of board feet. All of that pine proved to be very good for business. In the fall of 1880, Ingram, Kennedy and Company's Winona, Minnesota, wholesale yard established a profitable new outlet near the Missouri River railroad bridge at Pierre, in Dakota Territory. The future also looked very bright for the Empire Lumber Company's wholesale operation in Hannibal, Missouri. By mid-August 1881, Empire had shipped by rail eighty-five carloads of wood products, and orders for one hundred more remained unfilled.[20]

Most of the retail customers for lumber rafted down the Mississippi lived to the west. Therefore, cities on the west bank of the river benefited far more from the white-pine trade than did those on the east bank. Stevedores pulled the rafts from the water at places like Wabasha and Winona, Minnesota; Dubuque, Clinton, Davenport, Burlington, and Keokuk, Iowa; and Hannibal and St. Louis, Missouri. Lumber hauled from the river had to be washed, sorted, piled, and seasoned. Local mills reduced the saw logs to finished products. Wholesale yards then shipped dimension lumber, timbers, fencing, shingles, and lathe by rail to farmers living on the plains.[21]

The crushing depression of 1893 squeezed the vitality from the lumber industry. Other factors guaranteed that there would be no recovery. Unregulated cutting and uncontrolled wildfire had spared little of the once-extensive pineries. Then, too, the market for pine had shifted from the Great Plains to the growing cities, from the farmyard to the backyard. This changing market proved critical for two major reasons. First, demand from urban consumers was much less urgent than that from farmers. As historian Charles

20. Twining, *Downriver*, pp. 193–94, 237; George B. Hartman, "The Iowa Sawmill Industry," p. 75. For further information on the rafting of white pine, see Walter A. Blair, *A Raft Pilot's Log: A History of the Great Rafting Industry on the Upper Mississippi, 1840–1915.*

21. Twining, *Downriver*, pp. 116–18.

Table 1. Seasonal Capacity of Mills in Iowa River Towns (1877)

Town	Number of mills	Seasonal capacity in millions of board feet
Lansing	2	12.5
McGregor	1	15.0
Guttenberg	1	2.0
Dubuque	5	30.5
Bellevue	1	5.0
Sabula	1	3.5
Lyons	3	41.0
Clinton	4	113.0
Camanche	1	6.0
Davenport	5	54.0
Muscatine	3	41.0
Burlington	2	15.0
Fort Madison	2	20.0
Montrose	1	8.0
Keokuk	1	10.0
Total	33	376.5

Source: George B. Hartman, "The Iowa Sawmill Industry," p. 78.

Twining has explained, "The picket fence around a city house was not the same critical item as the corn crib on a pioneer farm." Second, intense competition in the pineries and general use of the Mississippi for transportation resulted in dirty, irregular, and improperly seasoned wood products. Urban consumers insisted on a higher grade of clean, white, finished lumber than the river towns had customarily shipped.[22]

While the lumber industry prospered, interest in waterpower from the Des Moines rapids had waned. Talk rather than action became the rule. Anyone who earned a living directly or indirectly from white pine had a vested interest in keeping the river free of obstructions, such as a dam, that would hinder the passage of hard-to-maneuver rafts. By the mid-1890s, the picture had changed considerably. With the demise of the white-pine industry, it no longer made economic sense to oppose construction of a power dam in

22. Ibid., pp. 128, 211–13, 265–90.

the river. Thus, the collapse of the pine boom revitalized the old dream of extracting energy from the Des Moines rapids. In Keokuk and Hamilton, business leaders continued to look to the river to save and sustain the economies of their towns. On 6 July 1899, a grocery dealer named C. P. Birge brought together twenty-five citizens of Keokuk and Hamilton "to organize a company and take up the work in earnest of utilizing the water power wasting at our doors." Birge and his associates formed the Keokuk and Hamilton Water Power Company. In so doing, they initiated the chain of events that led to construction of the Keokuk hydroelectric project.[23]

"Utilizing the water power wasting at our doors"

For most Americans who thought about such things in the early 1890s, hydroelectric power was still a curiosity or a promise. In 1894, news of the completion of a hydroelectric plant at Niagara Falls, New York, shattered this perception. Rated at over 100,000 horsepower, the Niagara facility attracted a cluster of factories and the attention of the nation's people. Within five years, the plant was prepared to double its electrical production. The Niagara project's success at attracting factories had a strong influence on the men who incorporated the Keokuk and Hamilton Water Power Company. In an interview with the *Keokuk Daily Gate City*, C. P. Birge explained, "The rapid growth and demand for power at Niagara Falls, conveyed twenty-five miles away to a great city like Buffalo, gives us a little idea of the possibility on the Des Moines rapids."[24]

In 1901, the company took two important steps. Keokuk and Hamilton's waterpower enthusiasts obtained a franchise from Congress to construct a wing dam and power canal on the eastern side of the river. They also paid for the counsel of Lyman E. Cooley, a respected Chicago hydroelectric engineer. Cooley's verdict on the wing dam proposal sentenced it to oblivion. He calculated that,

23. "Historical Review of the Great Keokuk Water Power Legislation and Construction." See also "Work Is a Product of the People." Mr. Birge's occupation is mentioned in H. S. Rogers, "Damming the World's Greatest River," p. 87.

24. Louis C. Hunter, *A History of Industrial Power in the United States, 1780–1930. Volume One: Waterpower in the Century of the Steam Engine*, pp. 138, 233; Joseph M. Petulla, *American Environmental History: The Exploitation and Conservation of Natural Resources*, p. 245. For Mr. Birge's remarks, see "In Two Weeks the Lid Will Be Taken off the Power Project," *DGC*, 25 May 1899, p. 6.

while the dam was technically possible, the cost could not be justified in terms of the power that would be produced. As a counterproposal, he suggested that the Keokuk and Hamilton Water Power Company embrace the far bolder proposition of building a dam all the way across the Father of Waters.[25] After a year's consideration, and probably substantial public debate and private anguish, the board of directors committed its company to this daring new plan. With this action, they broke through their nineteenth-century integument and began to nurture the approach that came to fruition in 1913.

For the next few years, the arena for important decision making shifted to Washington, D.C., with events proceeding rapidly and in a manner that pleased the stockholders of the Keokuk and Hamilton Water Power Company. Congress passed a resolution directing the secretary of war to survey the proposed Des Moines rapids dam. The report of the Corps of Engineers pointedly declared, "The interests of navigation at present require no improvements or alterations in the Des Moines Rapids Canal or its accessories." Although they found the canal and its three locks adequate, the engineers recognized that benefits, such as improved navigation over the Des Moines rapids, would result from combining the power dam with a navigation lock.[26] Physical compatibility was one thing and financial partnership quite another. The corps further reasoned that the government had already provided satisfactory facilities and should not be called upon for further expenditures. Convinced that the plan's promoters would pay for a suitable lock and other necessary navigational structures, the engineers recommended, "The Government should not oppose the private enterprise, and should permit the construction and operation of the

25. Accounts of the project's history between 1899 and 1913 vary primarily in the amount of detail provided. Unless otherwise noted, material for this summary is taken from the following: "Historical Review of the Great Keokuk Water Power Legislation and Construction"; Chester M. Clark, "Electric Power from the Mississippi River"; "Keokuk Hydroelectric Development"; "Celebrating the Inauguration of Keokuk Water-Power Plant"; and Don W. Hutchinson, "The Story of a Dream Come True." For information on Mr. Cooley's relationship with the Keokuk and Hamilton Water Power Company, see Hugh L. Cooper, "The Water Power Development of the Mississippi River Power Company, at Keokuk Iowa," pp. 224–25.

26. Executive Documents, *Annual Reports of the War Department. 1903, Report of the Chief of Engineers, Part 2*, appendix AA7, "Report of Maj. C.McD. Townsend, Corps of Engineers, Upon Examination of Mississippi River at the Foot of Des Moines Rapids . . . to Determine the Advisability of Constructing a Dam at the Foot of Said Rapids . . .," pp. 1506–7; see also 1500–1512.

lock and dam, subject to such conditions as shall safeguard the interests of navigation." [27]

At this point Congress reentered the picture and, early in 1905, unanimously approved the coveted franchise. The bill President Roosevelt signed on 9 February 1905 granted the Keokuk and Hamilton Water Power Company a perpetual franchise that conveyed the privilege of constructing a power dam at the foot of the Des Moines rapids. Capacious in the extreme, this waterpower grant sought only to guarantee development and protect the primacy of navigation. [28]

Several provisions of the act warrant mention because, within a few years, this franchise and the policy that fostered it would come under attack by conservationists. Congress demanded no user fee for the privilege of developing the franchise and made the concession transferable to ensure that *someone* would put the rapids to work. The senators and congressmen who voted for the bill wanted to encourage immediate use and discourage holding for speculation. Thus, the act would have become null and void if construction had not commenced in five years and if the project had not reached completion in ten years. Finally, Congress gave the secretary of war administrative control over the project. The statute directed him to approve all blueprints in advance and to appoint an army engineer to oversee the work. [29]

Between 1899 and 1913 three crucial events guaranteed the realization of the dream of developing the Des Moines rapids. The first took place in 1902 when the Keokuk and Hamilton Water Power Company committed itself to building a dam across the river; the second occurred in 1905 when the men from Keokuk and Hamilton employed Hugh L. Cooper as chief engineer; and the third transpired in 1908 when St. Louis utilities contracted for 60,000 horsepower upon completion of the dam.

It is clear that the Keokuk and Hamilton waterpower boosters recognized their own limitations. They intended to divest themselves of their franchise and the company's stock as soon as they found the right combination of skill and capital to see their project through to completion. True to this intent, the Keokuk and Hamil-

27. Ibid., p. 1507.
28. U.S. Congress, Senate, *Dam Across the Mississippi River*; U.S. Congress, House, *Dam Across the Mississippi River*; U.S. Congress, House, "Dam Across the Mississippi River," Debate over H.R. 15284.
29. "Dam Across the Mississippi River," pp. 1495–96.

ton Waterpower Company initiated a wide-ranging search for a chief engineer and for financial backing. Before 1905 ended, they had found an engineer. However, the quest for money continued for nearly four and a half years because financiers with risk capital considered the project a chancy investment.

In September 1905, H. L. Cooper journeyed to Keokuk and interviewed for the position of chief engineer. After a lengthy conference, several local men accompanied Cooper on an automobile journey to visit the waterpower plant he had under construction at Niagara Falls, Canada. Very impressed with the engineer's work, they signed a contract with Cooper and a group of Toronto investors giving them a two-year option on the company's stock and waterpower franchise. In 1907, the Toronto men backed out, and the Keokuk and Hamilton Water Power Company entered into a new contract with Cooper, which granted him the same option that the company had given the Toronto syndicate.

In 1907, many experts considered the building of a hydroelectric project in the Mississippi River an impossible or an impractical task. Forty-two-year-old Hugh L. Cooper may have been the only American engineer capable of proving them wrong. In the incipient field of hydroelectric engineering, Cooper possessed a rare and necessary blend of experience and professional reputation, vision and determination, leadership ability, business acumen, and luck. Like many engineers his age, Cooper was a self-made man whose formal education ended when he graduated from high school. Yet, by 1905, he had gained enough first-hand experience designing and constructing hydroelectric plants to become president of the New York-based Hugh L. Cooper and Company, Incorporated.[30]

Cooper's professional life and the new field of hydroelectric power matured together. In the first eight years of his company's existence, Cooper completed major installations at Winnipeg, Canada; McCall Ferry, Pennsylvania; Horseshoe Rapids (above Niagara Falls), Canada; and Keokuk, Iowa. Each advanced both the

---

30. Biographical material on Cooper comes from the following sources unless otherwise noted: *The National Cyclopedia of American Biography* (New York: James T. White & Co., 1947), 33:173–74; *Dictionary of American Biography* (New York: Charles Scribner's Sons, 1958), 22, suppl. 2, pp. 118–19; *New York Times*, 25 June 1937, p. 21; and Will P. Green, "Hugh Lincoln Cooper: The Man Who Built the Keokuk Dam Across the Mississippi." For further analysis of the process whereby colleges of engineering replaced the "school of experience," see David F. Noble, *America By Design: Science, Technology, and the Rise of Corporate Capitalism.*

science of hydroelectric engineering and Cooper's professional stature. When he died of arteriosclerosis in 1937, the *New York Times* reported that in his forty-five-year career Cooper had "designed and built works totaling more than 2,000,000 horse power and costing more than $200,000,000."[31]

In addition to Keokuk dam, Cooper's eulogists reserved their highest praise for two other endeavors. In the mid-1920s, he served as design and consulting engineer on the Wilson dam, which stoppered the Tennessee River at Muscle Shoals. This structure later became the first unit of the Tennessee Valley Authority's integrated, multiple-purpose river basin project. The Russian government also retained his services in 1926 as consulting engineer for the 756,000-horsepower Dnieperstroy hydroelectric project. When he turned the completed Dnieperstroy dam over to the Russians in 1932, the Soviet government made him the first foreign recipient of the Order of the Red Star.[32]

In 1907, chief engineer Cooper initiated a single-handed campaign to attract timid capital to his latest venture. Despite the chief engineer's formidable reputation, his task took nearly three years of grueling effort, an indication of the skepticism with which the financial community viewed the proposal. Without resorting to hyperbole, he claimed that "fifty-eight capitalists showed him out of their offices before one man could be found with the confidence to invest his money at Keokuk." Among the potential investors that turned Cooper down were the North American Company, J. P. Morgan & Company, Standard Oil Company, General Electric Company, and Westinghouse Electric Company.[33]

Potential investors had one major question: did a market for Keokuk energy exist in an area where electricity was generated from cheap, abundant coal? In an ingenious move calculated to win investors' confidence, Cooper located an advance market for 60,000 of the approximately 200,000 horsepower that the Keokuk and Hamilton Water Power Company would eventually have at its disposal. He negotiated a ninety-nine-year contract with the Mis-

31. *New York Times*, 25 June 1937, p. 21. For a more detailed look at the development of hydroelectric power, see Hunter, *A History of Industrial Power*.

32. *New York Times*, 25 June 1937, p. 21. See also *The National Cyclopedia of American Biography* and *Dictionary of American Biography*, as cited above.

33. Cooper is quoted in Green, "Hugh Lincoln Cooper," p. 366. For a list of the potential investors that rejected Cooper's proposal, see U.S. Congress, House, "Amendment of General Dam Act," Debate over H.R. 16053, Remarks of William C. Adamson. Adamson names only fifty-six.

sissippi River Power Distributing Company, which tied the price of Keokuk electricity to the cost of coal. In turn, the Mississippi River Power Distributing Company arranged for delivery of the Keokuk power to three St. Louis utilities in the following amounts: Union Electric Light and Power Company, 27,500 horsepower; United Railways Company, 27,500 horsepower; and Laclede Gas and Light Company, 5,000 horsepower.[34] The efficacy of this ninety-nine-year contract is readily apparent. It reduced the risk for investors to Cooper's ability to design and build a Mississippi River dam and powerhouse. The agreement created a lure that attracted capital and represented the third, decisive action that insured that the Keokuk dream would become a reality.

Thereafter, events moved quickly. For the sum of $20,000, Cooper exercised his option on the Keokuk and Hamilton Water Power Company's stock and franchise. The company officers resigned, a new board of directors was elected, and corporate headquarters were moved from Keokuk to New York City. On 8 January 1910, a telegram brought long-awaited news. After lengthy negotiations, the Boston-based Stone & Webster Group had agreed to provide the necessary financial support. Ultimately, 65 percent of the capital was subscribed outside the United States—in England, France, Canada, and Belgium. Cooper remained as chief engineer and, with the financial, technical, and managerial backing of Stone & Webster, had charge of all hydraulic design and construction in connection with the dam, the powerhouse substructure, and the lock and dry dock.[35]

Stone & Webster involved itself both directly and indirectly in the venture. Stone & Webster Engineering Corporation supervised the building of the powerhouse substructure, installation of the electrical equipment, and construction of the transmission lines. It also directed the operation of the accounting and financial departments. In early 1911, the Mississippi River Power Com-

34. "St. Louis to Take Large Amount of Hydroelectric Energy from Keokuk Development," p. 505. Laclede Gas withdrew before the project came on line, and the others bought its share. "Mississippi River Energy for St. Louis," p. 1289; "Keokuk Water-Power Development," pp. 1043–44; Cooper, "The Water Power Development . . . at Keokuk Iowa," p. 213; *Moody's Manual of Investments and Security Rating Service: Public Utility Securities* (1926):1473; "Cooper Speaks to Business Men," *DGC*, 13 November 1912, p. 5.

35. Green, "Hugh Lincoln Cooper," p. 366. For further information on Stone & Webster, see Thomas P. Hughes, *Networks of Power: Electrification in Western Society, 1880–1930*, pp. 386–91; *Report of the Commissioner of Corporations on Water-Power Development in the United States*, pp. 22–23, 163–67.

Building the cofferdam for the Keokuk dam, 2 January 1912.

Bird's-eye view from the end of the completed dam, 30 January 1912.

pany, managed by the Stone and Webster Management Association, replaced the Keokuk and Hamilton Water Power Company as proprietor of the hydroelectric project. Thus, Stone & Webster indirectly controlled every aspect of the undertaking both during and after construction.[36]

Construction began on 10 January 1910, one month before the franchise would have expired. Work continued at an accelerating pace until laborers poured the last load of concrete on 31 May 1913. The completed project represented the fulfillment of a long-standing dream, but it bore little physical resemblance to earlier, less ambitious proposals. Nineteenth-century waterpower advocates like John Bennett and Samuel Curtis would have stood in awe before one of the largest structures in the world taking form in the channel of the Mississippi. Contemporary observers watched with amazement as the dam, powerhouse, and navigation lock rose from the bed of the river. In each case, workmen constructed cofferdams and dewatered sections of the riverbed, in order to blast the necessary foundations. The limestone that made the Des Moines rapids so treacherous provided a very stable base for the hydroelectric project.

The complex comprised six major components: the dam, the powerhouse and turbines, the navigation lock, the dry dock, the transmission lines, and Lake Cooper. Keokuk dam began at the bluff on the Illinois shore. It then ran perpendicular across the current for about 4,500 feet, until it intersected the powerhouse at nearly a right angle. The dam was composed of 119 arched spans that gave the finished structure the appearance of a great concrete bridge. Between the arches, spillways regulated the level of Lake Cooper. Constructed roughly parallel to the Iowa side of the river, the powerhouse extended downstream from the dam for 1,400 feet. This massive, concrete edifice towered more than 130 feet above its foundation and occupied approximately twelve acres of the former riverbed. Specifications called for the plant to house thirty of the largest Francis-type turbines ever built. Each of these one-million-pound waterwheels had the capacity to generate 10,000 electrical horsepower. They had to be specifically designed to ac-

36. "The World's Largest Water-Power Plant," p. 1168; "The Greatest Thing in All Iowa History," pp. 42–43; "Water Power Development on the Mississippi River at Keokuk, Iowa," p. 355.

General view of Keokuk dam from the Iowa side of the river, showing progress on the final sections of the cofferdam, 6 August 1912.

Keokuk dam and its associated structures, the powerhouse, lock, dry dock, and the Corps of Engineers offices and buildings.

commodate the large volume of water and relatively low head characteristic of the Mississippi River.[37]

A navigation lock and dry dock joined the downriver end of the powerhouse to the bluff on the Iowa shore. Like the powerhouse and dam, the lock and dry dock were fabricated of unreenforced concrete. The Mississippi River Power Company constructed their facilities to replace the government canal, its three locks, and its dry dock, which would be flooded by Keokuk dam. Under the terms of the franchise granted by Congress, the power company donated the new lock and dry dock to the government. Both structures were the largest on the Mississippi River, and the lock ranked among the biggest in the world. It boasted interior dimensions of 110 by 400 feet and a lift of 40 feet. In width the Keokuk lock matched those in the Panama Canal, and it exceeded them in lift.[38]

The Mississippi River Power Company sold its electricity only to wholesale customers. In order to serve volume users, the Stone & Webster Engineering Corporation designed and built long-distance transmission lines north to Burlington, Iowa, and south to St. Louis, Missouri. Tall steel towers carried the 110,000-volt high-tension cable 144 miles from Keokuk dam to St. Louis. In the fall of 1913, this line distributed over 60 percent of the 120,000 horsepower offered for sale by the Mississippi River Power Company. In addition to the 60,000 horsepower purchased by St. Louis utilities, the Atlas Portland Cement Company took 10,000 horsepower from a substation at Hull, Illinois. Quincy and Alton, Illinois, and the Central Illinois Public Service Company contracted

37. "Six Big Features of Keokuk Power Plant," *DGC*, 15 August 1913, part 3, p. 10; "The World's Largest Water-Power Plant," pp. 1157–68; "Power-House for the Entire Mississippi," pp. 147–54. On the subject of the turbines, see Mississippi River Power Company, "Electric Power from the Mississippi River," *Bulletin number 5* (March 1912):19–31; "The Water Wheels at Keokuk," pp. 536–38; Chester H. Larner, "The 10,000-Horsepower Turbines at Keokuk: Description of the Design, Manufacture and Transportation of the Largest Water-Wheels Ever Built"; H. B. McDermid, "The Turbine Runners of the Mississippi River Power Co. at Keokuk, Iowa"; and "The Turbines of the Mississippi River Power Co. at Keokuk, Ia." The turbines had a 10,000-horsepower capacity at the normal head of thirty-two feet, a capacity of approximately 14,000 horsepower at the maximum head of thirty-nine feet, and an output of about 6,000 horsepower at the minimum operating head of twenty feet.

38. "Six Big Features of Keokuk Power Plant," *DGC*, 15 August 1913, part 3, p. 10; Mississippi River Power Company, "Electric Power from the Mississippi River," *Bulletin number 4* (November 1911):21–23; "Lock and Drydock at Keokuk"; "The Mississippi Lock at Keokuk"; "Mitering Lock Gate at Keokuk Presents Novel Features."

for lesser amounts. This line traversed bottomland, farm fields, and forested bluffs. It crossed and recrossed the Mississippi and spanned the Missouri. While not the longest line then in use, it added to the sense of monumental achievement associated with the Keokuk project and to the belief that American engineers had indeed subdued the forces of nature.[39]

In less than three years, H. L. Cooper had supervised the erection of the single largest hydroelectric plant in the world. In so doing, he helped make himself, Keokuk, and waterpower the objects of national and international interest. During the spring and summer of 1912, engineers and other experts from Switzerland, Germany, Russia, and Hungary inspected the dam. The Mississippi River Power Company and the Keokuk Industrial Association worked hard to create and mold project-related publicity. In order to fashion an image that would attract factories to the area, both organizations advertised extensively. Between October 1911 and September 1912, the association spent just over $10,500 for twenty-one advertisements in *The Saturday Evening Post, Outlook, Review of Reviews, Everybody's, Literary Digest, World's Work,* and *Factory.*[40]

The Mississippi River Power Company also promoted the undertaking by eagerly accommodating visitors and by filling many of the requests that it received for speakers. The company constructed two observation platforms, allowed access to the works on Sundays, and conducted tours. Led by chief engineer Cooper, officials of the Mississippi River Power Company frequently accepted

39. "Power Company States Its Policy," *DGC,* 5 February 1913, p. 5; Mississippi River Power Company, "Electric Power from the Mississippi River," *Bulletin number 9* (March 1913):25–31. The transmission line to St. Louis was not the longest then in service. That distinction went to another Stone & Webster Engineering Corporation project that spanned the 241 miles from Big Creek to Los Angeles, California. On the subject of the Big Creek line, see Hughes, *Networks of Power,* pp. 281, 390.

40. Examples of international interest may be found in "City News," *DGC,* 18 March 1912, p. 3; "Noted Germans Visit the Dam," *DGC,* 17 June 1912, p. 7; "Expert Russian Viewing the Dam," *DGC,* 17 June 1912, p. 8; "Noted Hungarian Engineer Here," *DGC,* 26 July 1912, p. 5; see also p. 3; and "Eng. Cooper Will Enjoy a Holiday," *HMJ,* 23 July 1913, p. 1. For further information on efforts to create and mold project-related publicity, see "City News," *DGC,* 2 April 1912, p. 8; "City News," *DGC,* 28 August 1913, p. 8; *Electric Power from the Mississippi River,* nine bulletins on the project issued by the Mississippi River Power Company between March 1911 and March 1913. The advertising campaign to promote the project is discussed in "[Report] . . . of Manager DeWitt," *DGC,* 21 January 1913, p. 4; "Much Advertising Given the City," *DGC,* 21 July 1913, p. 8; "Another Company Uses Local Pictures," *DGC,* 27 July 1913, p. 11; and "Best Boosters to Read of the Dam," *DGC,* 28 July 1913, p. 3.

invitations to talk about the project. Cooper's schedule during the fall and winter of 1911–1912 included sterioptiton-illustrated addresses in Boston; Ames and Des Moines, Iowa; St. Louis and Hannibal, Missouri; and Chicago and Nauvoo, Illinois.[41]

By the summer of 1912, Keokuk dam had become an important tourist attraction, particularly for people in the tri-state area of Iowa, Illinois, and Missouri. The "Gate City" regularly hosted crowds of one thousand or more on summer weekends in 1912 and 1913. On 9 March 1913, the Mississippi River Power Company permitted access to the riverbed work for the last time. An estimated twenty thousand visitors accepted an invitation to inspect the construction site before workmen allowed the river to reclaim its channel.[42]

Nearly every aspect of the project received wide-ranging coverage in newspapers, popular magazines, technical and scholarly journals, and silent newsreels. Between 1910 and 1913, technical publications such as *Electrical World*, *Engineering Record*, *Engineering News*, and *Power* printed over thirty-five articles on various aspects of the work at Keokuk. In September 1913, *Pathe's Weekly*, a silent newsreel, promised pictures of Harry K. Thaw, "views of the Keokuk Dam and the ceremonies at its dedication," scenes of an attempted arrest of Sylvia Pankhurst, "and many other equally interesting events." At times it seemed as though the attention of the region, of the nation, and even of the world had focused on the gigantic hydroelectric complex at the foot of the Des Moines rapids.[43]

Wealth and Vulnerability

Keokuk dam attracted attention because it promised both immediate and sustained economic growth, on a scale commensurate with its size. In the short run, the project stimulated a business boom in the area around the dam. Stone & Webster employed a workforce of from fifteen hundred to two thousand men. The skilled laborers were largely white Americans who paid for food

41. "Keokuk Water-Power Development"; "Chief Engineer Cooper Talks," *DGC*, 23 January 1912, p. 5.

42. "Thousands Visit the Water-Power," *DGC*, 10 March 1913, p. 5.

43. "Tomorrow-Pathe's Weekly," *HMJ*, 14 September 1913, p. 4. See also "Keokuk Dam Pictures at Orpheum," *DGC*, 23 January 1912, p. 3; "Pictures of the Dam," *DGC*, 11 February 1912, p. 4; "Keokuk Lock Seen Over the World," *DGC*, 24 June 1913, p. 8.

and lodging in nearby homes and boardinghouses. Most of the un-skilled workers were Italians, Austrians, and French-Canadians who purchased their own food but lived in company-owned bar-racks. In both cases, the men spent much of their pay in Keokuk and Hamilton. They shopped in retail stores, visited barbershops, and patronized a range of leisure-time businesses from restaurants, theaters, and showboats to taverns and bordellos.[44]

In addition to the direct effect of the workers' wages, the project provided numerous other local economic benefits. H. L. Cooper claimed in August 1912 that Stone & Webster had already given the Keokuk-based Taber Lumber Company $200,000 in business. The boom in Keokuk and Hamilton attracted large numbers of job-seekers and their families. The building trades industry labored overtime to keep up with the demand for both temporary and per-manent housing. In April 1912, the *Daily Gate City* reported, "A large force of men are busily engaged in putting in the foundations for the new apartment houses to be built at the corner of Fourth and Franklin." All the building created a brisk trade in real estate. Entrepreneurs in Keokuk and Hamilton also profited from tour-ism. An enterprising cigar manufacturer made a five-cent cigar dubbed the "Power City," while T. R. J. Ayres & Sons, jewelers and silversmiths, sold low-priced souvenirs of the dam and other "clever novelties."[45]

Regionally, the steamboat excursion trade received a windfall. The Hannibal, Missouri, organizations that sponsored 1912 river excursions to Keokuk dam included the 5th Street Baptist Sunday School, the Trades and Labor Assembly, the Presbyterian Sunday School, the Arch and Park Street methodist churches, the 1st Christian Church, the Broadway Methodist Church, and the Mis-souri State Editorial Association (in convention at Hannibal).[46] A

44. Most articles on the project have very little to say about the workforce. Some information may be found in "Water Power Development on the Mississippi River at Keokuk, Iowa," pp. 359, 362.
45. "The Hearing on Canal Closing . . .," *DGC*, 14 August 1912, p. 7; "City News," *DGC*, 14 April 1912, p. 11; advertisement for "Power City," *DGC*, 11 Feb-ruary 1912, p. 8; advertisement for "Dam Souvenirs," *DGC*, 17 March 1913, p. 2.
46. "Arranging for Big Excursion," *HMJ*, 20 April 1912, p. 1; "5th Street Baptist Sunday School," advertisement, *HMJ*, 29 May 1912, p. 8; "Excursion to Go Thro' the Locks," *HMJ*, 6 June 1912, p. 8; "1st Christian Church Excurs'n," *HMJ*, 7 June 1912, p. 1; "Methodist Excursion to Keokuk," *HMJ*, 12 July 1912, p. 1; "The Chris-tian Excursion," *HMJ*, 20 July 1912, p. 1; "Everybody Goes," advertisement, *HMJ*, 9 August 1912, p. 5; "Editors Entertained," *HMJ*, 22 August 1912, p. 1.

one-quarter-page ad in the 29 May 1912 edition of the *Hannibal Morning Journal* proclaimed:

> 5th Street Baptist Sunday School
> Day-Light Excursion
> On the Palatial Steamer G. W. Hill to
> See the Most Extensive Engineering Work
> Ever Produced in the World
>   'THE BIG DAM'
> at Keokuk, Iowa. Harnessing the Powers
> of the Great Mississippi. Now is Just
> the Right Time to See, for the Work
> Progressed Just Far Enough to See in
> Detail What You Cannot See Later[47]

More than one thousand people answered this call and paid to board the *G. W. Hill* for the upriver journey to Keokuk. Less than two weeks later, the Presbyterian Sunday School sponsored "the largest excursion ever given by a Hannibal Sunday school," when over two thousand people embarked for Keokuk on the steamer *St. Paul.*[48]

Excursionists came to Keokuk to satisfy their curiosity, enjoy a day on the river, follow the crowd, see friends, and share in the general excitement. Most visitors to the dam traveled aboard one of several excursion steamboats that served that portion of the river. The owners of these boats catered to the comfort and entertainment of their holiday-seeking passengers. The steamer *St. Paul* carried an orchestra onboard and was equipped with restaurants, electric fans, a soda fountain, and filtered drinking water. Private organizations frequently chartered excursion boats to Keokuk as a way to raise money. They attracted patrons by guaranteeing that the journey would be as much fun as the tour of the dam. When the Alpine Club of Hannibal, Missouri, sponsored a trip to Keokuk, promoters promised, "Everyone who enjoys good music and dancing should go on this excursion as it will be one of the best of the season."[49]

47. "5th Street Baptist Sunday School," advertisement, *HMJ*, 29 May 1912, p. 8.
48. "The Excursion Big Success," *HMJ*, 1 June 1912, p. 1; "The Excursion to Keokuk," *HMJ*, 12 June 1912, p. 4.
49. "First Excursion to Keokuk Dam," *HMJ*, 20 February 1913, p. 1; "Presbyterian Excursion to Keokuk," *HMJ*, 8 April 1913, p. 4.

In the long run, people who lived along the routes of the high-tension lines expected all that hydroelectric power to attract factories. This area between Burlington and St. Louis became known as the "Power Zone." Within the "Power Zone," cities and towns actively competed to lure factories. Yet optimism ran so high that few observers believed that anyplace within the reach of Keokuk power would be left wanting. Reflecting this confidence, headlines in the January 1912 number of *Iowa Factories* promised, "New Era in Industrialism of the Middle West Is Begun with the Great Keokuk Installation." Not to be out-boosted, the *St. Louis Globe Democrat* predicted, "It will be only a matter of a few years until the banks of the Mississippi will be lined with manufacturing plants for miles." Before the end of 1912, Stone & Webster and the Keokuk Industrial Association had each purchased property in Keokuk to be used for manufacturing districts. Across the river, Mr. R. O. Marsh announced plans to create a new industrial community between Hamilton and Warsaw, Illinois.[50]

This intense faith in industrialization had its origins in the historical tradition of the Des Moines rapids and in the collapse of the white-pine industry. White pine had brought both wealth and vulnerability to cities and towns along the upper river. During the 1870s and 1880s, lumber ports boomed. They also became economically addicted to white pine. By the 1880s, Hannibal, Missouri, had become "one vast area of saw mills and wholesale lumber yards," dangerously dependent on white pine for its economic health. In 1886, the Empire Lumber Company of Eau Claire, Wisconsin, delivered 23 million board feet of lumber to its wholesale yard in Hannibal. Gross receipts from the sale of this lumber totaled $379,732.20. Empire never recovered from the depression of 1893, however, and in 1898 ceased operations at Eau Claire and Hannibal. In that same year, a coterie of prominent citizens who had earned their wealth from white pine acted to save Hannibal's economy. They founded the Business Men's Association, which became the Commercial Club eleven years later.[51] The timing of

50. "The Greatest Thing in All Iowa History," p. 16; "St. Louis Is Taking Notice of Keokuk's Big Dam," reprinted from the *Globe Democrat* in *DGC*, 22 January 1912, p. 5; "Industrial Section Secured for Keokuk Manufacturing Industries," *DGC*, 12 May 1912, pp. 1, 11; "Great Industrial Plans Perfected for Keokuk," *DGC*, 1 October 1912, p. 5; "Marsh Taking Up Land Under Option in Illinois," *DGC*, 11 October 1912, p. 5.

51. "Low Freight and Power Rates Make It [Hannibal] Manufacturers' Mecca," *HMJ*, 27 June 1915, sec. III, p. 1; Twining, *Downriver*, pp. 363–64; "Hannibal's Wonderful Growth in Past 10 Years," *HMJ*, 9 April 1914, sec. IV, p. 3.

their action indicates that these men placed considerable emphasis on such organizations as a means of creating alternatives to white pine.

When the bust came, it forced business and financial leaders in river towns to confront their own vulnerability. Struggling to keep their economic lives afloat, these men clutched at industrialization, modernized transportation (especially river improvement), and the Keokuk hydroelectric project as a way to revitalize, diversify, and sustain the economy of the upper river. This impulse became institutionalized in the Keokuk and Hamilton Water Power Company, the Upper Mississippi River Improvement Association, and various commercial clubs. In company with several newspapers, these organizations became the banquet-table purveyors of official optimism. They saw their own ends, which they equated with the needs of the larger community, furthered by their advocacy of the Keokuk development. Their actions also heightened general expectations that contributed to escalating conflict after the project came on-line.

Both the Keokuk and Hamilton Water Power Company and the Upper Mississippi River Improvement Association had their origins in the post–white pine period of economic dislocation. The founders turned to the rapids in the belief that river development and cheap electrical power would bring industrial prosperity to their towns. They also acted as participants in a larger struggle to revive the economy of the upper river. When the Keokuk and Hamilton Water Power Company was established in the late 1890s, local support for the organization and its goals ran very high. Early in its history, the company needed money for surveys and promotional work. With the consent of the voters and taxpayers of the two communities, the city councils of Keokuk and Hamilton illegally appropriated the needed funds.[52]

In 1901, advocates of river development set up the Upper Mississippi River Improvement Association as an organized constituency for improving the upper river. During the first fifteen years of its existence, the association concentrated on two objectives. First, it helped persuade Congress to authorize a permanent six-foot channel for the upper river in 1907 and then it pushed for rapid completion of the project. Second, the association promoted modern municipal river terminals in order to integrate rail and water

---

52. Versions of the appropriations story may be found in "Work Is a Product of the People." Hutchinson, "The Story of a Dream Come True," p. 8.

transportation into an efficient, unified system.[53] An article re-printed from the *Quincy* (Ill.) *Herald* reflected the future that association members envisioned for the upper river:

> A big concrete building on the river bank at Quincy with railroad tracks running through it! Huge electric cranes picking freight off these cars and swinging it on to big steel barges at the dock! Tugs nosing about ready to take the barges off to New Orleans, to ships bound for the canal, to Australia, to South America, to the western coast of the United States, to Cuba, to India! Why not?[54]

Before World War I, the Hannibal Commercial Club, in company with many similar groups on the upper river, provided the main source of membership for the Upper Mississippi River Improvement Association. These same commercial organizations strongly supported the Keokuk hydroelectric project. They did so because the business and professional leaders who belonged to commercial clubs shared a view of progress that depended upon sustained economic growth. As the *Hannibal Morning Journal* reported, "Securing factories has been one of the main objects of the Commercial Club, because we must have business and make money before we can have parks, playgrounds, public buildings, etc."[55]

A June 1912 convention at Hannibal offers an excellent illustration of the fact that commercial club members considered the Keokuk project part of a larger effort to foster economic growth. Delegates from commercial organizations in six "Power Zone" cities—Hannibal, Quincy, Hamilton, Keokuk, Fort Madison, and Burlington—huddled at Hannibal "for the purpose of discussing matters in common pertaining to the cities along the river which are vitally interested in the big power plant at Keokuk." Keynote speaker Thomas H. Wilkinson, president of the Upper Mississippi River Improvement Association, "delivered a ringing address on the subject of 'River Terminals.'" After the applause had faded away, the convocation formally endorsed the association's work. The delegates then listened to speeches by George D. Clayton, chairman of the Good Roads Committee of the Hannibal Commer-

53. "The Convention in Hannibal," *HMJ*, 6 June 1913, pp. 1, 3. For more detailed information on the Upper Mississippi River Improvement Association, see *Proceedings of the Upper Mississippi River Improvement Association*, 1904, 1908, 1909, 1911, 1913.

54. "Possibilities of River Transportation," Editorial quoting from and commenting on an article from the *Quincy Herald*. *HMJ*, 6 February 1914, p. 4.

55. "The 'Livest' Commercial Organization in Missouri," *HMJ*, 27 June 1915, sec. I, p. 1.

cial Club; Maj. Montgomery Meigs of the U.S. Army Corps of Engineers; and A. J. Trawick of the Mississippi River Power Company. Thereafter the convention voted to adjourn with a promise to reassemble in August 1913 at Fort Madison, Iowa.[56]

For years, the memory of the white-pine experience remained an important motivation for the commercial clubs. The Hannibal Commercial Club sought to avoid readdiction to a single industry by attracting a variety of factories to the city. In 1915, the *Hannibal Morning Journal* published a retrospective article written by a member of the commercial club. The author expressed confidence that the club's policy had succeeded and boasted, "An industrial community that could survive the crash of the one industry period and emerge stronger and more prosperous than ever, will not be required to give any surety bond for the future."[57]

"Till the will of Man hath won"

In addition to providing a focus for economic growth, Keokuk dam also drew attention, and approbation, because of the ways in which it reaffirmed generally held views of the relationship between people and the river. Residents of the "Power Zone" clearly appreciated the beauty and recreational opportunities provided by the river. Their perceptions of the upper Mississippi could be both subtle and multifaceted. However, progress reigned supreme, and, from the vantage point of progress, the upper river was a collection of limitless resources that a hustling technological civilization could exploit to create economic growth and material well-being. Thus, the Keokuk hydroelectric project held out a promise of abundant, cheap power for industrialization. Together with improved navigation, it offered the hope of increased local prosperity. Designation of the area between St. Louis and Burlington as the "Power Zone" and Keokuk as the "Power City" represented a clear recognition of the perceived links between the Des Moines rapids, energy, industrialization, and quality of life.

Progress demanded that resources be used, that they be rendered productive. From this perspective, not to develop the po-

56. "Important Conference in Hannibal," *HMJ*, 18 June 1912, pp. 1, 4.

57. "Low Freight and Power Rates Make It [Hannibal] Manufacturers' Mecca." See also "Annual Meeting of the Hannibal Commercial Club," *HMJ*, 14 February 1913, pp. 1, 3, 6; "The Reports of Secretary Scheidker and Treasurer E. V. Settles of the Commercial Club, 1914, Submitted at the Annual Meeting Last Night," *HMJ*, 29 January 1915, p. 5.

tential energy of the Des Moines rapids was to allow profligate waste. As a contributor to *Independent* boasted in 1913, the Keokuk plant "will furnish sustenance to a million persons—and this new sustenance is developed out of nothing but scenery as surely as would be the discovery of a method for making omelets out of marsh mud."[58]

Because of its use of resources, Keokuk dam became caught up in the conservation movement that developed during the late nineteenth and early twentieth centuries. Therefore, it is important to note that much of the conservation debate that raged in this period focused on use—elimination of waste, coordination of various uses, and rationalization of development. In its 1911 report to the governor, the Iowa State Drainage Waterways and Conservation Commission explained, "Conservation means the wise use of any utility. . .in order to carry out its principles we must *use* these resources which we wish to conserve."[59]

Descriptions of the Keokuk project abounded with martial verbs because people believed themselves to be locked in a struggle for supremacy with the river. The contest pitted a wild, unpredictable, uncontrolled river against the technological order of modern industrial civilization. Keokuk dam infused people with the belief that technology had given them the ability to emerge victorious. A stanza from a poem entitled "The Mississippi Flood," published in the *Keokuk Daily Gate City*, conveys this sense of struggle and optimism:

> Still unconquered, still the monarch
>   Now as thy barren shores,
> From a thousand vassal rivers
>   O'er thy banks the death-tide pours.
> Swerveless as the fixed seasons,
>   Certain as the rising Sun,
> Ye shall 'tempt thy task eternal
>   Till the will of Man hath won.[60]

In the spring of 1912, the Mississippi River Power Company waged a determined struggle against a swollen, ice-clogged river. In order to blast and pour the foundation of the powerhouse, laborers had constructed a cofferdam that enclosed about thirty-five

58. G. Walter Barr, "Water Power for the Million," p. 1427. Barr headed the Mississippi River Power Company's publicity bureau.

59. *Report of the Iowa State Drainage Waterways and Conservation Commission*, p. 109; see also pp. 187–98.

60. Chester Firkin, "The Mississippi Flood," *DGC*, 10 April 1912, p. 4.

acres along the Iowa shore. Abnormally cold temperatures during the winter of 1911–1912 froze the upper midwest. Ice on the river above Keokuk reached thicknesses of up to thirty-two inches. In order to avert disaster when the ice let go in the spring, the company detailed workers to reinforce the cofferdam. On 24 March, the ice broke up with a roar. Great frozen slabs piled up against the cofferdam, crashed back upon the oncoming floe, and backed up the river for half a mile. As the company had predicted, the dam held, but the worst was yet to come. For the next two weeks, sandbag crews fought to stay ahead of rising floodwaters. Once again men bested the river. Victory in this contest added to the general conviction that the Father of Waters had indeed been forced to obey the will of man.[61]

Keokuk dam stimulated considerable regional pride and national patriotic spirit. Tri-state residents thought in terms of "their" dam, a fulfillment of a local historical tradition. People came to the dam to bask in the recognition that it brought to Keokuk and to the entire "Power Zone." Literature on the dam frequently linked its technical accomplishment with national greatness. It stood as a technological "city on a hill," a shining concrete monument to American skill and American superiority. Typical of this sentiment, a writer in the *Iowa Magazine* exclaimed, "American ingenuity had triumphed again." He assured his readers that the Keokuk project was "the most collossal [*sic*] engineering feat ever attempted not only rivalling, but actually surpassing, the ancient pyramids and the sphinx on the Nile."[62]

The unprecedented size of the project and the novelty of electricity drew people to Keokuk. Writing about Keokuk dam for *Scientific American Supplement*, an enthusiastic reporter declared, "The world is always interested in superlatives." In this case, his assessment proved to be true. With their curiosity piqued by the publicity, crowds of people surged into Keokuk to admire the single largest hydroelectric project in the world. Most tours steamed through the Panama Canal–sized lock and enjoyed a short ride on sixty-five-mile-long Lake Cooper.[63] In fact, sheer size was a nearly ubiquitous theme in accounts of the project. Contemporary descriptions abounded with powerful, size-oriented adjectives like

61. For two fairly standard accounts of the cofferdam struggle, see Mississippi River Power Company, "Electric Power from the Mississippi River," *Bulletin number 6* (June 1912):21–29; "Two Hundred Thousand Horse Power," pp. 30–31.
62. Hutchinson, "The Story of a Dream Come True," p. 5.
63. Rogers, "Damming the World's Greatest River," p. 87.

colossal, mammoth, enormous, spectacular, and *massive,* as well as a liberal sprinkling of superlatives—*greatest, largest, longest, highest,* and *boldest.* Of all the project's physical features, size intrigued both the popular and the technical mind. It served to validate the project by making it worthy of the mighty river it had subdued. *Electrical World* informed its largely professional readers, "Only 'the best' seems to have satisfied the builders, and the result is shown in a monumental installation, altogether worthy of the great 'Father of Waters' whose turbid tide it stems."[64]

When the Keokuk powerhouse came on-line in 1913, most residents of the "Power Zone" still regarded electricity as something of a mystery. Showboats churning up and down the river could attract patrons by promising "electrical effects" or a "spectacular Electrical display."[65] Newspapers occasionally printed articles that endeavored to make electricity more understandable. One particularly clever piece in the *Hannibal Morning Journal* asked: "What is a kilowatt?" The story explained,

> It is something you can't see, that you pay for according to what someone tells you who doesn't know what he is talking about and the meter that runs by guess and by thunder and is attached to the wall by a hired man with machine grease on his nose. You know just how many kilowatts you have had, just what they cost you apiece, but you don't know what they are, what they look like, who made them, or what shape they are.[66]

On the scale generated at Keokuk, electricity aroused nothing short of awe. A chance to see the powerhouse provided plenty of incentive for a journey to the work site. Pilgrims to Keokuk who thought beyond the novelty of electricity may have recognized that the project represented an important change in the nation's approach to energy. As they would soon discover, Keokuk dam also played a role in the evolution of the modern, integrated electric industry.

The Energy Context

During the latter half of the nineteenth century, America underwent a dramatic shift from solar energy to fossil fuel. In contrast

64. "The World's Largest Water-Power Plant," p. 1158.
65. Advertisements, *Canton News,* 6 June 1913 and 6 June 1914.
66. "Long Delayed Information," reprinted from the *Greenville* (Tenn.) *Sun, HMJ,* 14 February 1915, p. 4. See also "Why?" *DGC,* 19 February 1913, p. 4.

with solar energy, fossil fuel had fundamentally different attributes—it was nonrenewable, concentrated, constant, and easily stored and transported. In addition, fossil fuel vastly increased the amount of energy available for use and made it possible to own, control, and market energy on a large scale. Thus, the generalized switch to fossil fuel greatly expanded the limits on what people could accomplish. Fossil fuel ushered in a period of revolutionary change in nearly every aspect of life in America. As Henry Adams, a close observer of post–Civil War America, pointedly explained, "The historian needs not much help to measure some kinds of social movement; and especially in the nineteenth century, society by common accord agreed in measuring its progress by the coal output."[67]

While the Keokuk hydroelectric dam was not a fossil-fuel project, it did fit into the pattern of events brought about by the ascendancy of coal. Many Keokuk boosters recognized that progress based upon industrial prosperity required cheap energy in unprecedented amounts. This fact, coupled with a widely held belief that finite coal reserves might soon be depleted, injected a sense of immediacy into the development of waterpower sites such as the Des Moines rapids. In this context, conservation acquired a new shade of meaning: the inexhaustible energy potential of the Des Moines rapids must be used in order that finite coal reserves could be saved. The *Daily Gate City* quoted from a U.S. Geological Survey report that manifested this concern: "Our stock of coal is being rapidly depleted, and the cost of steam power is increasing accordingly. . . .Industrial growth—and, as a consequence, the progress of the United States as a nation, will cease if cheap power is not available. Water power affords the only avenue now open."[68]

Coal provided the energy that allowed Americans to concentrate in rapidly expanding urban and suburban areas. Between 1860 and 1900, the proportion of people living in cities with a population greater than 8,000 more than doubled, rising from 16 to 37 percent. Cities served as laboratories for the development of central power generation, electrical technology, and the phenomenal growth of the electric industry with its ever tightening control over technology, expertise, and capital. By the turn of the century, St. Louis boasted a population of just over 575,000 and had be-

67. Henry Adams, *The Education of Henry Adams*, ed. Ernest Samuels, p. 490; see also pp. 26, 33, 83, 237, 239–40, 330, 379–80, 415, 494, 496.
68. "Offers Cheap Factory Power," *DGC*, 8 April 1913, p. 5.

come the nation's fourth largest city. In 1908, when H. L. Cooper contracted to sell power to St. Louis, Union Electric and United Railways already controlled the electric light, power, and traction business in that city. Both corporations were wholly owned subsidiaries of a holding company called the North American Company. This situation permitted Cooper to take advantage of a fully articulated corporate structure with an aggressive marketing strategy, an integrated distribution system, and a growing demand from domestic and commercial consumers and public utilities.[69]

During the late nineteenth and early twentieth centuries, electricity became a mass production, mass distribution industry monopolized by a decreasing number of increasingly larger firms. Although Keokuk dam had long been considered almost a "birthright" by local people, its existence depended on two of these new electrical combines—the North American Company and Stone & Webster.[70] The North American Company provided a guaranteed annual market that in turn convinced Stone & Webster to finance the project. Both of these corporations chose to protect their investments and expand their spheres of influence by acquiring numerous formerly independent utility companies. Keokuk dam also provided power to the Central Illinois Public Service Company, a subsidiary of Samuel Insull's Middle West Utilities Company. During the 1910s, the Central Illinois Public Service Company was actively engaged in extending its control throughout the southern half of Illinois.

A closer examination of Stone & Webster, the North American Company, and the Middle West Utilities Company provides an opportunity to consider the energy context within which Keokuk dam came into existence. In 1912, the U.S. Bureau of Corporations published a study of waterpower in the United States. The bureau concluded that waterpower development had been characterized by concentration of ownership, interlocks among the leading companies, and affiliation between these corporations and local elec-

69. *Poor's Manual of Industrials* (1910):417–22; "Production and Sale of Electricity in St. Louis."
70. On the electric industry, see "Production and Sale of Electricity in St. Louis"; *Report of the Commissioner of Corporations on Water-Power Development in the United States*; "Unified Public Utilities in Central Illinois"; Thomas P. Hughes, "The Electrification of America: The System Builders"; Hughes, *Networks of Power*; Alfred Chandler, Jr., *The Visible Hand: The Managerial Revolution in American Business*, pp. 309–10, 426–33. For an example of Keokuk dam as a local "birthright," see "Work Is a Product of the People."

tric utilities. The report further noted that Stone & Webster, which had been founded in 1889, had become the second largest controller of developed and undeveloped waterpower in the country. Earlier plans for the Des Moines rapids had run afoul of insufficient private capital and the federal government's unwillingness to invest in waterpower development. With its family of fifty-five to sixty companies, Stone & Webster offered a private alternative to the unwilling federal government.[71]

Stone & Webster's influence followed closely on the heels of its money. In December 1913, four years after Stone & Webster committed itself to financing the Keokuk project, the company formed the Central Mississippi Valley Electric Properties under a trust agreement in Illinois. Managed by Stone & Webster Management Association, this holding company owned the electric light and power businesses in Keokuk, Fort Madison, and Dallas City, the electric light utilities in Hamilton and Warsaw, the gas company in Keokuk, and an interurban railroad that connected Keokuk, Hamilton, and Warsaw. The Mississippi River Power Company, also managed by the Stone & Webster Management Association, held contracts for the sale of electricity to utilities in St. Louis, Keokuk, Fort Madison, Burlington, Quincy, Alton, Hamilton, Warsaw, and Dallas City, and to the Central Illinois Public Service Company, which served a large number of central Illinois towns.[72]

The North American Company, incorporated in June 1890, had by 1909 grown into a large, diversified energy company. Through stock ownership, the North American Company controlled major utilities in Milwaukee and Detroit, a coal company in Kentucky, and a St. Louis County gas company, as well as the Mississippi River Distributing Company, United Railways, and Union Electric. In 1912, the North American Company purchased several St. Louis area utilities in order to provide an additional market for Keokuk electricity and to extend "the range of activity of this company's properties in the St. Louis district."[73] The next year, as part of a continuing effort to consolidate its holdings, Union Electric took over about thirty isolated power stations, including one of the largest independent block plants in St. Louis. The article that reported this last transaction concluded with the observation that

71. *Report of the Commissioner of Corporations on Water-Power Development in the United States*, pp. 1, 22–23, 163–67.
72. *Poor's Manual of Public Utilities* (1914):447–48, 469–70.
73. *Poor's Industrials* (1910):406; *Poor's Manual of Public Utilities* (1913):1450.

Union Electric would soon be supplied with Keokuk hydroelectricity, which would enable it to offer very attractive prices.[74]

The Middle West Utilities Company was established by Samuel Insull and his co-directors in 1912 as a holding company to acquire public utilities, especially in small cities and towns, and to organize state subsidiaries that would actually operate utilities acquired in their respective states. In 1913, the Central Illinois Public Service Company was one of sixteen Middle West subsidiaries located throughout the midsection of the country, Kentucky, and New England. Central Illinois controlled a variety of utilities in the southern half of Illinois that provided electric light and power, heat, gas, and electric street and interurban railway service.[75]

An article in the April 1913 issue of *Electric World* announced that the Central Illinois Public Service Company had begun carrying out an ambitious plan to unify small-town electric utilities in central, western, and southern Illinois. The Middle West subsidiary intended to purchase and replace ninety local electrical plants with a few central stations and a seven-hundred-mile grid of transmission lines that would tie together more than 125 communities. In addition to the takeover and rationalization of Illinois utilities, the plan called for stimulation of demand and load diversification through contracts with coal mines, drainage plants, electric railways, waterworks, and artificial-ice factories. Keokuk electricity facilitated the execution of these plans when Stone & Webster's Mississippi River Power Company contracted to deliver power to a Central Illinois substation located about ten miles east of Hannibal. By February 1917, Central Illinois Public Service Company had become the fifth largest user of Keokuk electricity, with an annual purchase of about 3,000 horsepower.[76]

Throughout this period, electric companies faced a constant problem: how to increase demand and at the same time diversify their load so as more fully to utilize peak winter capacity. One solution that the Central Illinois Public Service Company and other

74. "Block-Lighting Plant Absorbed in St. Louis"; "Extension of Central-Station Service in St. Louis"; "Production and Sale of Electricity in St. Louis."

75. *Poor's Public Utilities* (1914):1517–18, 1520–22.

76. "Unified Public Utilities in Central Illinois," pp. 1146–56; *Poor's Public Utilities* (1914):469–70; U.S. Congress, House, Committee on Rivers and Harbors, *Mississippi River—Impounding of Water Above Keokuk Dam: Hearings on the Subject of House Resolution 468 Directing an Investigation of the Alleged Impounding of Water Above the Dam in the Mississippi River at Keokuk and Its Effect upon the Navigation of the River*, p. 102.

electric utilities settled upon was the electrification of projects for draining wetlands. This tactic deserves examination because it played a direct, though perhaps not immediately apparent, role in the humanization of the environment of the upper river. During the 1910s, drainage of riparian wetlands progressed steadily along the upper Mississippi and Illinois rivers. Groups of farmers divided low-lying wetlands into districts, which they leveed, ditched, and pumped in order to lower the water table enough to permit agriculture.[77] In the early years, steam engines powered most of the pumps, which ran more or less continuously during the spring and early summer months. Once utility executives realized the market potential of drainage districts, they began to promote drainage and the conversion of steam-driven pumps to electrically powered ones.[78]

Encouraged by electric companies for economic and technical reasons, extensive drainage constituted a major alteration of the environment of the upper river, with wide-ranging and unanticipated consequences. Drainage raised flood levels as a result of constriction by levees and contributed to the destruction of overflow and marsh habitat, which had a marked effect on fish and wildlife populations. Drainage projects also frequently failed in their intended purpose of creating prime agricultural land. In an article entitled "Unwise Drainage," the chief of the U.S. Bureau of Biological Survey explained that one-sixth of the 65.5 million acres reported as drained actually proved to be worthless for agriculture. He concluded that this work had been destructive "since a great part of it eliminated water areas which were productive in their natural condition."[79]

Through the sale of power to the Central Illinois Public Service Company and the part it played in the growth and concentration of the electric industry, Keokuk dam contributed to the acceleration of drainage activities. In addition, the Mississippi River Power

77. S. H. McCrory, "The Drainage Movement in the United States," *Separate from Yearbook of the Department of Agriculture, 1918, No. 781,* entry 146, U.S. Agriculture Department, Bureau of Biological Survey, Record Group 22, Records of the Fish and Wildlife Service, National Archives Building, Washington, D.C. (hereafter cited as RG 22, NA.)

78. "Unified Public Utilities in Central Illinois," pp. 1140, 1151–54; "Lazwell Drainage-Pumping Plant"; "Electrical Drainage Pumping"; "Electricity Versus Steam in Drainage Pumping."

79. E. W. Nelson, "Unwise Drainage," *Bulletin of the American Game Protective Association* 13 (January 1924):8–9, 11, entry 146, RG 22, NA; Dilg, "The Drainage Crime of a Century," pp. 570, 600–601, 623.

Company contributed in a more direct manner to the drainage of upper Mississippi River wetlands. A *Daily Gate City* headline in March 1914 announced, "Power from Dam Will Work Pumps." The article revealed that a drainage district located on the Mississippi River near Quincy, Illinois, had contracted to purchase electricity generated at Keokuk dam. The Mississippi River Power Company also participated in the creation of a large drainage district situated north of Fort Madison, Iowa, on land drowned by newly created Lake Cooper. Known as the Green Bay district, this area was drained during the winter of 1917–1918. Undoubtedly, company officials recognized the market potential of such a development. There is also some indication that they wished to head off lawsuits that might have resulted from the inundation of farmland. During the 1910s, people who wrote about the Green Bay drainage district generally characterized it as having enhanced the economic and social value of the hydroelectric project. By the 1920s, however, scientists from the U.S. Bureau of Fisheries had become critical of the Green Bay district for the unintended impact it had had on the ability of the impoundment to sustain fish life.[80]

In 1925, the process of "Power Zone" utility consolidation reached its climax. The North American Company gained control over a vast area from Burlington to St. Louis when it purchased the Mississippi River Power Company and the Central Mississippi Valley Electric Properties from Stone & Webster. By the mid-1920s, Samuel Insull's Middle West Utilities Company had become one of the nation's largest utility holding companies. Middle West had subsidiaries in nineteen states and supplied 8 percent of the commercial power sold in the United States.[81]

The Keokuk hydroelectric project, which evolved out of a local dream for local prosperity, significantly accelerated the ongoing trend of concentration in the electric industry. By 1913 people had

80. "Power from Dam Will Work Pumps," *DGC*, 13 March 1913, p. 5. Indications that the Mississippi River Power Company formed the Green Bay district to head off lawsuits are contained in a petition from residents of Green Bay township to President Taft printed in U.S. Congress, House, Committee on Rules, *The Keokuk Dam: Hearings on H. Res. 390, a Resolution to Authorize and Direct the Committee on Interstate and Foreign Commerce of the House of Representatives to Make an Investigation as to the Keokuk Dam and Conditions Created by It*, p. 28. "The Greatest Thing in All Iowa History," p. 40; Rogers, "Damming the World's Greatest River," p. 90; Robert E. Coker, "Keokuk Dam and the Fisheries of the Upper Mississippi River," p. 116.

81. *Moody's* (1926):1455, 1471–72; Hughes, "The Electrification of America," p. 153.

begun to realize that Keokuk dam would not bring immediate prosperity to the "Power Zone." Their recognition of this fact fueled a sharp conflict that grew directly out of frustrated expectations. This crisis of unrealized expectations represents one of three important responses to the Keokuk project that will be examined in the following chapter.

The Keokuk, Iowa,
Hydroelectric Project
The Unanticipated Consequences
of River Development

Was it not the general opinion . . . that when the dam was completed we would have our light bills cut half in two?—letter to the
editor, *Daily Gate City*, 1913[1]

No where within recent years has attempt been made on such a
stupendous scale to monopolize natural resources of the highest possibilities in public benefits and convert them into a means of private profit. Its exploitation of the people's water power has lessons
for conservation. Its system of interlocked corporations has lessons
for finance as valuable as those of the Frisco.—*St. Louis Post-
Dispatch*, 1913[2]

For the people living around the Des Moines rapids, the work in
the riverbed should have represented the attainment of their special destiny, with electricity serving to extend the radius of prosperity. Yet, after construction started and especially once the project came on-line, the optimism that had united people began to
dissolve in the acids of frustration and anger.

Responses to the unanticipated consequences of this river-
development project took three forms. First, discontent swept the
"Power Zone" as people who had anticipated immediate benefits
from the dam instead found themselves paying the social costs of
development. In addition, concern extended beyond the immediate area. By the fall of 1913, congressional protagonists in a heated
debate over expanded federal waterpower regulation were unsuccessfully attempting to turn this unorganized protest to their own
ends. In this manner, the project became a debating point in the

1. "When Light Comes from the Dam," letter to the editor, *Keokuk* (Ia.) *Daily
Gate City*, 11 April 1913, p. 2 (hereafter cited as *DGC*).
2. "Investigate the Keokuk Grab," editorial, *St. Louis Post-Dispatch*, 24 November 1913, p. 12 (hereafter cited as *St. Louis P-D*).

continuing national discussion over the meaning of conservation. Finally, concern over the potential impact on the commercial fishery prompted the U. S. Bureau of Fisheries to undertake a series of investigations of the new impoundment. The knowledge gained from these studies contributed to a new understanding of the river that attempted to incorporate development and the consequences of development within the context of a complex, interrelated natural system.

Discontent in the "Power Zone"

Prior to the project's dedication in August 1913, recurrent publicity built up and reinforced sanguine expectations. Magazine and newspaper stories gushed with official optimism and drew much of their substance from public-relations material supplied by the Mississippi River Power Company and Keokuk Industrial Association. Both organizations maintained publicity departments. G. Walter Barr, the public-relations agent for the power company, was the author of at least five magazine articles between 1912 and 1914. An inveterate waterpower booster, Barr argued, "The object of all engineering work is the improvement of the country and the advancement of civilization." He predicted that Keokuk dam would meet his criteria by shifting the industrial center of the nation to the Mississippi valley and by attracting 1 million new people to the area served by the dam. In addition to Barr, the Mississippi River Power Company employed an official photographer whose pictures appeared in dozens of magazine articles. Many stories about the dam also drew heavily on a bulletin published by the power company.[3]

A common theme united most of the Keokuk-related literature: the huge hydroelectric project advanced the cause of progress. Never carefully defined, and meaning different things to different people, progress nonetheless had some standard characteristics. Article after article portrayed Keokuk dam as a technical solution

3. G. Walter Barr, "A Water Power of World-Wide Effects," p. 947. See also his "Harnessing the Mississippi to Electric Generators: The Power Achievement of the Century"; "Interesting Details about the Keokuk Dam"; "Water Power for the Million"; and "The Commercial Value of the Keokuk Dam to Iowa and the Mississippi Valley." Mississippi River Power Company, "Electric Power from the Mississippi River," *Bulletin Numbers 1–9* (March 1911–March 1913). The director of the Keokuk Industrial Association's publicity department was Will P. Green. See his "Hugh Lincoln Cooper: The Man Who Built the Keokuk Dam Across the Mississippi."

to a common problem—the quest for economic growth, prosperity, and material well-being. The *Daily Gate City* proclaimed, "This is peculiarly an age of progress on industrial and commercial lines."[4] Other publications echoed this sentiment, arguing that industrial and commercial growth depended on prompt development by private enterprise of natural advantages such as the Des Moines rapids. Repetition of the progress theme helped raise expectations in the "Power Zone" that cities served by the dam would become industrial centers of the Midwest. Close on the heels of the new factories would follow increased population and expansion of the commercial and service sectors of the economy.

By the summer of 1913, "The mighty Mississippi" had indeed "been hitched to the machinery and devices of civilization." It had been "harnessed to obey the commands of man."[5] The technology worked, but many of the expectations that developed in anticipation of the project's completion remained unfulfilled. The ensuing conflict that developed out of the derailment of the Keokuk dream manifested itself in dissatisfaction with the deteriorated quality of life in Keokuk, unhappiness at the failure of new factories to locate in the "Power Zone," anger over the price of power from the dam, frustration by local people over their loss of control, and discontent among river men who believed that navigation had gotten worse below the dam.

By 1912 Keokuk had become an energy boomtown. Opportunities to prosper abounded, but the benefits went largely to the business and commercial community, while others disproportionately paid the social costs. Huge, earth-wrenching, plaster-cracking blasts became a way of life, as did filthy, garbage-strewn streets and alleys, grossly insufficient sewage disposal, overcrowded and inadequate schools, and deplorable public health. Keokuk had a higher tuberculosis mortality rate than Chicago.[6] Real estate

4. "Keokuk and Her Future," *DGC*, 30 August 1912, sec. 3, p. 1. River development for navigation represented an obvious exception to the emphasis on private development.

5. "Power-House for Entire Mississippi," p. 154; F. G. Moorhead, "The Industrial Awakening of the Upper Mississippi," p. 472.

6. "Keokuk Needs a House Cleaning More Than It Needs New Factories," *DGC*, 28 February 1912, pp. 6, 7; "Trades and Labor Counc'l," *DGC*, 3 March 1912, p. 6; "Bombardment of the Blasts," *DGC*, 4 March 1912, p. 5; "Plain Words by Rev. Lilley," *DGC*, 11 March 1912, p. 5; "City News," *DGC*, 28 July 1912, p. 10; "City News," *DGC*, 20 September 1912, p. 8; "Heard About Town," *DGC*, 22 September 1912, p. 7; "Big Blasting Is Completed," *DGC*, 18 October 1912, p. 8; "City News," *DGC*, 13 December 1912, p. 10; "Sad Plight of Young Girl Disclosed," *DGC*, 20

View of the Keokuk dam powerhouse at night, 7 July 1913.

speculation and profiteering on rental property pushed the price of housing beyond the means of the poor and people on fixed incomes. Even for those who had the money, housing was in short supply, and complaints of shoddy construction and neglect indicated that some landlords turned the situation to their own financial advantage. In a letter to the editor, "A Working Man" insisted, "All property owners are not looking to the working man's interest." He then urged the community to "investigate the rotten plumbing and sewer work that is being done right now in the new houses that are being built."[7]

Slum development and crime accompanied the prosperity that had come to Keokuk. The Gate City had its "Rag Alley" populated largely by foreign and black workers. After having toured the tene-

December 1912, p. 8; "Must Decide on Sewer System," *DGC*, 10 March 1913, p. 5; "City News," *DGC*, 25 March 1913, p. 3; "Southern Iowa Editors in Keokuk," *DGC*, 18 July 1913, p. 4; "Safe, Sane, and Sensible Garbage Disposal," letter to the editor, *DGC*, 20 February 1914, p. 7.

7. The working man is quoted in a letter to the editor, *DGC*, 17 December 1912, p. 4. See also "Keokuk Needs a House Cleaning . . ."; "Golden Rule in Practice," *DGC*, 4 December 1912, p. 7; letter to the editor, *DGC*, 9 April 1913, p. 8; "City News," *DGC*, 27 May 1913, p. 3; "How Other Half Lives," *DGC*, 29 March 1914, part 2, p. 5.

ments of Philadelphia, a Keokuk Industrial Association member reported that he had "seen much more filthy and unsanitary dwellings in Keokuk."[8] Crime became epidemic in the city. Daily reports of thefts, assaults, drunkenness, gambling, and prostitution prompted one anguished citizen to express what many of his neighbors probably thought. "What are we going to do? Shall we let this go on or take steps to stop the riot of vice that is so patent to every man who walks the streets at any time of the day."[9]

The majority of Keokuk residents could not financially insulate themselves from the impact of development, and they felt betrayed by official Keokuk, which included the *Daily Gate City*, the Industrial Association, and the city administration. Workers resented the failure of elected officials and the Industrial Association to provide for the needs of ordinary people. At a March 1912 meeting of the Trades and Labor Council, the president of that organization declared that the mayor was "working against the laboring class of people." Another member "took a slap at the Industrial Association when he said it was composed of the so called aristocracy of the city."[10]

Not surprisingly, perceptions of the seriousness of conditions in Keokuk differed according to one's economic position in the community. Official Keokuk recognized that problems existed but tended to be optimistic and to focus on issues like cleaning up the streets, which affected the city's image and reputation. Others had a bleaker view and concentrated on things such as prices and living conditions, which directly affected their daily lives.[11]

Proposed solutions to Keokuk's problems varied in emphasis and

8. The Industrial Association member is quoted in "Worse Houses Here Than City Slums," *DGC*, 18 December 1912, p. 5. See also "No Evidence of Foul Play," *DGC*, 11 April 1912, p. 7; "City News," *DGC*, 18 December 1912, p. 5.

9. "What Are We Going to Do?" letter to the editor, *DGC*, 18 September 1912, p. 4. See also "Stray Negroes on Their Way," *DGC*, 9 July 1912, p. 5; "City News," *DGC*, 14 July 1912, p. 3; "Bunk Houses Are Robbed," *DGC*, 20 August 1912, p. 7; "Chief Says More Men Are Needed," *DGC*, 9 September 1912, p. 5; "Police Court Queer Mixture," *DGC*, 13 September 1912, p. 2; "The Recall," editorial, *DGC*, 22 August 1913, p. 4.

10. "Trades and Labor Counc'l."

11. Perceptions of official Keokuk may be found in "City News," *DGC*, 21 May 1912, p. 8; "City News," *DGC*, 13 December 1912, p. 10; "City News," *DGC*, 18 December 1912, p. 5; and "Southern Iowa Editors in Keokuk." For the bleaker view of other residents of Keokuk, see letter to the editor, *DGC*, 17 December 1912, p. 4; letter to the editor, *DGC*, 9 April 1913, p. 8; "When Light Comes from the Dam"; and "Citizens Meeting Arouses Interest," *DGC*, 8 March 1914, part 1, p. 5.

did not present a critique of the relationship between people and the river or of basic economic and political assumptions. Dissenters demanded a fairer division of material benefits and greater access to opportunity. Undoubtedly a great deal of unrecorded anger existed among Keokuk's working population. When expressed, however, it manifested itself in calls for officials to do their jobs, in statements of opposition, in an insistence on a moral housecleaning, and in a weak 1913 campaign to recall the entire city administration. Commenting on the recall effort, the *Gate City* editorialized, "The movement for the recall is unwise because of the reflection it casts upon the reputation of Keokuk."[12]

Official Keokuk clearly elevated making money above improving civic conditions. Keokuk's administration paid the Industrial Association $18,000 to promote the city but had a hard time coming to terms with a request for sewer construction. The Industrial Association spent $16,500 for a factory park and organized a drive for $75,000 worth of stock to build a new hotel. On the other hand, the association met human problems by forming committees to study them, hiring an expert planner, and holding a city clean-up day.[13] Official Keokuk's point of view was plainly stated in the January 1913 report of the Industrial Association:

> While the improvement of civic conditions is fundamentally the most important business of a commercial organization and in our articles of incorporation is given equal prominence with the securing of new industries, your officers and directors have fully realized that a large majority of those who have so generously supported the association have contributed to its support for the purpose of getting new factories and increasing the population through the influx of factory employees.[14]

Several other factors contributed to a rising level of anger in the "Power Zone." Keokuk and other cities in the area around the Des Moines rapids did not become instant urban industrial centers. The *Burlington Saturday-Evening Post* noted, "Not a single new

12. The *Daily Gate City*'s position is stated in "The Recall." On the subject of dissenters' opinions, see "Trades and Labor Counc'l"; "Plain Words by Rev. Lilley"; "Officials Should Enforce the City Laws or Resign," letter to the editor, *DGC*, 22 September 1912, p. 5; letter to the editor, *DGC*, 17 December 1912, p. 4; and letter to the editor, *DGC*, 9 April 1913, p. 8.

13. "City Planner Nolen Secured," *DGC*, 8 November 1912, p. 2; "[Report] of Manager John De Witt," *DGC*, 21 January 1913, pp. 4–5; "New Industrial Tract Purchased," *DGC*, 2 March 1913, part 2, p. 2; "Must Decide on Sewer System."

14. "[Report] of Manager John De Witt."

factory of consequence has moved into Hannibal or Quincy or Keokuk or Fort Madison or Burlington since the power was turned on." Keokuk also proved unable to achieve the expected sustained economic growth. Very few factories located in the city. Keokuk's population, which briefly swelled to sixteen thousand, had by 1920 returned to the preconstruction level of about fourteen thousand. By the end of 1914, the Gate City's industrial acquisitions stood at two: a small factory that manufactured cement machines and an electric smelter, which had yet to break ground. Throughout 1914, the Industrial Association found it necessary to defend itself publicly, in the face of rising popular scorn and large-scale desertion by its membership.[15]

While an increasingly squalid Keokuk brooded over its inability to lure factories, cries of protest over the price of power echoed from Burlington to St. Louis. The *Burlington Saturday-Evening Post* summed up the situation as seen from the editor's point of view: "All of the newspaper and banquet table talk about the 'cheap power' is the sheerest nonsense. The power is not being sold cheap." Discontent over power rates took three interrelated forms. First, consumers had expected considerably cheaper electricity. When their bills revealed this not to be the case, they felt betrayed. A letter in the *Daily Gate City* asked the key question, "Was it not the general opinion. . .that when the dam was completed we would have our light bills cut half in two?"[16]

Other protesters remembered that the government had granted the dam promoters a free franchise in 1905. They demanded to know why the electric customers, as former owners of the site, had not received the benefits of its development in the form of cheaper rates. The 29 October 1913 edition of the *Hannibal Morning Jour-*

15. *The Saturday-Evening Post* is quoted in U.S. Congress, House, Committee on Rules, *Keokuk Dam: Hearings . . . on H. Res. 390, a Resolution to Authorize and Direct the Committee on Interstate and Foreign Commerce of the House of Representatives to Make an Investigation as to the Keokuk Dam and Conditions Created by It*, p. 86. Keokuk's changing population is mentioned in *Moody's Manual of Investments and Security Rating Service: Public Utility Securities* (1919):794; *Moody's Public Utility Securities* (1926):1471; and "Keokuk Offers Many Advantages," *DGC*, 15 August 1913, part 2, p. 1. For information on Keokuk's industrial acquisitions and the problems faced by the Industrial Association, see "Keokuk Industrial Association Bulletin No. 14," ad, *DGC*, 22 February 1914, p. 5; "Industrial Association Bulletin No. 24," ad, *DGC*, 29 March 1914, part 2, p. 5; and "Officers of Association Reply to Local Critics," *DGC*, 20 January 1915, pp. 4–5.

16. *The Saturday-Evening Post* is quoted in *Keokuk Dam: Hearings*, p. 86; "When Light Comes From the Dam."

nal pointed out, "The government has made a valuable gift to the 'dam' promoters, the advantages of which to the people are not yet discernable [*sic*] to the naked eye."[17]

Finally, St. Louisans complained that they paid an artificially high price for Keokuk electricity. On 19 October 1913, the *St. Louis Post-Dispatch* ran a front-page story under the heading "Big Keokuk Dam Fails to Cheapen Electricity Here." Based upon a reporter's investigation, the paper contended that without government regulation the development would not cheapen St. Louis electric rates for two important reasons. First, the ninety-nine-year contract for 60,000 horsepower linked the price of hydroelectric power to the price of coal. It thereby eliminated competition between the two sources of electrical energy. A. C. Einstein, president of Union Electric, conceded, "The Keokuk current is costing more than the homemade power." The *Post-Dispatch* further blamed the corporate structure that delivered Keokuk energy to St. Louis for unnecessarily inflating the price of the hydroelectric power. The Mississippi River Power Company did not sell its power directly to the St. Louis utilities. Instead, it transmitted electricity from the dam to Florissant, about ten miles from the city, and there sold it for $18 per horsepower to the Mississippi River Distributing Company. The distributing company carried the current to the St. Louis city limits, where Union Electric and United Railways purchased it for $25 per horsepower. Union Electric, United Railways, and the Mississippi River Distributing Company were all subsidiaries of the North American Company. In effect, the North American Company bought the power at Florissant and sold it to itself at the St. Louis city line for a gross annual income of $420,000. This tactic angered St. Louis electric customers.[18]

Much of this discontent reflected a growing awareness that important decision-making authority, which affected employment, heat, light, and power, had been surrendered to Stone & Webster, the North American Company, and Middle West Utilities Company. Loud complaints over high prices, poor service, and heavy-

17. "The Great Power Dam," editorial, *Hannibal* (Mo.) *Morning Journal*, 29 October 1913, p. 4 (hereafter cited as *HMJ*).
18. "Big Keokuk Dam Fails to Cheapen Electricity Here," *St. Louis P-D*, 19 October 1913, pp. 1, 4. "St. Louis and the Keokuk Dam," reprinted from *St. Louis Star*, *HMJ*, 3 March 1915, p. 4.

handedness indicate that many electric customers did not place
the same high value on concentration, efficiency, and load diversification as did these three electric combines.[19]

A May 1913 strike by conductors and motormen who worked for
the Keokuk street railway provides a good example of a confron-
tation that centered around conditions of employment. Stone &
Webster owned the railway, as it did the other utilities in Keokuk.
The employees struck for more pay, shorter hours, and an end to
the "insulting" manner in which the new superintendent, J. P. Ingle, oversaw their collection of fares. Backed by the financial
strength and federal franchise of Stone & Webster, Ingle refused to
acknowledge that the workers objected to the way he supervised
them, and he quickly broke the strike by transferring men from
other Stone & Webster departments.[20]

The complaints directed at Stone & Webster, the North American Company, and Middle West Utilities were part of a larger national transition from entrepreneurial to corporate capitalism. Nationally, the Progressive era witnessed sustained attacks against
"soulless" corporations that put small companies out of business,
ran roughshod over consumers, and usurped decision-making
power that had formerly been exercised by local commercial elites.
Regionally, people in the "Power Zone" were aware of this trend
and its potential economic impact on their communities. An article
in the *Hannibal Morning Journal* urged readers to patronize Hannibal merchants rather than large mail-order houses. In this manner, consumer dollars would remain at home to stimulate the local
economy. The article concluded that healthy Hannibal businesses
would aid the city by paying taxes and license fees and contributing to community development programs.[21]

Empirically, most informed residents of Keokuk recognized that
large corporations had made major advances at the expense of independent, small-town entrepreneurs. Emotionally, these citizens
of post-Victorian America fervently believed in an economy composed of freely competing individuals. Many proponents of the
dam realized that inviting Stone & Webster to town had subjected
the local economy to decisions made in distant boardrooms. Advo-

19. *Keokuk Dam: Hearings*, pp. 72–90, contains newspaper clippings from
"Power Zone" communities.

20. "Street Car Men Keokuk Strike," *HMJ*, 16 May 1913, p. 4; "Walkout of
Street Car Men," *DGC*, 14 May 1913, p. 5.

21. "Patronize Hannibal Merchants," *HMJ*, 17 December 1914, p. 10.

cates of the project tried to reconcile this conflict by arguing that close cooperation with Stone & Webster would allow them to control the corporation to the point that Keokuk would receive its expected benefits. Several factors made this point of view seem plausible. Most important was the presence of Hugh L. Cooper.

Cooper helped many boosters of Keokuk dam settle the clash between their heads and their hearts. Local people admired the chief engineer. He was one of Horatio Alger's self-made men come to life. Cooper represented the classic American story of a man with little formal education who achieved success through his own hard work. He also worked for one of the largest electric power syndicates in the nation. While Cooper remained in Keokuk, he frequently spoke for Stone & Webster in its dealings with the city. On several occasions, he sincerely promised that a big corporation could be a good citizen provided it obeyed the "golden rule." An article in the *Daily Gate City* declared, "His sincerity in this may be measured by the fact, known to everybody around here, that he has constantly been using the golden rule as his controlling guide of action." [22]

Steamboat owners, captains, and pilots, who had expected vastly improved navigation, constituted a final source of dissatisfaction with the dam. Among the factors that disturbed the river men was an administrative ruling that the Corps of Engineers promulgated in 1908, allowing the Mississippi River Power Company to store part of the river's flow at night, in order to meet early morning power demands. [23] This ruling angered river navigators for two reasons. First, because they did not learn of its existence until January 1913, river users reasoned that the decision had been kept secret in an attempt to forestall their objections. The *Hannibal Morning Journal* announced, "River men from St. Louis to St. Paul are excited over the discovery, just made, in regard to the great water project at Keokuk." Second, once the dam began operations, river interests complained that overnight storage, which the power company denied ever doing, caused repeated groundings and de-

22. "Work Is a Product of the People," *DGC*, 30 August 1912, sec. 4, p. 5.

23. *Keokuk Dam: Hearings*, pp. 41–60, contains letters and memoranda from officers and other employees of steamboat companies. See also U.S. Congress, House, Committee on Rivers and Harbors, *Mississippi River—Impounding of Water Above Keokuk Dam: Hearings on the Subject of House Resolution 468 Directing an Investigation of the Alleged Impounding of Water Above the Dam in the Mississippi River at Keokuk and Its Effects upon the Navigation of the River*, pp. 69–72.

lays. In October 1913, C. P. Martin, pilot of the *Dubuque*, contended that storage lowered the river below Keokuk about one and a half feet "and in so doing has caught the steamer *Dubuque* a number of times on the bank" while at the Keokuk landing overnight.[24]

River users also strongly objected to daily fluctuations in the river level below the dam, which they claimed resulted from regular operation of the facility for power generation. Steamboat men suspected the Corps of Engineers of being more sympathetic to the needs of power generation than the requirements of navigation. As a result, irate river men remained unconvinced when the corps conducted tests to prove that routine functioning of the dam did not harm downriver navigation.[25] A final factor convinced navigational interests that the promise of improved navigation had indeed been broken. After construction had already begun, the Keokuk Industrial Association persuaded the Keokuk and Hamilton Water Power Company to span the forebay at the head of the navigation lock, in order to allow use of the dam as a railroad bridge. River men disapproved of this plan on the grounds that the alignment and proximity of the pilings placed in the forebay represented a serious safety hazard.[26]

River users, then, added their voices to those of others who objected to the quality of life in Keokuk, the paucity of new factories, the price of power, and the loss of control. Their disordered cries of protest reverberated from one end of the "Power Zone" to the other. Beginning late in 1913, congressional proponents of a more comprehensive federal waterpower policy attempted to forge these disenchanted interests into an organized, friendly constituency.

The Progressive Era Conservation Movement

While Keokuk dam was still in the planning stage, the issues of waterpower and conservation became united in a multiple-purpose

24. "River Men Planning to Protect Interests of Navigation," *HMJ*, 26 January 1913, p. 1; *Keokuk Dam: Hearings*, p. 52.

25. "River Tests Made at Keokuk, Ia.," *HMJ*, 5 December 1913, p. 1; *Keokuk Dam: Hearings*, pp. 57–60.

26. U.S. Congress, House, Committee on Interstate and Foreign Commerce, *Bridges at Keokuk: Hearings on bills H.R. 26559 and H.R. 26672*, pp. 5–8; *Keokuk Dam: Hearings*, see especially p. 5; "Must Widen Draw Span," *HMJ*, 28 January 1913, p. 1; "Mississippi River Power Company Must Make Changes in Dam and Bridge at Keokuk," *HMJ*, 29 January 1914, p. 1; "New Bridge Authorized at Keokuk," *HMJ*, 6 March 1914, p. 6.

concept developed by conservationists in the Roosevelt administration. In this form, the issues became the subject of an unresolved national conflict that lasted until passage of the 1920 federal
Water Power Act. The fact that Keokuk became embroiled in this
controversy imbued it with historical significance but, at the
same time, practically ensured that local complaints would not be
resolved.

Samuel P. Hays's *Conservation and the Gospel of Efficiency,* the
best existing analysis of the Progressive-era conservation movement, provides a good starting point in an effort to place the Keokuk project into a larger conservation context. Hays dates the Progressive conservation movement as extending from 1890 to 1920
and argues that it was neither of popular origin nor an attack
against private corporations. Instead, he characterizes it as a "scientific movement" orchestrated by a small group of professionals
who held appointive positions within the executive branch. They
shared a deep faith in applied science and advocated rationally
planned, efficient resource development that would provide the
"greatest good for the greatest number." These scientists and technicians equated the greatest good (in terms of national or social
progress) with economic growth and a rising material standard of
living—goals attainable through the application of science and
technology to the nation's tremendous resource base. They further
believed resource management to be a complicated task that
should be handled administratively by experts like themselves
operating within general congressional guidelines.[27]

Hays asserts that federal interest in conservation began with the
planning of reclamation projects designed to promote family farms
in the arid West. He dates the beginning of government involvement to a water-resource investigation authorized by Congress in
1888. Thereafter, mutually attracted by the idea of efficiency, government hydrographers and foresters united to promote reclamation and scientific forestry. From this beginning, conservationists
turned their attention to range management, other public land resources, and finally to multiple-purpose river-basin development.
As the Roosevelt conservation program evolved, it developed proposals designed to promote wise use, such as federal ownership of

27. The analysis in this and the next four paragraphs is based upon material from
Samuel P. Hays, *Conservation and the Gospel of Efficiency: The Progressive Conservation Movement, 1890–1920,* pp. 3, 22, 60–65, 71–81, 90–105, 122–23, 127,
133–38, 261–76.

natural resources, a limited-duration lease to block speculation, and a user fee designed as a control measure and as a means of raising revenue.

The multiple-purpose concept can be traced to two dissimilar ancestors. First, waterway organizations, such as the Upper Mississippi River Improvement Association and the Lakes-to-the-Gulf Deep Waterway Association, provided an enthusiastic, dedicated constituency for river development. Spearheaded by merchants and manufacturers from Chicago and St. Louis, business interests from the Mississippi River valley formed the Deep Waterway Association in 1906 to lobby for federal funding of a fourteen-foot channel from Chicago to New Orleans via the Illinois and Mississippi rivers. Second, conservation leaders in the Roosevelt administration had already started to think of rivers as one resource with many uses. Efficient development required that engineering works be created to accommodate more than one use. They had also begun to conceive of rivers in basin-wide terms that necessitated federal, rather than local or state, management. WJ McGee, the "geologist, anthropologist, philosopher" who was regarded as "the chief theorist of the conservation movement," brought these two groups together.

Raised in Dubuque County, Iowa, McGee, like Hugh L. Cooper, learned his science at the school of experience. Between 1903 and 1907 he served as head of the St. Louis Museum, a position to which he brought impressive credentials as a scientist, thinker, and organizer. McGee had been a former member of the U.S. Geological Survey, head of the federal Bureau of Ethnology, and a founder of the National Geographic Society. He was elected to a one-year term as president of the National Geographic Society in 1904.

While in St. Louis, McGee became actively involved with river-development enthusiasts, in particular a businessmen's organization known as the Latin American Club. Members of the club viewed improvement of the Mississippi, in conjunction with the future Panama Canal, as a way to enhance the commercial fortunes of St. Louis (and presumably themselves) through trade with the Southwest, Latin America, and the Orient. By 1906, McGee had become a spokesman for the Latin American Club. In that year, the club appointed him a delegate to the first meeting of the Lakes-to-the-Gulf Deep Waterway Association.

McGee's vision of river development transcended the limited

goals of the Lakes-to-the-Gulf Association. He thought boldly in terms of "artificializing" and controlling entire river systems and recorded these views in a 1907 article that focused on the multiple-purpose potential of the Mississippi River. He argued that the Mississippi had two significant characteristics. It was "as lawless as a monster of the jungle and not yet brought under human control," and it was composed of interrelated parts arranged into an interdependent system.[28]

McGee saw the river as composed of physical characteristics— a "self-moving" body of fluid that could float a vessel, transport silt, erode and deposit, and fluctuate in level. Successful, complete development, therefore, required the cooperation of scientists from various disciplines who could, through the application of their combined expertise, tame the river by bringing all its interdependent parts under at least partial control. Full, efficient utilization also necessitated that engineering works be integrated into a multiple-purpose development. For McGee, and for others who shared this perspective, single-purpose engineering works seemed wasteful and inadequate in the face of a wild, uncontrolled river.[29] Therein lay the seeds of conflict with the Army Corps of Engineers.

McGee's theory called for the use of applied science to transform natural rivers into efficient, productive, controlled systems. Efficient use directed toward the pragmatic objective of enhanced material progress formed the core of the multiple-purpose concept. Efficiency had certain standard characteristics: the fullest possible use of natural resources, elimination of waste in resource development, faith in science rationally applied to resource exploitation, and centralized planning directed by experts seeking to promote their vision of the common good. McGee and other Roosevelt conservationists thought of the general welfare in terms of material prosperity and national manifest destiny. Writing about his contemplated multiple-purpose development of the Mississippi River, McGee declared, "The end is the manifest destiny of North America."[30]

Roosevelt conservationists also saw themselves as leaders of the

28. WJ McGee, "Our Great River: What It Is and May Be Made for Commerce, Agriculture, And Sanitation—The Largest Inland Project of Our Time," pp. 8579–80.
29. Ibid., pp. 8579–84.
30. Ibid., p. 8584. See also Hays, *Conservation and the Gospel of Efficiency*, pp. 122–27; Gifford Pinchot, *The Fight for Conservation*, chap. 4; WJ McGee, "Water as a Resource," pp. 521–23.

contemporary movement to foster efficiency in every phase of life. Gifford Pinchot, head of the U.S. Forest Service and probably the best known of the Roosevelt conservationists, clearly articulated the potential social significance of the conservation movement:

> The outgrowth of conservation, the inevitable result, is national efficiency. In the great commercial struggle between nations which is eventually to determine the welfare of all, national efficiency will be the deciding factor. So from every point of view conservation is a good thing for the American people.[31]

McGee advocated the creation of a presidential waterways commission as a first step toward redirecting the federal river policy along multiple-purpose lines. In January 1907, his plan gained important support when the Corps of Engineers issued an unfavorable report on the fourteen-foot-deep waterway advocated by the Lakes-to-the-Gulf Deep Waterways Association. River improvement boosters in the association and in St. Louis businessmen's organizations threw their support behind a presidential commission as the best way to circumvent the hostile corps. On 10 February 1907, McGee left St. Louis bearing petitions that asked President Roosevelt to appoint such a commission. At an early March meeting, he presented his petitions to a president already receptive to the multiple-purpose concept. Shortly thereafter, Theodore Roosevelt appointed the Inland Waterways Commission with McGee as secretary, charging it to conduct its investigation along multiple-purpose lines.[32]

Early in 1908, President Roosevelt received the commission's report, with the only dissenting voice coming from commission member Brig. Gen. Alexander Mackenzie, chief of the Army Corps of Engineers. Shortly before completion of the final report, Sen. Francis Newlands of Nevada, another commission member, took the first step in a long and ultimately unsuccessful struggle to persuade Congress to develop the nation's rivers along multiple-purpose lines. Newlands introduced a bill that would have created a permanent, presidentially appointed agency with the authority to plan, authorize, and supervise construction of projects. Congress would have financed the commission's work by setting up an

31. Pinchot, *The Fight for Conservation*, p. 50.
32. The material on the national debate over conservation and waterpower in this and the next three paragraphs is from Hays, *Conservation and the Gospel of Efficiency*, pp. 81, 102–46, 175–98, 208–30, 271–76.

inland water fund of $50,000,000 that the president could replenish whenever the balance fell below $20,000,000. The commission could have used this fund as it saw fit without having to ask Congress for annual authorizations.

For over ten years, Congress wrestled with one form or another of the Newlands bill and the multiple-purpose concept it embodied. The Army Corps of Engineers actively opposed Newlands's proposal and officially denied the efficacy of the multiple-purpose concept. Corps officials saw multiple-purpose use as a threat to the primacy of navigation, to their close working relationship with Congress, and to their administrative autonomy. This stand placed the corps in opposition to the Forest Service, the Geological Survey, and the Reclamation Service. Sensitive to the issue of states' rights and jealous of its authority to act on individual projects, Congress opted for logrolling in place of the rationalized approach advocated by Senator Newlands. Not until 1917 did both houses approve an attenuated version of the commission proposed by Newlands, limiting its powers to investigation. The Army Corps of Engineers, however, capitalized on the exigency of World War I and easily blocked appointment of the nearly powerless commission.

Hydroelectricity played an important part in the plans of Roosevelt conservationists: it was to be the financial keystone of the multiple-purpose structure. The conservationists reasoned that the sale of power would provide the revenue to finance river development independent of continuous congressional appropriations. By the spring of 1908, President Roosevelt had worked out a set of criteria that waterpower bills would have to meet in order to receive his signature. He insisted that franchises would have to provide for a user fee, rate regulation, and a limited duration, recoverable grant. Thus capacious, perpetual franchises such as the Keokuk concession of 1905 would henceforth be subject to his veto. Yet Roosevelt's waterpower policy met no greater success in Congress than did Newlands's proposed waterways commission.

By 1912 Congress had become as deadlocked over waterpower as it had over multiple-purpose river-basin development. This impasse brought a hiatus to hydroelectric development in navigable rivers, including a plan to build a Keokuk-type project at the foot of the Rock Island rapids. In the spring of 1912, Rep. Irvin Pepper of Iowa introduced a bill in the House that authorized construction of a power dam just below the rapids near Davenport, Iowa. Excitement flared briefly in Davenport only to be doused by the determined opposition of Secretary of War Henry L. Stimson and Rep. Henry T. Rainey of Illinois. Both men objected to waterpower bills that contained sweeping privileges of the sort granted at Keokuk. After years of congressional conflict, the Water Power Act of 1920 again permitted construction, but in so doing it divorced hydroelectric projects from a more comprehensive multiple-purpose program.[33]

The Water Power Act of 1920 marked the end of the Progressive-era conservation movement. Its ultimate failure, however, lay in the inability of Roosevelt conservationists to forge a constituency from among the nation's disparate resource-user groups. The concept of multiple-purpose development offered little to attract single-purpose organizations such as the National Rivers and Harbors Congress or the Upper Mississippi River Improvement Association. Further, the emphasis on administrative planning and control by experts cut across the pluralism that was rapidly developing in the American political system. True to these generalizations, the gospel of efficiency made few converts among the proponents of Keokuk dam. Most advocates of the project thought of conservation as almost interchangeable with use. They argued that to conserve the Des Moines rapids it was necessary to use them and thereby prevent the waste of their potential energy. From this perspective, federal regulations that mandated coordinated development, user fees, or limited-duration leases were undesirable because they slowed the rate of exploitation and thereby discouraged use.

Conservation defined in this manner served as both a justification for and a defense of the Keokuk project. Maj. Montgomery Meigs, the army engineer in charge of the river at Keokuk, included this widely held point of view in an impassioned defense of the dam. Meigs argued, "Congress authorized this because it was seen to be a conservation of something going to waste and valuable to the whole of this country. It is saving right now a thousand tons of coal daily."[34] As a general rule, people in the "Power Zone" be-

33. For information on the proposed dam near Davenport, see "Davenport Has the Dam Fever," *DGC*, 7 April 1912, p. 14; "Davenporters at Keokuk Dam," *DGC*, 7 May 1912, p. 7; "Davenport Dam Strikes a Snag," *DGC*, 24 May 1912, p. 3; "Davenport Dam Has Been Blocked," *DGC*, 16 July 1912, p. 8; "Davenport Dam Being Pushed," *DGC*, 2 March 1914, p. 7.

34. Major Meigs is quoted in "Dam Not Harmful to Navigation, Says Meigs," *DGC*, 16 October 1913, p. 4. See also "First Missouri River Harnessed to Make Electricity," *St. Louis P-D*, Sunday Magazine, 14 December 1913, p. 6; "The White Coal Age," *HMJ*, 25 November 1913, article reprinted from the *Burlington Hawkeye*, p. 4; "More Dams to Be Constructed," *HMJ*, 8 December 1912, section

lieved the Keokuk dam to be a conservation measure. When conflict broke out in 1913, it had far more to do with unrealized economic expectations than with unattained conservation goals.

A National Conservation Issue

A dramatic reversal of editorial position by the *St. Louis Post-Dispatch* brought the Keokuk situation to the attention of a Congress already stalemated over water resources policy. Before the bills for Keokuk power began to come due, the *Post-Dispatch* published several stories that flattered the undertaking and spoke favorably of its potential impact on the city's economic future. A June 1913 editorial considered the significance of "cheap power, available in enormous quantities." In this context, it described the transmission lines as "a route over which gold will flow into the city . . . an avenue for the entrance of new opportunities." Keokuk electricity became available to St. Louis customers during the third week of July. Three months later, the *Post-Dispatch* published a report on its investigation of rates charged for the electricity. The paper now accused the North American Company of monopolizing the fruits of the river's labor while neither gold nor opportunity accrued to the people of St. Louis.[35] Metropolitan electric users who agreed with this point of view quickly brought the rate situation to the attention of Congress.

In October and November 1913, two St. Louis groups cited the *Post-Dispatch's* findings when they formally called for federal involvement. One of those organizations was the People's League, which had come into existence in the midst of a bitter fight over a new St. Louis city charter. In January 1911, a coalition of labor organizations and Progressive civic groups formed the People's League to defeat the charter at the polls. Organizers believed that the charter represented the interests of corporations at the expense of citizen participation and the needs of workers. After a one-month voter-mobilization campaign, the league won an overwhelming victory on election day.[36] During the fall of 1913, revela-

2, p. 1; "Father of Waters to Work," *DGC*, 21 March 1912, article reprinted from *Santa Ana* (Calif.) *Register*, p. 4; "Saving the Fuel of the Nation," *DGC*, 21 June 1912, article reprinted from *Scribners*, p. 4; "Work Is a Product of the People."

35. "Keokuk Dam's Completion," editorial, *St. Louis P-D*, 9 June 1913, p. 10; "Big Keokuk Dam Fails to Cheapen Electricity Here."

36. On the origins of the People's League, see *St. Louis Labor*, 7 January 1911, p. 1, and 14 January 1911, p. 1; and "Organized Labor's Glorious Victory in Anti-Charter Battle," *St. Louis Labor*, 4 February 1911, p. 1.

tions about the sale of Keokuk electricity to St. Louis brought the People's League back to life. The league sent letters to three St. Louis-area representatives seeking an investigation of the original franchise, the construction and operation of the project, and the price of power. League members wanted to know why rates had not been set low enough "to give material benefits to the people" served by the dam. The league also filed a complaint with the Missouri Public Service Commission in conjunction with the United Engineers' Association and the Engineers' Incitation Club.[37]

The second group calling for federal involvement was the Progressive Party Club of St. Louis. At its November meeting, the club unanimously passed resolutions denouncing the Mississippi River Power Company and the North American Company. The club forwarded these resolutions to two Progressive congressmen, Sen. Miles Poindexter of Washington and Rep. Victor Murdock of Kansas, for presentation to both houses of Congress. St. Louis Progressives condemned false advertising by the Mississippi River Power Company, which had promised that hydroelectricity would be cheaper than steam-generated power. They censured the contract that tied the price of Keokuk electricity to the cost of coal. The Progressives further accused these two corporations of "violating a moral obligation," "betraying a public trust," and "usurping the God-given rights of the people" by creating subsidiaries that practiced extortion, by exercising arbitrary authority, and by agreeing not to compete within a thirty-mile radius of St. Louis. St. Louis's Progressive Party Club appealed for an investigation of its charges and legislation that would better regulate private development of publicly owned waterpower sites.[38]

Congressional reaction followed swiftly but ultimately proved ineffective because the issue involved much more than regional dissatisfaction. Congressmen responded as a result of pressure from "Power Zone" voters and also because some of them recognized that the Keokuk situation provided a new twist to a continu-

37. Information on the league's protest of electric rates may be found in "Inquiry in Keokuk Dam Rates by Congress Asked," *St. Louis P-D*, 23 October 1913, p. 7; and "Getting After Keokuk Dam," *HMJ*, 25 October 1913, p. 1. See also "Union Electric Rates Not Unfair," *Canton News*, 7 May 1915; "Service Board Reverses Self," *Canton News*, 22 October 1915.

38. The Progressives' changes are detailed in U.S. Congress, Senate, "Keokuk Dam Co. and North American Co.," Senator Poindexter introduces the Progressive Party Club's resolutions, p. 5962. See also "Progressives to Ask Investigation of Keokuk Dam Co.," *St. Louis P-D*, 28 October 1913, p. 6; "Progressives Ask Investigation of Keokuk Dam Rates," *St. Louis P-D*, 11 November 1913, p. 13.

ing debate over federal waterpower policy. On 30 October 1913, Richard Bartholdt became the first St. Louis representative to declare that he would ask for a congressional inquiry into the rates charged for Keokuk power. In a letter to the People's League, Bartholdt stated, "If the company has not kept its promises as to prices there must be found some authority that can bring them to terms." The specific authority he envisioned was that of the secretary of war. He therefore drafted and introduced a bill that conferred the power to regulate the price of Keokuk electricity upon the secretary of war.[39]

At the end of November 1913, St. Louis Rep. William Igoe submitted a bill that would have empowered the Interstate Commerce Commission to regulate "corporations engaged in interstate business of generating, furnishing and transmitting electricity." Although Igoe's bill was aimed directly at the Mississippi River Power Company, Igoe regarded it as a first step in extending federal control over the interstate sale of electricity. Congressman Igoe had originally thought in terms of a far more comprehensive solution—a federal public service commission with nationwide regulatory authority over waterpower sites and other publicly owned resources. He narrowed the scope of his proposal because he realized that a broadly conceived waterpower bill would be doomed in a Congress badly divided over conservation-related issues.[40]

Late in November 1913, Senator Poindexter introduced the resolutions adopted by the Progressive Party Club of St. Louis and vowed to press for an investigation of Keokuk electric rates. He declared his intention to use the dam as "an object lesson in my fight against the water power monopoly" and an illustration of the inadequacies of existing federal law as it applied to waterpower development.[41]

39. Representative Bartholdt is quoted in "Bartholdt to Ask Congress to Act on Keokuk Rates," *St. Louis P-D*, 30 October 1913, p. 10. See also "Bartholdt to Ask Congress to Act on Keokuk Rates," *St. Louis P-D*, 27 November 1913, p. 1; "Bill Aimed at Keokuk Water Power," *DGC*, 28 November 1913, p. 2; "Bill Offered to Fix Power Rate," *DGC*, 1 December 1913, p. 7.

40. "Igoe Introduces Bill to Regulate Keokuk Dam," *St. Louis P-D*, 30 November 1913, part 1, p. 11. See also "Bill Offered to Fix Power Rate"; "Igoe Bill Would Give US Control of Keokuk Dam," 2 November 1913, *St. Louis P-D*, part 4, p. 12.

41. "Senate Investigation of Keokuk Dam to Be Asked," *St. Louis P-D*, 21 November 1913, p. 1. Further information on Senator Poindexter's position on Keokuk dam may be found in "Poindexter Opens Senate Fight on Keokuk Dam Rate," *St. Louis P-D*, 22 November 1913, p. 1; "Investigate the Keokuk Grab," *St. Louis P-D*, 24 November 1913, p. 12.

The efforts of Representatives Bartholdt and Igoe and Senator Poindexter met quiet deaths in committee. Two other congressmen, William C. Adamson of Georgia and Henry Rainey of Illinois, put up a greater struggle before their proposals, too, became casualties of the waterpower debate. Representatives Rainey and Adamson occupied opposing positions in the controversy over water resources policy. Rainey thought of himself as a conservationist, and that title fit in the sense that he favored many aspects of the Roosevelt conservation program. He particularly championed federal regulation of waterpower development. Adamson, on the other hand, could not have qualified as a conservationist except under the broadest interpretation of the word: he favored use. Adamson considered conservationists of Rainey's type obstructionists. He believed that turning the waterpower sites over to private developers with minimal regulation best served the public interest. Both of these men, and others who shared their points of view, attempted to use the crisis of unrealized expectations as an opportunity to rectify what they saw as shortcomings in federal waterpower policy.

Five days before Christmas 1913, Rainey became the final member of Congress to respond directly to the Keokuk situation when he sponsored a House Resolution that called for an investigation of the Mississippi River Power Company. He asserted that the dam had proved to be a hindrance to navigation, had fostered a concentration of electric utilities, and had resulted in higher electric prices for less than efficient service. Rainey wanted an investigation that would determine whether the 1905 franchise should be repealed or amended to allow for a financial return to the national government and for federal regulation of power rates.[42] Congressman Rainey proved to be the most persistent of any of the big dam's critics. Between 1913 and 1917, he introduced three resolutions that requested investigations of the Keokuk situation. Two of his resolutions resulted in hearings before the House Rules Committee in April 1914 and the Rivers and Harbors Committee in February 1917. He also introduced a bill to amend the General Dam Act in order to provide for greater federal regulation in the development of waterpower sites.[43]

42. "U.S. May Investigate Keokuk Dam," *HMJ*, 20 December 1913 p. 1; "Attacking the Keokuk Monopoly," *St. Louis P-D*, 21 December 1913, p. 2; "Keokuk Dam Up for Discussion," *DGC*, 21 December 1913, part 2, p. 2.

43. U.S. Congress, Henry T. Rainey, 63d Cong., 2d sess., *Congressional Record*, 51:Index; U.S. Congress, House Resolution 468, 64th Cong., 2d sess., *Congressional Record*, 54:Index.

In December 1913, the *Daily Gate City* reported that some members of Congress had in mind a revision of the General Dam Act. Passed in 1906 and amended in 1910, this act established the conditions under which dams could be constructed across navigable streams. The article quoted William C. Adamson, chairman of the House Committee on Interstate and Foreign Commerce, as saying, "The development of the Keokuk enterprise . . . seems to bring the water power question to a head."[44]

Throughout the fall and winter of 1913–1914, Adamson's committee considered several bills, including those of Representatives Bartholdt and Rainey, which called for closer federal regulation of waterpower concessions.[45] Then, on 27 April 1914, the committee approved and sent to the full House H.R. 16053, a bill to amend the General Dam Act. H.R. 16053 reflected Adamson's position in favor of private development with minimal regulation. When introduced into an already polarized House, the Adamson committee bill touched off a debate that raged on and off for months and occupied several hundred pages of the *Congressional Record*. This controversial piece of legislation was ultimately passed by the House and rejected by the Senate. In the process, however, the complaints of disgruntled individuals in the "Power Zone" were absorbed into the larger issues and then disregarded.[46]

The House debate over the Adamson committee bill provides an opportunity to contrast the attitudes of the contestants and to illustrate the relationship of Keokuk to the national conservation controversy. In a probable attempt to sidestep thornier issues, apologists for H.R. 16053 presented it as chiefly a navigation bill. They argued that profits from the sale of hydroelectricity would lure private capital to construct dams and simultaneously to improve navigation without expense to the federal treasury.[47] The issues that

44. "Government May Fix Power Rates," *DGC*, 10 December 1913, p. 5.

45. "Congressmen See Keokuk Dam; Rate Inquiry Is Next," *St. Louis P-D*, 13 January 1914, p. 3; U.S. Congress, Richard Bartholdt, 63d Cong., 1st sess., *Congressional Record*, 50:Index; U.S. Congress, Keokuk Water, Power, Henry T. Rainey, 63d Cong., 2d sess., *Congressional Record*, 51:Index.

46. U.S. Congress, House, General Dam Act, debate over H.R. 16053, 63d Cong., 2d sess., 27 April 1914–5 August 1914, *Congressional Record*, 51:7350, 7404, 7598, 11068–71, 11401–5, 11413–32, 12283–84, 12328–40, 12406–8, 12568–99, 12657–716, 12748–78, 12892–12909, 13016–41, 13237–76 (appendix 767), 13296; Hays, *Conservation and the Gospel of Efficiency*, p. 81. Hays states that passage by the House and rejection by the Senate was the typical pattern for waterpower bills at the time.

47. "Bill to Construct Dam Across Navigable Waters," *Congressional Record*, 51:7350, 11069, 11403–4, 11417, 11421–22.

soon dominated the debate proved that the House considered H.R. 16053 to be both a waterpower and a conservation bill.

Rep. Irvine Lenroot of Wisconsin, an opposition speaker, pointedly stated, "The bill before us, both in its present form and with the amendments proposed, is a water-power bill in fact." Lenroot characterized Chairman Adamson as "utterly opposed to the ideas and policies of the conservationists." He blamed the anticonservationist federal policy of the not-too-distant past for reckless, criminal waste of natural resources and their monopolization by private interests. Congressmen like Lenroot who spoke against the bill usually identified themselves as conservationists. These men expressed concern lest poorly written legislation deny future generations their resource legacy. They warned that they could not support H.R. 16053 unless it was amended to include rate regulation, financial return to the government through user fees, and a limited-duration, recoverable lease.[48]

Advocates, on the other hand, believed that the regulatory hand of government should rest lightly on private capital. Adamson and other defenders of H.R. 16053 adhered to the traditional nineteenth-century point of view that government could best foster material progress by creating opportunities for individuals to prosper through the transfer of public resources to the private sector. Proponent Oscar Underwood contended that true conservation required that the commercial potential of resources be used. He reminded his colleagues, "For seven years Congress has continued its debate upon this question, and while we talk about the conservation of our waterpower resources other countries build dams and conserve their water powers, while ours go on to waste."[49]

Champions of the Adamson committee bill denounced House conservationists for frustrating progress by blocking waterpower development. In an obvious reference to conservationists, Adamson sarcastically stated, "Certain patriotic and benevolent persons, whose motives were no doubt good . . . raised objections which have retarded progress" by discouraging investment in hydroelectric plants.[50]

Keokuk dam was definitely on the House's mind, and both sides took advantage of the Keokuk situation to bolster their cases. Chairman Adamson turned to Keokuk as an example of the diffi-

48. Ibid., 51:12328,33; see also 11424–26, 11429–32, 12328–34, 12568–70:
49. Ibid., 51:12338.
50. Ibid., 51:11069; see also 11068–70, 11417–24, 12334–38.

culties involved in attracting private capital "to do this important work for us free of cost." Adamson promised that H.R. 16053 would make waterpower a more attractive investment.[51] Foes of the bill used the widespread unrest in the "Power Zone" to illustrate the evils of free, perpetual, Keokuk-type waterpower concessions. Victor Murdock of Kansas told the House that ever since completion of the project the area served by the dam had been "in revolt" against the excessive rates charged for hydroelectricity. Murdock informed his listeners that his mail as well as that of "every other Member of this House has been filled at times with protests against the exactions of that company which enjoyed its great grant free of charge."[52]

Despite obvious divisions, House debate also revealed a broad area of agreement between the opponents and the advocates of H.R. 16053. Congressional prerogative was not an issue. By unspoken agreement a majority of House members preferred logrolling rather than surrendering the right to act on each franchise to an administrative resource agency. Disagreements over river development also took place within a larger framework of accord. In this case, Congress reflected attitudes toward the upper Mississippi expressed in "Power Zone" newspapers. Representatives aligned on both sides of H.R. 16053 placed overwhelming emphasis on material progress. Discussion focused on how to develop the commercially exploitable qualities of rivers. Multiple-purpose conservationists advocated the coordination of uses, rationalization of the conflict with nature, and control of entire river basins. Opponents had no quarrel with the concepts of use, rationalization, and control, their differences being matters of emphasis and degree. Both sides also viewed river improvement as largely a technical problem, and both sides were confident they knew enough to manipulate river environments to their own ends.

Changes in the Life of the River

Conservation had a somewhat different meaning for scientists in the U.S. Commerce Department's Bureau of Fisheries than it did for most participants in the congressional waterpower debate. These fisheries experts thought in terms of managing the production of useful species. From this perspective, they recognized that

51. Ibid., 51:11417–18, 11421; see also 11426, 12335–36.
52. Ibid., 51:11429–30; see also 11431–32, 12329, 12331.

the Keokuk impoundment could have a potentially serious though as yet unknown impact on the fish life in the river. Their attempt to understand the conditions created by the dam represented another important response to the Keokuk hydroelectric project.

In 1913, Robert E. Coker, director of the bureau's Biological Station at Fairport, Iowa, published a preliminary investigation of Lake Cooper. He began his report in predictable fashion by praising the project as "an epoch in man's utilization of the greatest North American river." Coker interested himself primarily in commercially exploitable fish and mussel resources, and he justified concerns over the dam in terms of the present and future economic value of the river fishery. Coker suggested two scenarios in which the waterpower development could have a major impact on the fishery of the upper river. On the one hand, the dam might have a negative influence by shutting off the upstream passage of migratory fish. On the other hand, the project could be of significant benefit by artificially creating shallow overflow areas that favored the propagation of useful fish life. On balance, Coker saw Lake Cooper as a tremendous opportunity for fish culture. After conceding that waterpower should not be "sacrificed to fisheries," he argued that it would be shortsighted not to consider ways to minimize possible damage and to enhance potential benefits.[53]

Although Coker's report had much in common with the great body of literature on Keokuk, it differed in several important ways, thereby establishing lines of inquiry that matured in the 1920s. Undoubtedly because of his professional interest in fish and mussel life, Coker's investigation focused on new habitat conditions created by the dam and their direct and indirect effects on the river fishery.[54] Coker's article thus joined at least one other in raising questions about the long-range consequences of damming the river. On 15 July 1913, the *Hannibal Morning Journal* reported that J. A. S. Ebert, who resided in a summer home overlooking the Mississippi, had noticed a remarkable decrease in the river's current since the construction of the dam. The brief story concluded with a subtle and atypical observation:

> The building of the great power dam at the foot of the Des Moines rapids and the subsequent forming of great Cooper lake are produc-

53. Robert Coker, "Water-Power Development in Relation to Fishes and Mussels of the Mississippi," *U.S. Bureau of Fisheries Annual Report With Appendixes, 1912/13*, pp. 5–6; see also pp. 1–29.
54. Ibid., pp. 6–10.

ing changes in the very life of the old Mississippi which are being watched with interest by her lovers and which few now are able to predict in their ultimate results.[55]

Coker's report stands out in other ways as well. He assumed that not enough information existed to permit either the full conservation (utilization) of fish and mussels or a complete understanding of the impact of waterpower development on river fisheries. Coker saw the creation of Lake Cooper as an opportunity for systematic, long-term studies that would augment the inadequate existing knowledge. He maintained that such studies might supply information upon which to base decisions concerning future river development.[56] Studies of the Keokuk impoundment did, in fact, play an important role in the planning of the nine-foot navigation channel constructed in the 1930s.

After 1913, the Bureau of Fisheries maintained a commitment to the study of the upper river and of the conditions created by the dam. Statistical studies revealed that the commercial fish harvest from the Keokuk impoundment peaked in 1917 and thereafter began a long downward slide that reached bottom in the early 1930s. In 1917, the total catch equaled about 1.8 million pounds, while in 1930 fishermen reported taking slightly less than 242,000 pounds. Before construction of the dam, a thriving mussel fishery in the Des Moines rapids had supplied huge numbers of shells to the pearl-button industry. After the creation of Lake Cooper, the mussel fishery soon ceased to exist.[57]

Two reports by scientists in the bureau published during the late 1920s and early 1930s drew upon and added to the growing body of knowledge about the upper river. These articles also give some insights into the bureau's attitudes toward the use and development

55. "Changes in the Mississippi," *HMJ*, article reprinted from the *Fort Madison* (Ia.) *Gem City*, 15 July 1913, p. 2.

56. Coker, "Water-Power," pp. 22–25.

57. Fishery statistics are available in the annual reports of the Bureau of Fisheries. See, for example, "Fisheries of the Mississippi River and Tributaries," *U.S. Bureau of Fisheries Annual Report With Appendixes, 1931* (Washington, D.C.: GPO, 1931), pp. 522–34. The 1931 *Report* is especially useful because it provides data for 1914, 1917, 1922, and 1927–1930. After 1930, the commercial fish harvest in Lake Cooper gradually recovered to a level of 1.1 million pounds in 1937. It then fell off to 611,100 pounds in 1939. By way of comparison, Lake Pepin peaked at 3.6 million pounds in 1922, hit a low of 388,010 pounds in 1930, and made a weak recovery to 944,700 pounds in 1935. Production from the river between the two lakes ranged from 3.6 million pounds in 1930 to 5.4 million pounds in 1932, and 4.7 million pounds in 1939.

of the river. With some interruptions, Robert Coker's study of the Keokuk impoundment and the upper Mississippi River continued from 1914 through 1927. Coker published a second report on Keokuk in 1929, and a comparison with his 1913 report reveals a remarkable shift in emphasis. He had begun his 1913 assessment of the project by singing its praises and by carefully stating that waterpower should not be sacrificed to fish. He also expressed considerable optimism that the conditions created by the dam would prove beneficial to the fishery. Coker introduced his 1929 report by arguing that the consequences of various changes made in the name of progress had diminished the ability of rivers nationwide to support fish and mussel life. Deforestation, agricultural land clearance, and drainage speeded up runoff, while swamp reclamation and navigational improvements caused rivers to flow more rapidly to the sea. As a result, river levels fluctuated more rapidly and widely than they had in their unaltered state. Coker argued, "The trend of the changes in our rivers wrought indirectly by man's alteration of the face of the land has been in a direction generally unfavorable to the growth and multiplication of fish."[58]

A shift is also evident in the tenor of the remarks that Coker addressed directly to the Lake Cooper situation. Gone was his early optimism that damming the river would boost fish production. He now strongly leaned toward the conclusion that the drainage of overflow lands had destroyed the productivity of the impoundment. By 1930, as a result of several breaches of the levees during high water, the Green Bay drainage district north of Keokuk had failed. Farmers were leaving the community, and local commercial fishermen wanted to see portions of the levees removed in order to restore overflow habitat.[59] Coker recognized that the fishery problems of Lake Cooper and the upper river were a part of the very fabric of progress. He stopped short, however, of making recommendations to mitigate the situation.

M. M. Ellis, the scientist from the bureau who conducted the other investigation of interest, did not demonstrate a similar reluc-

---

58. Robert Coker, "Keokuk Dam and the Fisheries of the Upper Mississippi River," *Bulletin of the U.S. Bureau of Fisheries, vol. 45, 1929*, pp. 88, 87–91; See also, Robert Coker, "Studies of Common Fishes of the Mississippi River at Keokuk," *Bulletin of the U.S. Bureau of Fisheries, vol. 45, 1929*, pp. 141–225.

59. Coker, "Keokuk Dam and the Fisheries," pp. 91–107, 116, 126–27, 129–30, 132–34, 136; Thomas K. Chamberlain to Assistant in Charge Division of Inquiry, 12 February 1930, entry 121, Record Group 22, Records of the Fish and Wildlife Service, National Archives Building, Washington, D.C. (hereafter cited as RG 22, NA).

tance. A brilliant scientist, Ellis was respected by his colleagues as a much-published expert on freshwater mussels and water quality. People who knew Ellis personally described him as a devoted family man who enjoyed the company of his wife, mother, and daughter on research trips. Acquaintances also found him to be a stern, no-nonsense individual who could be exasperatingly secretive about his work. Professionally, Ellis had few equals. During the late 1920s, he held appointments as a professor of physiology at the University of Missouri School of Medicine, as a special investigator in mussel culture for the U.S. Bureau of Fisheries, and as a research fellow for the American Button Manufacturers Association. From 1930 until 1947, he directed a water-quality investigation unit jointly sponsored by the University of Missouri and the Bureau of Fisheries. Pollution surveys carried out by Ellis and his staff represented some of the most comprehensive and innovative water-quality research conducted during the first half of the twentieth century.[60]

In May 1930, Ellis attended a conference called by the Army Corps of Engineers to discuss its plans to construct a series of locks and dams between Alton, Illinois, and the Twin Cities. The intention of the corps to use fluctuating water levels in the pools behind the navigation dams had evoked a strong protest from groups interested in fish and wildlife. When the U.S. Bureau of Biological Survey and the U.S. Bureau of Fisheries joined the protest, the corps responded to this official concern by asking for a joint conference. At this meeting, the corps requested that each bureau conduct a study of the Keokuk impoundment with an eye toward mitigating the impact of the nine-foot channel on fish and wildlife. Ellis headed up the investigation undertaken by the Bureau of Fisheries. In 1931, he published an article that contained the highlights of the bureau's report to the Corps of Engineers.[61]

60. Ellis's appointments during the late 1920s are listed in a letter of introduction from Henry O'Malley, Commissioner, to Director, Die Biologische Station (Kupelivieserche), Lunz, Nied Ostreich, 8 March 1928, entry 121, RG 22, NA. Personal information on Ellis was obtained from Dr. Wesley Platner and Mary McConathy Platner, interview, Columbia, Missouri, June 1983. Dr. Platner studied under Ellis and assisted in water-quality investigations from 1942 until 1947. Mary McConathy Platner served as Ellis's secretary from 1930 until 1945. Further information on Ellis may be found in Chapters 3 and 5.

61. F. M. Uhler, "Report on a conference with U.S. War Department Engineers . . . ," 6 May 1930, entry 162, United States Agriculture Department, Bureau of Biological Survey, RG 22, NA; M. M. Ellis, "A Survey of Conditions Affecting Fisheries in the Upper Mississippi River," *U.S. Bureau of Fisheries, Fishery Circular Number 5*. Ellis also studied the river between the head of Lake Keokuk and the Twin Cities.

Ellis argued that, in common with other natural resources, the upper Mississippi River was subject to "new and larger demands" from "the ever-increasing needs of our complex civilization." Along its entire course, the river came into contact with and was modified by a wide range of human activities. The Mississippi also transported downstream the consequences of activities that would otherwise have been of only local significance. During the late nineteenth and early twentieth centuries cities along the upper river constructed sewer systems that drained into the Mississippi, and these sewer systems became the single largest contributors to serious, generalized pollution of much of the upper river. From Ellis's perspective, difficulties that had developed as a result of the Keokuk dam, or that might arise in conjunction with the nine-foot channel, had to be considered within the larger context of man-induced change in the environment of the entire upper river.[62]

Ellis identified a number of factors, including silt from erosion, pollution, wetlands drainage, navigational improvements, and shoreline construction, that had helped bring about undesirable changes in the fauna of the upper Mississippi. He further singled out erosion silt as being the most responsible for creating the conditions that had brought about the destruction of the fisheries of Lake Keokuk and the entire upper river. In the summer of 1930, Ellis found that for five or six miles behind Keokuk dam the bottom of Lake Cooper was covered with three to six feet of fine, brown silt. This silt, which had increased significantly in the few years before 1930, overwhelmed bottom-dwelling plants and animals faster than they could adapt to the new conditions. Silt also exacerbated an increasingly serious pollution problem. In combination with silt, organic pollution was carried farther downstream and decayed more slowly than it would have in clear water. When deposited on the river bottom, this mixture of silt and sewage had a high oxygen demand that dramatically reduced the quantity of dissolved oxygen in the water. Ellis's analysis revealed that the bottom fauna of Lake Keokuk consisted almost entirely of species that could tolerate low oxygen conditions. He considered such species to be "indices of a polluted or biologically unfavorable body of

62. Ellis, "A Survey of Conditions," pp. 1–4. On the subject of sewer systems see, for example, Judson L. Wicks, "Pollution of the Upper Mississippi River," pp. 286–87; *Report of the Pollution of the Mississippi River Minneapolis to La Crosse, Inclusive by the Minnesota State Board of Health in Collaboration with the Minnesota Commissioner of Game and Fish and the Wisconsin State Board of Health*, pp. 3, 9–12.

water." Ellis carefully pointed out that these conditions were not unique to the Keokuk impoundment. Indeed, they existed anywhere on the upper river that a natural or man-made obstruction slowed the current and permitted the sewage-laden silt to settle out.[63]

Ellis's recommendations contained elements of the ecosystem perspective that began to find favor in various segments of the postwar scientific community and environmental movement. He characterized the upper Mississippi River as a complex, interdependent system that included the river's physical characteristics as well as life and the ability to support life. More than remote control manipulators, people fit into his system in a number of ways: they made demands on the river, they depended on the river, and they modified the river. Ellis concluded that fixed water levels behind a series of navigation dams could benefit the river fishery. First, however, some basic changes had to take place in the way people used the river. Overflow lands had to be protected from drainage through the establishment of fish refuges. Erosion silt and pollution also had to be removed from the upper Mississippi. He told the Army Corps of Engineers, "These are problems facing the fisheries interests, regardless of the construction work of the War Department." Ellis called for changes not only in practices but also in underlying attitudes and values.[64]

Keokuk dam provided scientists from the Bureau of Fisheries with an opportunity for long-term study of the conditions created by artificial impoundment of the upper Mississippi River. Their conclusions differed markedly from conceptions of the river that had prevailed two decades earlier when the Keokuk dam was constructed. In common with Robert Coker and other scientists, M. M. Ellis blamed the undesirable consequences of progress for the degradation of the fishery of the upper river. In large part, the scientists' sensitivity to the consequences of river use and development evolved out of the failure of an ambitious program for the propagation of freshwater mussels. For this reason, the mussel fishery and the pearl-button industry provide vehicles for analyzing the changing attitudes of fisheries scientists toward the upper Mississippi River.

63. Ellis, "A Survey of Conditions," p. 8; see also pp. 4–9, 15–17.
64. Ibid., p. 18.

3 Shells, Sewage, and Silt
The Bureau of Fisheries and the Pearl-Button Industry, 1890–1930

> By far the chiefest use of mussel shells is . . . for the manufacture of pearl buttons, now worn by nearly every individual from the cradle to the shroud. —Robert Coker, 1919[1]

Before white settlement, Indians living in what is now the United States gathered immense numbers of freshwater mussels, using these mollusks as a source for food and for highly prized freshwater pearls. After extermination or removal of the Indians, mussels reproduced practically undisturbed in the nation's rivers and streams. By the late nineteenth century, these waterways teemed with hundreds of species of freshwater mussels. With few exceptions, those species with shells suitable for making buttons inhabited the Mississippi River system.[2] The pearl-button industry experienced rapid development in the quarter century after 1891 by cashing in on this accumulated biological capital.

In 1891, a single, tiny factory in Muscatine, Iowa, pioneered in the manufacture of buttons from the shells of freshwater mussels. Within ten years, the pearl-button industry had become an economic mainstay of towns all along the upper river. In 1899, mussel fishermen working the Mississippi River from north of Prairie du Chien, Wisconsin, to south of Canton, Missouri, harvested almost twenty-four thousand tons of mussel shells. These shells provided the raw material for sixty button factories located in Missouri,

1. Robert E. Coker, "Fresh-Water Mussels and Mussel Industries of the United States," *Bulletin of the U.S. Bureau of Fisheries, vol. 36, 1917–18*, pp. 15–16. The bureau also published this study as *U.S. Bureau of Fisheries, Document Number 865* (1919).
2. George F. Kunz, "A Brief History of the Gathering of Fresh-Water Pearls in the United States," *Bulletin of the U.S. Fish Commission for 1897, vol. 17*, pp. 321, 326–27; Coker, "Fresh-Water Mussels," p. 16. Coker states, "There are approximately 500 species of fresh-water mussels in the United States."

Iowa, Illinois, and Wisconsin.[3] Intense, unregulated shelling soon threatened to exhaust the once-abundant beds of mussels. By 1907, the U.S. Bureau of Fisheries had committed itself to a policy of assisting the industry by guaranteeing the supply of mussels. Artificial propagation, supplemented by state regulations, formed the keystone of this supply-oriented policy.

The Bureau of Fisheries and its predecessor, the U.S. Fish Commission, fought for over forty years to sustain and enhance mussel production. The upper Mississippi River was a major front in that struggle. Hugh M. Smith, a Fish Commission scientist, fired the first shot in the prolonged conflict when in 1898 he conducted an investigation of the mussel fishery and button industry at the request of "interested persons." Smith's study strongly implied that the interested persons were button manufacturers who already feared "the early exhaustion of the mussel beds in that part of the Mississippi River which is in Iowa and Illinois."[4] By the early 1930s, the bureau's program of artificial propagation had failed in the face of man-caused changes in the environment of the upper river. This failure forced the Bureau of Fisheries to confront the issue of habitat degradation. It also helped to bring about important changes in the attitudes of fisheries scientists, in the composition of the agency's constituency, and in the policies of the bureau toward the use and development of the upper river.

"Mein buddons vill make you all rich"

Exploitation of mussels by white Americans began with geographically scattered, frenzied hunts for freshwater pearls. In 1857, someone removed a mussel from Notch Brook near Patterson, New Jersey, pried it open, and discovered a magnificent pearl that weighed ninety-three grains. Tiffany and Company purchased the pearl and resold it for $2,500 to Empress Eugénie of France. Pub-

3. C. H. Townsend, "Statistics of the Fisheries of the Mississippi River and Tributaries," *U.S. Commission of Fish and Fisheries, Commissioner's Report, 1901,* pp. 664, 678, 707–8, 714–15, 722–23. Shell production from states along the upper river in 1899 breaks down as follows: Illinois, 8.9 million pounds; Iowa, 20.4 million pounds; Missouri, 2.1 million pounds; and Wisconsin, 16.3 million pounds; for a total of 47.7 million pounds, or nearly 24,000 tons. In a table on p. 670, Townsend lists "mussel shells used" at 11,800 tons. The difference is most likely accounted for by shells shipped by rail to factories in New York, Pennsylvania, New Jersey, and other nonriver states.

4. Hugh M. Smith, "The Mussel Fishery and Pearl-Button Industry of the Mississippi River," *Bulletin of the U.S. Fish Commission for 1898, vol. 18,* p. 289.

lication of the selling price set off the first great pearl rush of the nineteenth century. Fortune seekers converged on Notch Brook and other streams throughout the area. Pearl fever proved to be extremely contagious, and it spread rapidly to other parts of the country. Within a few seasons, the furor abated, but not before the lucky ones had discovered pearls worth approximately $50,000. For the remainder of the nineteenth century, pearl fever broke out about every ten years in various parts of the nation. Pearl hunters rushed to Ohio's Little Miami River in 1868. Eight years later a pearl craze broke out in the vicinity of Waynesville, Ohio. In 1889, the discovery of large numbers of beautifully colored pearls made Wisconsin the next location for a headlong dash to the streams. Eight years of searching creek beds yielded about $300,000 worth of pearls and nearly exterminated mussels in many Wisconsin rivers and streams.[5]

Activity in Wisconsin gradually subsided only to be replaced in 1897 by a fresh outbreak of pearl fever on the White River in Arkansas. Arkansas's waterways abounded with mussels, and rural residents had actually found pearls from time to time, without being cognizant of their value. They apparently regarded the pearls as lucky stones and children's playthings. In 1897, visitors from St. Louis and Memphis discovered some pearls and sent them home to determine their value. Before long, word got out, setting off the last great nineteenth-century pearl craze. People flocked to the White River, and the excitement quickly extended into large sections of Arkansas, Kansas, Missouri, and the Choctaw Indian Territory. In the first year, Arkansas produced many fine pearls, including some that sold for more than a thousand dollars apiece. Newspapers nationwide printed sensational stories of the Arkansas Klondike, which caused an epidemic of pearl fever to sweep through Iowa, Tennessee, Georgia, New York, and Connecticut.[6]

Pearl seekers quickly established a pattern of exploitation that became standard practice into the twentieth century. Pearl hunting was conducted like a game of chance in which the participants wagered that if they opened enough mussels they would eventually hit the jackpot. Most pearl hunters were men and boys who located the beds of mussels by wading into the water and feeling

5. Kunz, "A Brief History," pp. 322, 330.
6. Ibid., pp. 322, 323, 330. For further information on the pearl excitement, see George F. Kunz, "The Fresh-Water Pearls and Pearl Fisheries of the United States," *Bulletin of the U.S. Fish Commission for 1897, vol. 17*, pp. 394–402.

along the bottom with their bare feet. They collected, tore open, and destroyed millions of mussels, gambling that they could beat the odds and find a pearl that would make them rich. By the late 1890s, a few observers had begun to condemn these practices, comparing them to the decimation of timber, fish, and wildlife that had been carried out with little regard for the future productivity of the resources. In Europe, where mussel populations were much more limited than in the United States, various tools had long been used that allowed gatherers to partially open a mussel and inspect it for pearls without killing the animal. In the United States, with its apparently limitless beds of mussels, few pearl seekers employed these simple, inexpensive devices.[7]

The expectations and practices of pearl hunters were extremely destructive when incorporated into the systematic, intense shelling characteristic of the button industry. Repeated episodes of pearl mania had conditioned many residents of the Mississippi River valley to regard mussel gathering as a treasure hunt—a chance to get something for nothing. In 1898, three species of mussels accounted for more than 99 percent of the shells used by the button makers. Over the next thirty years, the number of species regularly used to make buttons gradually expanded from three to seventeen. Yet mussel gatherers customarily cooked out the entire river run, regardless of size or species, in the hope of finding pearls. During the early years of the industry, when Muscatine exhibited both the spirit and look of a goldrush town, people crowded to the riverbank and watched the mussel fishermen at places where pearls had been found. Enterprising clammers sometimes sold their catches unopened, at inflated prices, to onlookers willing to bet that one of the mussels they bought would contain a valuable pearl.[8]

7. Charles T. Simpson, "The Pearly Fresh-Water Mussels of the United States: Their Habits, Enemies, and Diseases, with Suggestions for Their Protection," *Bulletin of the United States Fish Commission for 1898, vol. 18*, p. 287; Kunz, "A Brief History," pp. 323–25, 330; Kunz, "Fresh-Water Pearls," p. 381.

8. Smith, "Mussel Fishery," pp. 289–92, 303; Coker, "Fresh-Water Mussels," pp. 16, 36, 38, 60; Michael G. O'Hara, "The Founding and Early History of the Pearl Button Industry," *Proceedings of the UMRCC Symposium on the Upper Mississippi River Bivalve Mollusks* (Rock Island, Ill.: Upper Mississippi River Conservation Committee, July 1980), p. 8; "Pearls Hidden in Mussels Always Lure to Sheller; Pearls Found Worth $5,000," *Muscatine Journal and News-Tribune*, 31 December 1928, p. 8, entry 121, Record Group 22, Records of the Fish and Wildlife Service, National Archives Building, Washington, D.C. (hereafter cited as RG 22, NA).

The pearl-button industry had emerged by the early 1890s, when three factors converged to create the context within which the industry experienced almost explosive growth. First, in 1890, Congress passed the McKinley Tariff, which raised the duty on imported buttons and gave American-made buttons a competitive advantage. Second, a proliferation of ready-made clothing created a market for large numbers of durable, inexpensive buttons. Prior to 1891, manufacturers made buttons from a wide variety of materials including marine shells, wood, metal, agate, vegetable ivory, glass, and bone. Buttons manufactured from marine shells were of high quality but expensive, while those crafted from other substances were less expensive but prone to rust or breakage or warping. The shells of f·eshwater mussels, however, produced excellent, affordable buttons that were ideally suited for the marketing requirements of the ready-to-wear clothing industry. Finally, a German immigrant named John Boepple possessed the knowledge, vision, and persistence to weld the various pieces together and give the industry its start.[9]

Boepple had been a button worker near Hamburg, Germany. One day, probably in the early 1880s, a friend brought him some shells of American freshwater mussels, which he told Boepple had been collected from a river about two hundred miles southwest of Chicago. Boepple experimented with these shells and found them to be superior button-making material. In 1887, Boepple sold his business and emigrated to the United States, where he sought his fortune in freshwater mussels. He settled first in west central Illinois, where he worked for a time as a farm laborer. That summer Boepple cut his foot while bathing in the Sangamon River. When he looked for the object that had inflicted his injury, Boepple discovered that the riverbed was carpeted with mussels. He wrote in an autobiographical account, "At last I found what I had been looking for; yet there still was a problem before me. I was without capital in a strange land among strange people and unfamiliar with the language."[10]

Boepple seemed equally strange to ethnocentric, native-born

9. For more detailed information on the materials used to make buttons, see U.S. Department of Commerce, *Census of Manufacturers, 1914, vol. II*, pp. 843–44. See also Robert E. Coker, "The Protection of Fresh-Water Mussels," *Bureau of Fisheries Annual Report with Appendixes, 1911/12*, p. 3; Coker, "Fresh-Water Mussels," pp. 67–69.

10. Coker, "Fresh-Water Mussels," p. 65. Coker quoted from an account of the industry's beginning written by Boepple.

Americans who saw only millions of worthless clams (or potential pearls) where Boepple envisioned a fortune in buttons. They laughed with delight when he insisted that "mein buddons vill make you all rich." Boepple continued to search for mussels and located several more beds, including one in the Mississippi near Muscatine, Iowa. After the tariff increase in 1890, Boepple moved to Muscatine, which was still a busy lumber town, and solicited money so that he could establish a button factory. Following numerous rejections, in 1891 he persuaded two Muscatine men to provide financial and mechanical assistance. Boepple and his partners then opened the first freshwater pearl-button factory in the basement of a Muscatine cooper's shop.[11]

Once Boepple had blazed the way, other Muscatine entrepreneurs saw the commercial potential of "buddons." The mussels were plentiful, free, and easy to collect. In less than a decade, Muscatine became the capital city of a new and rapidly expanding industry. Boepple, however, failed to succeed as a manufacturer of buttons. By 1907, his financial situation had deteriorated to the point that he unsuccessfully sought employment with the U.S. Bureau of Fisheries. Three years later, under pressure from button interests, the bureau hired Boepple as a shell expert and assigned him to its Fisheries Biological Station at Fairport, Iowa. John Boepple died in a Muscatine hospital in 1912. Despite his personal economic tragedy, Boepple lived to see the fabulous success of the industry he had founded. He also witnessed the development of a pattern of exploitation that threatened to kill the resource that gave the industry life.[12]

Patterns of Exploitation

After 1891, the pearl-button industry sustained itself by continually expanding into new areas. Exploitation began at Mus-

11. Edward Mott Woolley, "Buttons: A Romance of American Industry," p. 114. While it is not at all certain that Boepple said these words, they do reflect people's perceptions of him. Coker, "Fresh-Water Mussels," pp. 65–66.

12. Woolley, "Buttons," pp. 113–17; Coker, "Fresh-Water Mussels," pp. 64–66; O'Hara, "Founding," p. 5. Boepple's attempt to secure employment with the bureau in 1907 is discussed in Barton W. Evermann, Assistant in Charge, U.S. Bureau of Fisheries, Division of Scientific Inquiry, to W. C. Curtis, 31 May and 18 June 1907, Collection Number 2528, Curtis, Winterton Conway Papers, 1892–1962, Western Historical Manuscripts, Ellis Library, University of Missouri–Columbia (hereafter cited as 2528, Curtis Papers, WHM).

catine, but gatherers quickly moved up and down the river, lured by the promise of unworked streams and driven by the exhausted mussel beds that they left behind. In the mid-1890s, someone discovered a large concentration of mussels just south of Muscatine near New Boston, Illinois. During three years of intensive exploitation, mussel collectors harvested nearly ten thousand tons of shells from a section of river about one and a half miles long and three hundred yards wide. By 1898, the New Boston bed, which was one of the most productive in that part of the river, had been mined to exhaustion. Mussel gatherers responded to depletion by extending their quest. Between 1891 and 1897, shellers enlarged the range of their activities to encompass a 167-mile stretch of the river between Sabula and Fort Madison, Iowa. By the turn of the century, they had penetrated north into southwestern Wisconsin and south to the mouth of the Illinois River near Grafton, Illinois.[13]

Between 1898 and 1916, the boom years of the industry, shelling spread through a large part of the Mississippi basin and into a few streams that drained into the Great Lakes and the Gulf of Mexico. At various times in this period, three midwestern rivers (the Illinois, the Wabash, and the Ohio) and three Arkansas rivers (the White, the Black, and the St. Francis) temporarily reigned as centers of the mussel fishery. Parts of the Mississippi continued to be important sources of shells until the mid-1920s. Output from Lake Pepin, a widened portion of the river between Minnesota and Wisconsin, peaked at three to four thousand tons in 1914–1915 and at two thousand tons in 1924. In its bulletin for 1917–1918, the Bureau of Fisheries published an important analysis of the pearl-button industry in which the author explained, "Unquestionably Lake Pepin . . . has recently been yielding a greater quantity of shells per linear mile than any other stream or portion of a stream." As late as 1930, Muscatine remained a center of manufacturing, even though shells had to be shipped there by rail and barge from as far away as Arkansas.[14]

While differences did exist, the process of shelling for the button industry exhibited considerable consistency over time and

13. Smith, "Mussel Fishery," pp. 298–300; Coker, "Fresh-Water Mussels," p. 39; Townsend, "Statistics," pp. 678, 722.

14. Coker, "Fresh-Water Mussels," pp. 38–40; "The Fresh-Water Pearl Button Industry and the Relations of the Bureau of Fisheries Thereto," 5 April 1930, entry 269, United States Commerce Department, Bureau of Fisheries, Division of Scientific Inquiry, RG 22, NA; "List of Fresh-Water Button Manufacturers," circa 1930, entry 269, RG 22, NA.

Loading mussels on scows at LeClaire, Iowa, for transportation to Muscatine.

throughout the Mississippi River basin. Very early in its development, the pearl-button industry took on a nomadic character. Even though local people did gather mussels to supplement their incomes, a class of itinerant shellers rapidly developed, which followed the mussel frontier in shantyboats. Temporary cutting plants often became established in areas of greatest activity, only to move on as mussel beds gave out. These establishments usually cut only blanks and shipped them to larger, permanent plants for the final processing into buttons. Mussel gatherers customarily lived and worked in makeshift riverbank camps. At these riverside locations, the shellers steamed open their catches in large, flat pans and then removed and discarded the soft inner parts of the mussels. They then proceeded to wash, sort, and market the commercially useful shells.[15]

Most mussel camps combined elements of a boomtown with the sensory insults of an unregulated rendering plant. An article in a March 1931 issue of the *Grand Rapids* (Mich.) *Chronicle* described the angry response of local people to the stink that emanated from nearby mussel camps. The paper reported, "For some

15. Coker, "The Protection of Fresh-Water Mussels," p. 6; Smith, "Mussel Fishery," pp. 292–93. Coker, "Fresh-Water Mussels," pp. 59–61.

time now various citizens who attain no aesthetic delight from the masterful odor of huge mounds of steaming, dessicating [sic] clams have been urging that the clam fishers be eliminated." Itinerant shellers had a reputation for being shiftless, lawless, and even dangerous. Permanent residents in areas of active mussel gathering did not welcome the presence of either the camps or their inhabitants. In December 1932, M. M. Ellis observed, "Numerous conversations with landowners and others, have shown . . . disapproval and oftentimes fear of mussel fishermen to be wide-spread and serious." Ellis went on to explain that observations of mussel camps by members of his staff confirmed that "violations of ordinary laws and common decency are all to [sic] frequent." [16]

In 1919, Robert Coker, the bureau's assistant in charge of scientific inquiry, generalized about the pattern of exploitation that sustained the industry and hastened its doom. When shelling commenced in a new area, large, old mussels predominated in the catch. After a few years, the average size gradually decreased until in the final phase of exploitation very small shells formed the majority of the take. At this point two factors accelerated the rate of exhaustion: First, gatherers had to collect two or three mussels to equal the amount of shell formerly obtained from just one. Second, as production fell the price often rose, a fact that tempted the sheller to work harder and keep every mussel no matter how small. Finally, when an area became severely depleted, nomadic professional gatherers abandoned it in favor of new locations. As a general rule, however, local people continued to work the depleted beds for extra cash. Coker concluded, "The cases of natural recuperation are therefore conspicuous by their rarity." [17]

Mussels were a "common property" resource—publicly owned and free to anyone who wished to collect them. Until the mid-1910s, the harvesting of these valuable bivalves was largely unregulated. These factors trapped gatherers and manufacturers in a cycle of competition that contributed in a major way to the exhaustion of the resource. As the supply of mussels in any given area plummeted and their value increased, a powerful monetary incen-

16. "Care-Free Clams," *Grand Rapids* (Mich.) *Chronicle,* 13 March 1931, typescript, entry 269, RG 22, NA; Letter of Transmissal, M. M. Ellis to Henry O'Malley, Commissioner, U.S. Bureau of Fisheries, 14 December 1932, 15 pages, entry 269, RG 22, NA.

17. Coker, "Fresh-Water Mussels," pp. 44–45; H. M. Smith, Commissioner, U.S. Bureau of Fisheries, to State Conservation Commission, Wisconsin, 29 December 1917, entry 121, RG 22, NA.

tive urged shellers to work ever harder to recover the increasingly scarce mollusks. Even when an individual gatherer recognized that depletion was well advanced, he could see little reason to stop collecting and permit a rival to get his share. For their part, manufacturers reasoned that if they refused to purchase small shells a competitor would buy them anyway. State laws passed after 1914 helped to regulate the conduct of the fishery. Nonetheless, as late as 1929 the head of the bureau's Fairport, Iowa, research station reported that it would be difficult to enforce a size limit in already overfished Arkansas waters. He contended, "The button association is so inclined toward cut throat competition that I doubt whether it will prove possible to keep the grading system in force."[18]

Two additional factors—perceptions of abundance and the development of technology—complicated the pattern of exploitation. Particularly during the two or three decades after 1891, mussel fishermen and manufacturers engaged in extremely wasteful practices. Hugh Smith pointed to "the disregard for the future which has come to be regarded as characteristic of fishermen" as one of the major reasons for the depletion of the mussel beds. Records of the attitudes of mussel fishermen are rare. In 1908, however, a Prairie du Chien, Wisconsin, sheller addressed the subject of depletion in a letter to the commissioner of fisheries. The man, J. P. Albee, contended, "There is not the slightest danger" of commercially useful mussels becoming extinct. Albee based his assessment on the fact that "some beds are literaly [sic] alive with young clams, too small for commercial uses." In 1921, Robert Coker surveyed thirty years of pearl-button manufacturing and explained the destruction of mussel beds as part of a larger pattern of U.S. resource development. He argued that the pearl-button industry had "a history similar to many other American industries in that the pioneers wasted large quantities of good material through lack of knowledge and experience . . . secure in the thought that the supply was inexhaustible."[19]

Technological developments that speeded up the gathering and the processing of shells also contributed to the destruction of the

18. Thomas K. Chamberlain, Director, U.S. Biological Station, Fairport, to Lewis Radcliffe, 8 April 1929, entry 269, RG 22, NA; Garrett Hardin, "The Tragedy of the Commons," pp. 250–64.

19. Smith, "Mussel Fishery," p. 300; J. P. Albee to Commissioner of Fisheries, 10 June 1908, 2528, Curtis Papers, WHM; Coker, "Fresh-Water Mussels," p. 16.

mussel fishery. In 1898, Hugh Smith noted the recent invention of a device for taking mussels called the "crowfoot." This piece of equipment consisted of an iron bar to which the fishermen attached numerous four-pronged hooks. The crowfoot took advantage of the fact that mussels usually rested on streambeds partially buried in the bottom material. Mussels so positioned oriented themselves upstream with their shells ajar in order to allow a free circulation of the water from which they derived food and oxygen. If touched, the mussels snapped shut and held fast to any foreign object that happened to be between their valves. Mussel collectors lowered the crowfoot from a boat, floated downstream with the device dragging the bottom, and retrieved it covered with mussels closed tightly on the hooks. In Lake Pepin, which had very little current and an extraordinary abundance of mussels, shellers used motorboats to scour the riverbed with two to four crowfoot bars at the same time.[20]

When first introduced into a new area, the crowfoot provided significant short-term benefits to those who used it. From the gatherers' perspective, the crowfoot had numerous advantages: it was easy to make, it was cheap and efficient, and in comparison with other kinds of gear it was less labor-intensive and permitted coverage of a greater area. Hugh Smith reported that the crowfoot, which cost from seventy-five cents to one dollar, had become the most popular form of mussel-gathering apparatus. He enthusiastically explained, "Any one who has not witnessed the use of this apparatus can scarcely realize how remarkably effective it is. Often when the mussels are abundant almost every prong will have a mussel on it, and two or three are sometimes caught on one prong." By 1914, the crowfoot accounted for 70 percent of the total catch and almost 94 percent of the mussels taken from the Mississippi River.[21]

In the long run, the unanticipated consequences of this new technology proved to be very destructive to the mussel fishery.

20. Smith, "Mussel Fishery," pp. 294–96; Coker, "Fresh-Water Mussels," pp. 46–52. Coker discusses the adaptation of the crowfoot to conditions found in Lake Pepin on p. 51.

21. Smith, "Mussel Fishery," pp. 295–96; "Fresh-Water Mussel Fishery," *U.S. Bureau of Fisheries Annual Report with Appendixes, 1915–16*, p. 50; Coker, "Fresh-Water Mussels," pp. 39, 59. In a table on p. 59, Coker states that the crowfoot accounted for 70 percent of the total catch. His data base consisted of three surveys conducted by the Bureau of Fisheries in 1912, 1913, and 1914. These surveys are discussed on p. 39.

Fishermen could work deeper water with the crowfoot than they could with most other kinds of apparatus. Deep water, therefore, failed to protect some beds of mussels that could have served as breeding populations. General use of the crowfoot meant that shellers repeatedly dragged thousands of hooks through a bed of mussels. Fisheries scientists suspected that this practice caused gravid females to abort. They knew that the crowfoot readily hooked very small mussels and frequently injured them so seriously that they died even if the gatherers returned them to the water.[22]

The constituent relationship between the bureau and the button industry made it extremely difficult to control the use of the crowfoot. Along with other agencies in the evolving federal bureaucracy, the Bureau of Fisheries cultivated a constituency composed of compatible private organizations. In the case of the button industry, the bureau worked out a symbiotic relationship with individual manufacturers and with their trade association, the National Association of Button Manufacturers. The button interests looked upon the bureau's program of artificial propagation as the salvation of their industry. In turn, they assisted the agency in its work by lobbying for congressional appropriations and by subsidizing the research of scientists employed by the bureau.[23]

By 1919, the bureau had clearly identified the crowfoot as a pernicious device. The agency, however, lacked the authority to regulate the mussel fishery, and the success of its mussel conservation activities depended upon the goodwill and cooperation of the pearl-button industry. This situation placed the bureau in a serious dilemma: it encouraged mussel fishing and promoted the industry at the same time that it cautioned careful use and advocated regulation. An article published in 1919 in the *Bulletin of the U.S. Bureau of Fisheries* reflected this quandary. The study explained exactly how to make a crowfoot, discussed its effectiveness, and then

22. Coker, "Fresh-Water Mussels," pp. 52–53.
23. The button manufacturers supported the research of Lefevre and Curtis. In 1908, they purchased and donated the land for the site of the bureau's Fairport, Iowa, biological station. See, for example, Winterton C. Curtis, unpublished autobiography, chapter on "The Joys of Research," pp. 7–16, 2528, Curtis Papers, WHM. The button men also financed and supported some of the research conducted by M. M. Ellis. Ellis to Dean Guy L. Noyes, 30 January 1928, Collection number 3651, School of Medicine Records, University of Missouri, Western Historical Manuscripts, Ellis Library, University of Missouri–Columbia (hereafter cited as 3651, School of Medicine Records, WHM).

counseled against its use. The author did not recommend that the crowfoot be banned. He merely suggested that mussel gatherers be educated to accept less destructive types of apparatus.[24]

More than twelve years later the bureau still had not officially proposed that the crowfoot be declared illegal. In 1933, M. M. Ellis analyzed some proposed recommendations for regulating what remained of the mussel fishery. He explained that, unless the crowfoot was banned, undersized mussels would continue to be caught and killed in large numbers. He also recognized the political reality of the situation and argued that it would be unwise for the bureau to propose regulations limiting the use of the crowfoot. Ellis pointed out, "Such a recommendation would surely bring about a violent protest from both the industries and the shellers."[25]

While the crowfoot improved the efficiency with which mussels could be harvested, advances in the technology of button production speeded up the manufacturing process and increased the demand for shells. In the very early years of the industry, the making of buttons required tremendous amounts of hand labor. The process of manufacturing buttons began with a cutter, who sawed blanks one at a time from the shells of freshwater mussels. The blanks then went from the cutter to another operator who used an emery wheel to grind a smooth surface on the back of each one. After the blanks had been backed, a different worker shaped the face of the button on a lathe, and then someone else drilled the holes. Once they had been backed, faced, and drilled, the buttons received their final polish in bulk. Then, the final sorting and the carding were accomplished by hand.[26]

By 1901, automatic machinery had begun to replace most of the handwork that had formerly been required to manufacture buttons. The sawing of blanks remained hand labor, while backing, facing, and drilling became automated. One of the most significant developments in the technology of button production occurred in 1903 when two Muscatine men invented the double automatic machine. This new device dramatically improved the speed and efficiency of button manufacturing. In the days of hand labor, a facer could turn out about twenty gross of partially completed buttons

24. Coker, "Fresh-Water Mussels," pp. 46–53.

25. M. M. Ellis to Elmer Higgins, In Charge Division of Scientific Inquiry, 1 March 1933, entry 269, RG 22, NA.

26. Smith, "Mussel Fishery," pp. 305–8; Coker, "Fresh-Water Mussels," pp. 69–70.

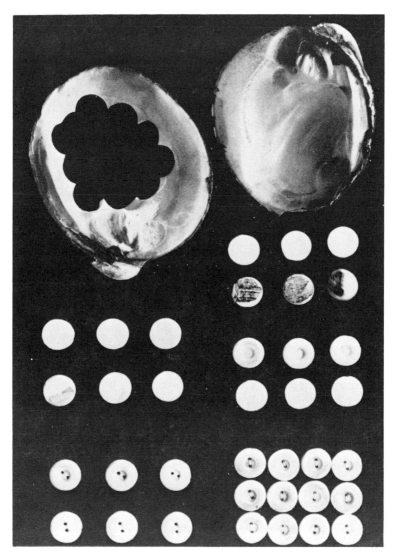

A mussel shell in its natural state (top right) and (from top to bottom and left to right) the shell with "blanks" cut from it; the blanks ground but not polished; the blanks after the central depressions have been made; the blanks with the holes drilled; a dozen finished buttons as fastened on a card for sale.

per day. The facer's work then had to be passed along to a driller, who could handle about fifty gross per day. One double automatic machine, attended by one person, could face and drill from one hundred to one hundred and ninety gross per day. Mechanization speeded production, increased output, and lowered costs, thereby establishing the manufacture of buttons from the shells of fresh-water mussels as an economically significant American industry.[27]

From Boom to Bust

During the industry's period of emergence, which lasted from 1891 until 1897, button manufacturing experienced slow growth and an uncertain future while entrepreneurs scurried to locate markets for their new product. By 1897, their efforts had paid off, and orders from across the nation poured into button factories located along the upper river. Beginning in 1898, these orders initiated a boom that lasted for about seventeen years. Between 1897 and 1898, the number of button factories operating in Iowa and Illinois nearly quadrupled, from thirteen to forty-nine.[28] After 1901, the introduction of automatic machinery served to accelerate the pace of development. Output of completed buttons shot up from 11.4 million gross in 1904 to 21.7 million gross in 1914 and peaked at about 40 million gross in 1916. Thereafter, the industry entered a mature phase, during which production fell off to 20.2 million gross in 1929. Finally, in the 1930s, faced with rising prices, basin-wide depletion of the mussels, and habitat deterioration, the industry slipped into a rapid decline.[29]

Regionally, the pearl-button industry had established itself along the upper river and in several northeastern states by the late

27. Coker, "Fresh-Water Mussels," pp. 66, 69–80; "Story of Button Industry in Pre-Muscatine Era and Early Days Here Written by Willis," *Muscatine Journal and News-Tribune*, 31 December 1928, p. 9, entry 121, RG 22, NA. One gross equals twelve dozen. However, according to Hugh Smith, "Mussel Fishery," p. 308, manufacturers counted fourteen dozen as one gross "in order to make allowance for the imperfect or defective buttons that are liable to be produced at every stage of the business."

28. Smith, "Mussel Fishery," pp. 292–93, 305, 310, 313.

29. "Button Production of Past Years Is Shown by Figures," *Muscatine Journal and News-Tribune*, 31 December 1928, p. 8, entry 121, RG 22, NA; *Census of Manufacturers, 1914*, p. 844; H. M. Smith, Commissioner, U.S. Bureau of Fisheries, to Geo. F. Turner, 24 November 1917, entry 121, RG 22, NA; "The Fresh-Water Pearl Button Industry and the Relations of the Bureau of Fisheries Thereto." Figures for button production must be considered approximate, as some variation existed among the sources that reported such information.

1890s. In 1899, Iowa, Illinois, Missouri, and Wisconsin had sixty button factories, in which 1,917 workers turned out about $336,000 worth of finished buttons. Most of these firms were "saw works" that only cut rough blanks and shipped them to New York and other eastern cities for processing into completed buttons. Eastern factories, many of which already manufactured buttons from oyster shells, had also begun to purchase Mississippi River mussel shells in carload lots. Hugh Smith reported that, in the winter of 1898–1899, a shell buyer at Leclaire, Iowa, had a contract to ship one thousand tons of shells to New York.[30]

From boom to bust, mussel shells served as the raw material for an industry that paid wages to thousands of factory workers and shellers. At the height of the boom in 1916, the freshwater pearl-button industry employed about twenty thousand persons in the fisheries and factories and manufactured $12.5 million worth of buttons. In 1929, when the industry had already begun to slide toward its nadir, it still provided work for over five thousand people who produced $5.8 million worth of buttons. These workers labored in seventeen major factories situated in Iowa, Wisconsin, Missouri, New York, and Massachusetts, as well as numerous smaller plants located throughout the Mississippi River basin.[31]

Locally, the economic importance of the button industry loomed even larger than it did regionally. By the late 1890s, button manufacturing had begun to replace the lumber industry as the most important business of many Mississippi River towns in Iowa and Illinois. Coincident with the end of the white-pine era, Muscatine rapidly established itself as the headquarters of the new pearl-button industry. According to the *Muscatine Journal and News-Tribune*, button manufacturing "saved the industrial life" of the city because it provided "employment to hundreds" just as "the large lumber mills began to wane." In 1898, Muscatine, with a population of about 11,500, had thirty-three button factories, five of them complete plants and the other twenty-eight saw works,

30. Smith, "Mussel Fishery," p. 302. Smith also reported uncut shells being shipped to factories west of the river, but their value was much less than that of shells sent east, and this trade declined in importance. Townsend, "Statistics," pp. 670, 714–15. In 1899, Iowa had forty-one factories, Illinois eleven, Missouri six, and Wisconsin two.

31. "The Fresh-Water Pearl Button Industry and the Relations of the Bureau of Fisheries Thereto"; John M. Curran, "Prices in the Button Industry," *War Industries Board Bulletin Number 29*, pp. 6–8; "Button Production of Past Years Is Shown by Figures."

which employed 829 workers. The city had also developed an important ancillary industry that manufactured and supplied button-making machinery. At the end of the 1920s, Muscatine, which had grown to a city with more than 16,500 residents, retained its position as the capital of the pearl-button industry. In 1927, Muscatine factories produced 11 million gross of buttons valued at $4 million, or about half of all freshwater pearl buttons made in that year. During the following year, workers in the city's button factories earned about $2.5 million in annual wages, while the eight largest operators paid approximately $20,000 in taxes.[32]

Canton, Missouri, which had a population of 3,217 in 1910, provides an example of what a single factory could mean to the economy of a small river town. On 13 February 1913, after considerable negotiation with Canton's commercial club, the Hawkeye Button Company of Muscatine opened a subsidiary plant in Canton. Led by the commercial club, Canton celebrated the coming of the new factory in grand style. The mayor issued a proclamation that called upon all businesses to close for the afternoon so that people could attend an open house at the factory. Crowds of townspeople dressed in their Sunday best toured the facility; in the evening, the commercial club sponsored a banquet in the new factory attended by a sellout crowd of 240 people. Canton's weekly paper described the banquet as "the biggest affair of the kind ever pulled off in Canton." The primary reason for all the excitement, especially on the part of the commercial club, was that the factory created jobs for about seventy-five men and women. Girls and women operated the automatic finishing machines and sorted buttons, while about fifty men were needed to run the saws that cut blanks from the shells. The wages paid to these workers, about $700 per week in October 1914, provided considerable stimulation to the local economy.[33]

Thousands of people who found work in the button factories and the mussel fisheries depended upon button manufacturing for all or part of their annual income. Data on wages and employment are

32. Smith, "Mussel Fishery," pp. 304–5, 308; "11 Million Gross Buttons Made Here in 1927," Clipping, probably from the *Muscatine Journal and News-Tribune*, early 1929, entry 121, RG 22, NA; "Mean Millions Paid In Wages," *Muscatine Journal and News-Tribune*, 31 December 1928, entry 121, RG 22, NA; U.S. Department of Commerce, *Thirteenth Census of the U.S., 1910, Population, vol. II*, p. 598; *Fifteenth Census of the U.S., 1930, Population, vol. III, Part 1*, p. 810.

33. "Big Banquet at New Button Factory," *Canton* (Mo.) *News*, 14 February 1913; "A Visit to the Button Factory," *Canton News*, 10 October 1913; article about button factory, *Canton News*, 16 October 1914; *Thirteenth Census*, p. 1078.

hard to come by, but the *Census of Manufacturers* for 1914 does illuminate an otherwise murky subject. In 1914, 121 button factories in Iowa, Illinois, and Missouri employed a yearly average of 3,384 workers who earned a total of approximately $1,420,000. This workforce, which was roughly 75 percent male and 25 percent female, performed piecework and was paid by the gross, according to a sliding, job-related scale. The highest-paid wage earners in a button factory were the cutters, who were exclusively male. In 1914, they could expect to make from ten to twenty dollars per week. Nearly all of the machine work, which required proportionately fewer employees than hand labor, was done by girls or women. In most factories, women operated the double automatic machines. These machine tenders took home a weekly pay envelope that contained from seven to eleven dollars. The girls who hand-sorted the finished buttons received from five and a quarter to twelve dollars per week, while those who ran the sewing machines that stitched the buttons to cards earned between six and ten dollars each week.[34]

In contrast with the wage earners on the payrolls of the button factories, shellers were largely self-employed. Because of the transient, seasonal, and often part-time nature of this occupation, accurate estimates of the number of mussel gatherers are rare. Nonetheless, it is evident that during the industry's boom years, which lasted from the late 1890s to the late 1910s, tens of thousands of gatherers harvested mussels at one time or another. According to Hugh Smith, in 1897 over three hundred shellers were engaged in dredging mussels from the bottom of the Mississippi between Burlington and Clinton, Iowa. The next year as many as one thousand gatherers crowded to the river between Fort Madison and Sabula, Iowa. In these early years of the mussel fishery, shellers who found a productive bed could earn thirty dollars or more per week, although the average weekly earnings were about one-third of that amount.[35]

34. *Census of Manufacturers, 1914*, p. 845. In 1914, Iowa had eighty-one button manufacturing establishments; Illinois, thirty-one; Missouri, nine; Minnesota, three; and Wisconsin, two. The 3,384 employees included only wage earners and excluded clerks, salaried managerial personnel, and proprietors. The census did not give employment and income data for Minnesota and Wisconsin. Information on job classification and wage scales may be found in Coker, "Fresh-Water Mussels," pp. 71–80. For a brief look at factory hands and their wages for 1897 and 1898, see Smith, "Mussel Fishery," pp. 308–9, 312. Employment statistics for 1899 may be found in Townsend, "Statistics," p. 670.

35. Smith, "Mussel Fishery," pp. 292–93.

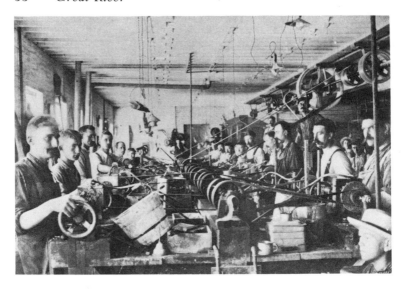

Workers sawing the rough blanks in a button factory.

Workers grinding the blanks in a button factory.

The U.S. Bureau of Fisheries conducted three of the most detailed and useful surveys of the mussel fishery in 1912, 1913, and 1914. In each of these years, the bureau surveyed separate segments of the Mississippi River drainage, so that by the end of 1914 the agency had covered almost the entire Mississippi basin. The bureau's annual report for 1915–1916 combined statistics from these surveys in order to create a composite picture of the mussel fishery between 1912 and 1914. This report concluded that, for the period in question, 9,746 shellers found employment in the Mississippi River system. These gatherers collected millions upon millions of mussels that yielded shells worth $825,776 and that contained pearls that sold for $376,284. Indeed, pearls continued to be one of the attractions of mussel fishing. Most shellers never found a valuable pearl, but for a lucky few the twist of a knife could reveal a treasure equivalent to their earnings for many months or even for many years.[36]

Mussel fishing, then, was of great economic importance to thousands of gatherers and to the communities where they spent their hard-earned dollars. Concomitantly, the legions of eager, unregulated shellers were one of many factors that contributed to the decimation of the resource and to growing demands that something be done to protect and sustain the mussel fishery.

Controlling the Waste of Nature's Seeding

In the late 1890s, Hugh Smith expressed considerable alarm over the accelerating destruction of the mussel fishery. He recommended a range of statutory controls to ameliorate the damage, including a prohibition against the gathering of small shells, a minimum size limit, and a ban on shelling during the mussels' spawning season. Other investigators associated with the U.S. Fish Commission argued in favor of artificial propagation, a solution that was consistent with the agency's history and nineteenth-century attitudes toward resource exhaustion. Congress had established the

36. Coker, "Fresh-Water Mussels," pp. 38–40. On p. 38, Coker explained, "Generally the value of the shells is considerably greater than the return from the pearls; the usual ratio is about 2 to 1." "Fresh-Water Mussel Fishery," p. 57. The surveys for 1912, 1913, and 1914 reveal that in addition to 9,746 shellers the mussel fisheries provided work for 91 transporters and 494 shoremen, for a total of 10,331. Of this number, 427 were women. See also, Smith, "Mussel Fishery," p. 299. Smith estimated that 10,000 tons of shells represented "not less than 100,000,000" mussels.

U.S. Fish Commission in 1871 and charged it with investigating the depletion of food fishes in coastal and interior waters. Within a few years, the commission had dedicated a large portion of its budget to raising useful species and distributing the fry nationwide. When the Bureau of Fisheries superseded the Fish Commission in 1903, many of the commission's personnel continued to work for the new agency. They retained and augmented the commission's fish-culture program.[37]

Anxious to sustain the button-based economic vitality of communities along the upper river, the Bureau of Fisheries invited two University of Missouri zoologists to find out if anything could be done to prevent the "commercial extinction" of freshwater mussels. Early in 1907, George Lefevre and Winterton Curtis agreed to head up an investigation directed toward developing a method of artificial propagation. In 1910, the two scientists announced their success in an article in *The Journal of Experimental Zoology*. Following a period of experimentation at its Fairport, Iowa, laboratory, the bureau began commercial-scale propagation in 1912. The agency concentrated its efforts on the upper Mississippi River, the Wabash River in Indiana, the Ohio River, and the White and Black rivers in Arkansas. In so doing, the bureau committed itself to saving an economically important, highly competitive industry from self-destruction.[38]

Mussel propagation found favor with the bureau and with the industry because it promised greater control over supply and because it did not interfere with commercial use of the resource. In conformity with nineteenth-century attitudes toward nature, propagation emphasized production rather than regulation. It made no attempt to prevent exploitation or to interfere with private enterprise. Rather, the government wanted to help individuals to prosper. They, in turn, would benefit society by converting otherwise worthless material into commercially useful products.[39]

37. Smith, "Mussel Fishery," pp. 313–14. Simpson, "Pearly Fresh-Water Mussels," p. 288, suggests both regulation of the fishery and "mussel farming." Kunz, "Fresh-Water Pearls and Pearl Fisheries," p. 426, recommends "artificial culture of Unios." On the subject of fish culture, see Susan L. Flader, "Scientific Resource Management: An Historical Perspective," pp. 5–8.

38. H. F. Moore, Acting Assistant in Charge of Scientific Inquiry, to George Lefevre, 21 March 1907, 2528, Curtis Papers, WHM; George Lefevre and Winterton C. Curtis, "Reproduction and Parasitism in the Unionidae"; "The Relation of the Bureau of Fisheries to the Fresh-Water Pearl Button Industry," January 1923, entry 121, RG 22, NA.

39. For further information on the relationship among government, resource development, and economic growth, see James Willard Hurst, *Law and the Conditions of Freedom in the Nineteenth Century United States*, chap. 1.

Despite its emphasis on propagation, the bureau experienced many of the changes that transformed a traditional nineteenth-century society into a modern twentieth-century nation. During the early twentieth century, the bureau became increasingly professional and science-based. The agency supported the work of university-trained experts, in the expectation that their investigations would yield results with a practical application to economically significant fisheries problems. However, fisheries experts in the bureau soon concluded that success in the laboratory did not translate into salvation for the button industry. Even though it lacked statutory authority to regulate the fishery, the agency moved to control an ever-increasing number of natural and human variables that interfered with artificial propagation. In so doing, it sought to extend scientific management to the life cycle of the mussels, to the practices of the shellers, and to the manufacturing techniques of the industry.

Soon after the bureau committed itself to artificial propagation, fisheries experts in the agency concluded that it made little sense to stock unregulated waterways. In 1914, the bureau used an article by Robert Coker, director of the U.S. Biological Station at Fairport, Iowa, to launch a campaign for state regulation of the mussel fisheries. Mindful of the bureau's constituency, Coker insisted that state statutes be framed so as not to interfere with the productivity of the pearl-button industry. He also warned his readers, "Ultimate benefits can scarcely be obtained without some temporary sacrifice." Coker pointed out that shelling had spread to about twenty states but that only a few had taken any action to protect the resource. He urged that state laws be drafted so as to include two essential provisions. First, Coker suggested that state regulations should impose a minimum size limit, in order to prevent the capture and waste of juvenile mussels with shells too small for the button industry. Second, he recommended that states devise some plan for dividing waterways into sections that could be alternately opened and closed to shelling. Such a system would allow the periodic recovery of mussel beds through both natural and artificial propagation.[40]

Effective regulation of the upper Mississippi River required cooperation among the four states that shared jurisdiction over the river's most important mussel-producing regions. With this in mind, the bureau persistently lobbied state officials and industry

40. Coker, "Protection of Fresh-Water Mussels," pp. 8–10.

representatives for the passage of uniform laws by Minnesota, Wisconsin, Iowa, and Illinois. By 1919, the bureau could congratulate itself for playing a major role in persuading four state legislatures to approve relatively congruous regulations. Each of the statutes provided for size limits, restrictions on the ways in which mussels could be collected, license fees, and the temporary closure of segments of the state's waterways. Fisheries experts in the bureau considered the closure provisions the most important powers of the new regulations. During the next few years, they cajoled and pressured the states into implementing a coordinated system for alternately opening and closing jointly administered sections of the Mississippi River. By the early 1920s, Minnesota, Wisconsin, Iowa, and Illinois had enacted and enforced nearly uniform laws that complemented the bureau's efforts at artificial propagation.[41]

Events in the Lake Pepin area soon appeared to demonstrate the efficacy of coupling a state-sponsored closure system with artificial propagation. After 1912, Lake Pepin was one of the centers of the bureau's propagation work. Despite the agency's efforts, output plummeted from over three thousand tons of shells in 1914–1915 to two hundred tons in 1919. Confronted with this economic disaster, Minnesota and Wisconsin agreed to ban shelling in segments of Lake Pepin, in order to give mussel populations an opportunity to recover. In March 1924, the states reopened the closed sections, and in the first year thereafter gatherers harvested two thousand tons of shells. Even though the catch fell off precipitously in subsequent years, the bureau claimed a major victory in its war against overuse. In 1925, twenty-one local gatherers questioned the effectiveness of the states' laws when they petitioned to have the entire lake reopened to shelling. Officials in the bureau bristled at this challenge, the acting commissioner arguing, "The evidence of the benefit of the closure system seems incontrovertible."[42]

41. A. F. Shira, "The Necessity of State Legislation in the Conservation of Fresh-Water Mussels." See also Hugh M. Smith, "Fresh-Water Mussels: A Valuable National Resource Without Sufficient Protection," *U.S. Bureau of Fisheries, Economic Circular Number 43.* The files of the U.S. Bureau of Fisheries contain considerable correspondence on the subject of state regulations. See especially "mussel legislation 1916–22" and "mussel legislation 1916–25," entry 121, RG 22, NA.

42. Lewis Radcliffe, Acting Commissioner, to Mr. Albert C. Klancke, Supervisor, Bureau of Commercial Fishing, Game and Fish Department, St. Paul, Minn., 28 May 1925, entry 121, RG 22, NA; Petition to the State Game and Fish Commissioner, St. Paul Minnesota, undated but probably April 1925, entry 121, RG 22, NA. See also, Henry O'Malley, Commissioner, to Mr. A. C. Klancke, 19 May 1925, entry 121, RG 22, NA; Albert C. Klancke to Henry O'Malley, 28 April 1925, entry

Fisheries scientists interested in providing a reliable supply of shells for the industry believed that natural reproduction was inefficient because it depended to an unacceptable degree upon chance. In nature, larval mussels (or glochidia) are discharged from the female's marsupial pouches into the open water and must quickly attach themselves to a suitable host fish. During a period of parasitism on a fish, the glochidia undergo metamorphosis and take on the appearance of adult mussels. The young mussels then drop off the fish and begin an independent existence. From the perspective of fisheries scientists interested in supply, this natural reproductive process contained two periods of great risk. Considerable numbers of larval mussels perished before they could become encysted on a host fish, and a high percentage died because they dropped off the fish over an unsuitable bottom. Lefevre and Curtis eliminated the first great period of uncertainty by putting the glochidia and host fish together in a tank and then releasing the "infected" fish into a river or stream.[43]

Artificial propagation dovetailed nicely with another of the bureau's production-oriented fisheries programs. Each spring the Father of Waters overflowed its banks and spread its arms over the adjacent lowlands. River fish found these temporary shallows to be attractive spawning areas. When the flood tide receded, it stranded millions of fingerlings in slowly evaporating backwaters. From the perspective of scientific resource managers, the death of these fry represented a tremendous loss of potential human food. During the first decade of the twentieth century, the bureau attempted to exert a measure of control over this wasteful natural phenomenon by rescuing as many of these landlocked fish as money and manpower would allow. Rescue crews returned most of the fish to the nearby river, where presumably they would reach maturity, be caught by commercial fishermen, and find their way to markets throughout the nation. Before their release, many of these fish were infected with glochidia. By forcing the fish to perform a double duty, the bureau improved the cost effectiveness and increased the efficiency of both rescue and propagation.[44]

121, RG 22, NA; George H. Hammond to State Game and Fish Commissioner, St. Paul, Minn., 23 April 1925, entry 121, RG 22, NA.

43. Robert Coker et al., "Natural History and Propagation of Fresh-Water Mussels," *Bulletin of the U.S. Bureau of Fisheries, vol. 37, 1919–20*, pp. 135–37, 160–63; "The Fresh-Water Pearl Button Industry and the Relations of the Bureau of Fisheries Thereto."

44. C. F. Culler, "Fish Rescue Operations" and "Depletion of the Aquatic Resources of the Upper Mississippi River and Suggested Remedial Measures." Brief

During the quarter-century after 1912, the bureau annually stocked public waters with an estimated 1 billion glochidia safely encysted on host fish. Although this may seem like an awesome number, under the best conditions only about 2 percent of the juvenile mussels survived to reach commercial size. An analysis by the bureau explained that conditions in the open water "are uncontrollable on account of their character and immensity." Fisheries scientists cherished the hope that someone would find a way to artificially supply the glochidia of useful species with "the food materials and other conditions necessary for the metamorphosis, so that it might become possible to rear mussels without the use of fish."[45]

In 1925, M. M. Ellis began a series of experiments designed to eliminate the glochidia's parasitic stage. Ellis realized that, despite widespread use of the technique developed by Lefevre and Curtis, the supply of mussels in the upper Mississippi drainage had continued to decline. He blamed two factors for the steady decrease in mussel populations: constantly growing domestic and foreign demand for shells and "changes in the environment brought about by stream pollution from the large cities along the rivers and by channel changes made necessary by navigation demands." By the late 1920s, Ellis had succeeded in developing a nutrient solution that allowed the glochidia to undergo metamorphosis without the use of a host fish. His accomplishment made it possible to raise mussels under controlled conditions and release them in suitable bodies of water directly on favorable bottoms. All Ellis's process required from nature was a supply of healthy glochidia from gravid female mussels and an appropriate place to stock young mussels after they had undergone metamorphosis in the nutrient solution. His technique did away with nearly all the risk associated with the natural reproduction of mussels.[46]

Ellis had made it possible to raise mussels with the dependabil-

---

accounts of the rescue operations for the 1910s and 1920s may be found in "The Report of the Commissioner of Fisheries," located in the *U.S. Bureau of Fisheries Annual Report with Appendixes.* Although the bureau conducted rescue operations from Minnesota to Mississippi, it concentrated of its efforts along the upper river. Construction of the navigation dams in the 1930s stabilized water levels and ended the rescue program.

45. "A Brief Resume of the Life History and Propagation of Fresh-Water Mussels," circa winter 1922–1923, entry 121, RG 22, NA; "The Fresh-Water Pearl Button Industry and the Relations of the Bureau of Fisheries Thereto"; Coker et al., "Natural History," p. 157.

46. M. M. Ellis, "The Artificial Propagation of Freshwater Mussels," pp. 220, 222.

ity and efficiency of farm crops. A 1930 memorandum published by the bureau observed that juvenile mussels could be raised to "planting size," stocked in suitable locations, "centralized for economic exploitation," and harvested in much the same manner as agricultural crops. Ellis's procedure could also be used to propagate mussels selectively based upon desirable commercial characteristics such as the color and thickness of their shells. Thus, the bureau memorandum boasted that "the prodigal waste of nature's seeding" could now be avoided, since "absolute control" of supply had been placed in the hands of fisheries scientists.[47]

"There ain't no good in spoiling a river"

In June 1929, the Bureau of Fisheries felt confident enough to arrange a demonstration of Ellis's work for button manufacturers at its Fairport, Iowa, biological station. Yet, just when triumph seemed at hand, man-caused environmental change dealt the bureau's supply-oriented policy a fatal blow.

For some time, scientists from the bureau had generally recognized the significance of habitat degradation. Hugh Smith expressed considerable anxiety over the impact of pollution on the mussel fishery as early as 1898. In succeeding years, employees of the bureau continued to manifest similar concerns. Many of the agency's fisheries experts regularly contributed to the journal of the American Fisheries Society and participated in the society's annual conventions. At the 1910 convention, Dr. C. H. Townsend, director of the New York Aquarium, delivered a paper that among other subjects considered the topic of pollution. In the ensuing discussion, the first speaker cogently stated the dilemma faced by many of the society's members when he pointed out, "Though we can hatch the fish and place them in the water, if the water is polluted all the fish culturists in Christendom cannot make it productive." The assembled delegates passed a resolution that called upon the society and its members to work for effective state and federal legislation. At periodic intervals thereafter, the society approved resolutions condemning water pollution and printed articles on the subject in its journal.[48]

47. "The Fresh-Water Pearl Button Industry and the Relations of the Bureau of Fisheries Thereto."

48. C. H. Townsend, "The Conservation of Our Rivers and Lakes"; "Report of Committee on Resolutions," *Transactions of the American Fisheries Society* 40 (1911): 55.

Eleven years later, in June 1921, the Bureau of Fisheries hosted a conference on interior waters at Fairport, Iowa. The approximately 120 delegates represented a wide range of interests, including the Bureau of Fisheries, commercial fishermen, the Corps of Engineers, several universities, state fish and game departments, and the pearl-button industry. Three independent delegates also registered as either sportsmen or conservationists. Most of the discussion focused on the destruction of habitat and the depletion of useful aquatic species, particularly as a result of pollution and wetlands drainage. Several speakers argued that river problems had an important social dimension; solutions depended as much on changes in popular values as they did on technical expertise, regulation, and adjustment of conflicts among users. At the same time, the sense of the convention seemed to be that really serious water-quality degradation was confined to the eastern part of the country. Winterton Curtis, a University of Missouri professor of zoology, told his listeners, "It always impresses me, as I go east . . . mile after mile of those streams in the manufacturing district of the east [are] evidently unfitted for many of the forms of life which formerly populated them."[49]

In the decade after the Fairport conference, the bureau's awareness of habitat degradation in the upper river increased appreciably. In 1926, at the request of a joint interim committee of the Wisconsin and Minnesota legislatures, the bureau detailed A. H. Wiebe to survey the water quality of the upper river. The citations in the bibliography of Wiebe's report indicate that Wiebe conducted the pioneering scientific study of pollution in the upper river. In this report, Wiebe revealed that for about forty-five miles below the Twin Cities the river suffered from a serious pollution problem during periods of low water. In June 1928, the bureau directed Wiebe to attend a meeting of the pollution committee of the Minnesota Division of the Izaak Walton League of America. The major topic of discussion at that gathering was cleaning up the river below the Twin Cities. Yet, even with this growing body of knowledge about habitat degradation at its disposal, the bureau continued to assign a high priority to its plans for artificially increasing the supply of mussels in the upper river.[50]

49. "Conservation Conference for Resources of Interior Waters, Held at United States Fisheries Biological Station, Fairport, Ia., June 8–10, 1921," p. 14, typescript, entry 121, RG 22, NA.

50. A. H. Wiebe, "Biological Survey of the Upper Mississippi," *Bulletin of the U.S. Bureau of Fisheries, vol. 43, Part II, 1927*, pp. 137–38, 152, 162–67; A. H.

During the 1920s, domestic sewage, industrial waste, and erosion silt had entered the upper river in ever-increasing amounts. Sewage and industrial waste originated in growing urban areas located along the banks of the river, especially Minneapolis/St. Paul. In 1931, Ellis observed that the silt load of the upper Mississippi River system had increased significantly during the previous decade "as a result of deforestation, current methods of tilling the land, and various improvements incident to commercial progress." He emphasized that silt presented perhaps the most serious fisheries problem in inland waters. Separately, pollution and silt degraded water quality. Together, they produced synergistic results. Sewage combined with fine silt was carried farther downstream than it would have been in clear water. Thus a local problem became regional in scope. Any natural or man-made obstruction that caused the current to slacken permitted the sewage-laden silt to settle to the bottom, where it decayed slowly and severely depleted the oxygen supply.[51]

By the late 1920s, natural reproduction of commercial mussels had practically ceased in the upper Mississippi and in many of its tributaries. Erosion silt smothered a large portion of the mussel population under a layer of mud. Ellis and other investigators found that in polluted waters the marsupia of gravid female mussels were "heavily infested with bacteria and infusoria." This effectively sterilized the mussels because most of the glochidia contained therein were either dead or in a weakened state. Sampling carried out by fisheries experts in the bureau revealed this condition to be so pervasive as to make it difficult to obtain breeding stock for propagation work. While conducting studies directed toward the commercial-scale application of his method of propagation, Ellis also discovered that glochidia and juvenile mussels were very sensitive to habitat change. They succumbed much more readily than did the adult bivalves to pollution, to siltation, and to lowered oxygen levels in the water. Ellis concluded, "The present

Wiebe to Chief, Division of Inquiry, Bureau of Fisheries, "Report on Minneapolis Pollution Meeting," 16 June 1928, entry 121, RG 22, NA.

51. *Second Annual Report of the Metropolitan Drainage Commission of Minneapolis and St. Paul on the Subject of Sewage Disposal of Minneapolis, St. Paul, and Contiguous Areas*, pp. 44–45, 54–55; Ellis, "Survey of Conditions Affecting Fisheries," p. 15–18; C. G. Bates and O. R. Zeasman, "Soil Erosion: A Local and National Problem," *Wisconsin Agricultural Experiment Station Research Bulletin*, pp. 30, 32, 95–96; M. M. Ellis, "Some Factors Affecting the Replacement of the Commercial Fresh-Water Mussels," *U.S. Bureau of Fisheries, Fishery Circular Number 7*, p. 5.

problem of mussel culture is not one of propagation, either natural or artificial, but the maintenance of a suitable habitat."[52]

In 1930, two factors combined to seal the fate of the bureau's mussel-restocking program. First, as a result of environmental degradation, much of the upper river drainage could not fulfill the simple needs of Ellis's method: a supply of healthy glochidia and a suitable body of water in which to stock the young mussels. Second, the Corps of Engineers announced its intent to construct navigation dams in a river already heavily burdened with silt and sewage. The dams would slow the current and cause the sewage/ silt mixture to settle out and blanket the bottoms of the newly created pools. Faced with this major alteration of the upper river, the bureau began to reanalyze the relationship between long-accepted river use and development practices and aquatic life. Scientists in the bureau did identify scattered rivers and streams that they believed could be managed so as to produce the twenty to twenty-five thousand tons of shells annually used by the industry.[53] Nonetheless, with the heart of the mussel region doomed, it was only a matter of time until the extremities expired as well.

The failure of artificial propagation forced the Bureau of Fisheries to pay more serious attention to man-induced changes in the river. After a February 1930 conference in Washington, D.C., the bureau abandoned its propagation activities in the upper river and decided to urge the five states along the upper Mississippi to repeal their protective legislation. The report of that meeting bluntly stated, "It appears that the mussel fishery of the Mississippi River is doomed to economic exhaustion." On 26 January 1932 the commissioner of fisheries recommended to the Minnesota commissioner of game and fish that his state's mussel protection laws be rescinded so that the industry could harvest the remaining mussels before they were killed or buried by silt and pollution.[54]

52. M. M. Ellis, "Memorandum on Propagation and Natural Replacement of Fresh Water Mussels," undated, but position in file indicates winter 1931–1932, entry 269, RG 22, NA; "Fisheries Situation and Bureau's Program, Mississippi River Area," 17–21 February 1930, entry 269, RG 22, NA; "The Fresh-Water Pearl Button Industry and the Relations of the Bureau of Fisheries Thereto."

53. The bureau's hopes for maintaining the industry are discussed in "Fisheries Situation and Bureau's Program, Mississippi River Area."

54. Ibid.; Henry O'Malley, U.S. Bureau of Fisheries, to Mr. Wm. D. Stewart, Commissioner of Game and Fish, Minnesota, 26 January 1932, entry 269, RG 22, NA; Henry O'Malley, Commissioner, to W. P. Fickett, President, National Association of Button Manufacturers, 2 March 1932, entry 269, RG 22, NA.

Officials in the bureau redefined the mussel depletion problem from simple overuse to habitat destruction. Concomitantly, the agency shifted its emphasis from controlling the propagation of a few useful species to understanding and mitigating the impacts of "commercial progress" and "civilization" on aquatic life. During the 1930s and 1940s, the bureau maintained a friendly liaison with the survivors of the pearl-button industry and continued to administer a much-abbreviated mussel-propagation program. Nonetheless, the devastation of the mussel fishery and the bureau's subsequent modification of policy shattered the effectiveness of the decades-old constituent relationship between the agency and the industry. This dissolution freed the Bureau of Fisheries to move in a new direction. Loss of the manufacturers' support also helped persuade the bureau to develop a new constituency. The agency began to frame press releases and other publicity to appeal to sportsmen and conservationists who would back a policy that stressed maintaining the biological productivity of water.[55]

Water pollution quickly emerged as one of the bureau's most important new concerns. A memorandum distributed by the agency in April 1930 argued that up until that time studies of water pollution had focused on the recovery of trade wastes and sanitation but had done little to determine the affect of pollution on aquatic life. To remedy this shortcoming, the bureau in 1930 established a jointly sponsored Field Station for Interior Fisheries Investigations at the University of Missouri in Columbia and appointed M. M. Ellis as director.[56] It would be incorrect to conclude that this increased concern over water quality immediately altered the bureau's focus on improving the commercial productivity of inland waters. Rather, over the next thirty years the agency's research on water pollution contributed to a trend that became increasingly important within the bureau and among segments of the public.

Ellis and his staff at the Field Station for Interior Fisheries Investigations conducted a wide-ranging analysis of stream pollution. They used a floating laboratory for studies of the Mississippi

55. For an early example of the bureau's appeal to a new constituency, see Elmer Higgins, Chief, Division of Scientific Inquiry, "U.S. Bureau of Fisheries Warns Conservationists of Industrialization and Pollution of Mississippi River," fall 1931, typescript, entry 269, RG 22, NA. Higgins summarized Ellis's "A Survey of Conditions Affecting Fisheries in the Upper Mississippi River."

56. "The Fresh-Water Pearl Button Industry and the Relations of the Bureau of Fisheries Thereto"; M. M. Ellis to Dean Edgar Allen, Medical School, University of Missouri, 24 April 1930, 3651, School of Medicine Records, WHM.

and its tributaries and motorized laboratories to extend their field observations nationwide. In 1937, the bureau published Ellis's "Detection and Measurement of Stream Pollution." The agency intended this work to establish standards for evaluating water pollution and to serve as a "yardstick" for measuring pollution hazards throughout the country so that "steps for the correction of existing evils may be based on accurate knowledge."[57]

The bureau employed the knowledge generated by Ellis's studies to attempt to change ingrained attitudes toward river pollution. Late in 1936, for example, Ellis wrote an article intended for a popular audience, which he titled "Trailing Stream Pollution." In this article, Ellis used a refugee from the world of Huck Finn to pique his readers' interest and to introduce his theme. In the first paragraph, one of Ellis's pollution investigation teams is startled by a shouted warning. "Hey! Don't put your hands in that water! It'll eat your fingers off!" At that point, a "river rat" pushes his way through the willows that grow along the shore. Having captured the crew's attention, this "worn but contented" individual mutters half to himself and half to them, "There ain't no good in spoiling a river." His purpose fulfilled, the river rat wanders off through the willows so that Ellis can explain the social and biological costs of spoiling a river. He argues, "Conspicuous among the obstacles to a clean-up of existing conditions is the apathetic tolerance of stream pollution in the United States." Ellis contended that this attitude resulted from two widely held but incorrect assumptions: first, that pollution "is the necessary companion of municipal and industrial progress" and, second, "that no feasible remedial measures exist."[58]

By the late 1930s, the bureau's quest for knowledge about pollution and its attempt to change attitudes on the subject had evolved into support for national water-pollution-control legislation. Fisheries scientists insisted that such legislation be designed to protect water quality at a level sufficient to support aquatic life. This specification necessitated the setting of standards more stringent than those required to protect human health, because water that would

57. "Detection and Measurement of Stream Pollution—A Publication Every Conservationist Should Have," *The Progressive Fish Culturist* (December 1937): 950; M. M. Ellis, "Detection and Measurement of Stream Pollution," *Bulletin of the U.S. Bureau of Fisheries, vol. 48, 1937*, pp. 365–437.

58. M. M. Ellis, "Trailing Stream Pollution," typescript, December 1936, entry 269, RG 22, NA.

not sustain a diversity of aquatic life could still be treated to make it potable.[59]

Between 1898, when Hugh M. Smith published his investigation of the mussel fishery, and the late 1920s, some significant changes took place in the way scientists from the Bureau of Fisheries defined the problem of mussel depletion, in the policies they formulated to address the mussel shortage, and in the attitudes toward the river that undergirded their policy decisions. For approximately the first third of the twentieth century, the bureau singled out overuse as the main reason for the exhaustion of mussel beds in the upper river. After the Bureau of Fisheries replaced the Fish Commission in 1903, it designed its initial series of policy responses—investigation, advice, propagation, and advocacy of regulation—to guarantee a supply of mussels for the pearl-button industry.

Scientists from the bureau shared a number of attitudes with multiple-purpose conservationists such as Gifford Pinchot and WJ McGee, who emphasized scientific management of marketable resources. Fisheries specialists advocated supply-oriented conservation in order to ensure the future availability of mussels and the continued productivity of the industry. They counseled gatherers to eliminate wasteful harvesting practices and urged the industry to adopt the most efficient techniques for the manufacture of buttons from shells. The bureau also conducted stream surveys in order to locate new mussel beds and made a long-term commitment to artificial propagation.[60]

From this perspective, the highest use of the river was the commercial exploitation of mussels by private enterprise to create material progress and an improved quality of life. As Hugh Smith explained, the Mississippi River button industry transformed "a hitherto useless product into a valuable commodity" and marketed it at a reasonable price.[61] Scientists from the bureau also had a view of the river that emphasized conquest and control, through the application of specialized knowledge. A clearly stated objective of the bureau's mussel-propagation program was to control the

59. The bureau's position on national water-pollution-control legislation is discussed in Chapter 5.
60. "A Brief Resume of the Life History and Propagation of Fresh-Water Mussels"; "The Fresh-Water Pearl Button Industry and the Relations of the Bureau Thereto."
61. Smith, "Mussel Fishery," p. 304.

supply of mussels by eliminating the uncertainty associated with natural reproduction in rivers.

The bureau's investigators applied a narrow, somewhat reductionist method to their general research and their work on freshwater mussels. That is to say, they studied the component parts of living organisms in an artificial, laboratory environment. M. M. Ellis had practiced this approach, as had most other researchers who worked for the bureau during the first third of the twentieth century. From the inception of the cooperative research laboratory established by the bureau at the University of Missouri–Columbia, Ellis had insisted that his primary interest was in "pure science." This contention was borne out by a 1935 report on the progress of his work, in which he stated, "From the investigations completed in this laboratory publications have appeared or are now in press which show the application of physiological and biochemical work to fisheries problems, and conversely the correlations of these investigations with pure science and medical physiology."[62] The reductionist method used by the bureau's investigators and their emphasis on artificial propagation had the potential to give them a narrow focus on the river.

Another important factor worked in the opposite direction. These men had an interest in perpetuating aquatic life that eventually contributed to a more comprehensive understanding of the river. Beginning with Hugh Smith's 1898 article, scientists from the bureau studied the river environment and expressed concern over unfavorable man-induced changes in aquatic habitat. Smith had cautioned, "The effect on animal life—especially that on the bottom—of the discharge of city and factory refuse into streams has hardly been considered by those interested in the preservation of the mussels, but it constitutes, perhaps, the most serious menace to the industry, in that the destruction wrought is inevitable and complete." His warning turned out to be remarkably accurate.[63]

In the three decades after Smith completed his seminal investigation, the resource problems of the pearl-button industry stimulated considerable scientific research. By 1930, fisheries sci-

62. Ellis to Noyes, 30 January 1928; M. M. Ellis, "Organization and Function of the United States Bureau of Fisheries Cooperative Research Laboratories at the University of Missouri," 12 December 1935, 3651, School of Medicine Records, WHM.

63. Smith, "Mussel Fishery," p. 314.

entists had conducted numerous studies of the upper river that sensitized them to the importance of environment and the significance of habitat change. This line of inquiry matured into an understanding of the river as a complex, interdependent system. The system included people who expected the river to provide a range of social benefits and who altered the river in the process of fulfilling their various demands. These fisheries experts began to realize that material progress and man-caused changes in the environment of the upper river were interrelated aspects of the process of national development. They recognized that the undesirable consequences of modernization had diminished the river's capability to sustain a diversity of aquatic life and to meet the demands placed on it by society.

As a result of its new concern over the consequences of progress, the Bureau of Fisheries placed increasing emphasis on the biological productivity of rivers. Scientists such as Ellis concentrated on understanding the impact of man-caused change on the environment of inland waters. Acting upon the knowledge gained from these investigations, the bureau endorsed national water-pollution-control legislation, with standards designed to protect aquatic life. Officials of the bureau realized that a change in public values would have to precede effective federal action. These positions offered both an implicit and an explicit critique of those aspects of the modernizing process that had degraded the nation's rivers and streams. Increasingly, during the 1930s, fisheries scientists aligned themselves against corporate and municipal polluters and with conservationists and sportsmen who shared the belief that "there ain't no good in spoiling a river."

4 Conservation Crusade
The Izaak Walton League of America

I AM weary of civilization's madness and I yearn for the harmonious gladness of the woods and of the streams.

I AM tired of your piles of buildings and I ache from your iron streets.

I FEEL jailed in your greatest cities and I long for the unharnessed freedom of the big outside. —Will Dilg[1]

In January 1922, fifty-four Chicago fishing enthusiasts formed the Izaak Walton League of America—defender of the out-of-doors. Within two and a half years the fifty-four had become more than one hundred thousand, and the league had scored an important national conservation victory with the creation of the Upper Mississippi River Wildlife and Fish Refuge. The Izaak Walton League demonstrated considerable vigor in the cities and towns along the upper Mississippi River, where it found eager converts among businessmen and professionals. A decade earlier, these residents of "mainstreet" had joined commercial clubs and had routinely boosted river-development projects such as wetlands drainage, navigational improvements, and Keokuk dam. Their mass conversion to active conservationism reflected an underlying fear that qualities of the river they had long prized, but had taken for granted, might soon cease to exist.

"The Moral Equivalent of War"

In 1910 William James wrote an essay titled "The Moral Equivalent of War," in which he suggested that military conscription be

---

1. Will Dilg, "City Worn," reprinted in *Outdoor America* 6 (October 1927):21 and 2 (January 1937): 5 (hereafter cited as *OA*). Even though *Outdoor America* underwent some changes of name between 1922 and 1935, it is referred to as *Outdoor America* throughout this manuscript.

replaced by mandatory service in a war on nature. This essay and the Izaak Walton League sprang from a common cultural response to the development of an urban, industrial society. James suggested that an army of young men should march to productive employment in coal and iron mines, fishing fleets, factories, and construction projects. As a pacifist, he was repelled by the militarism of early-twentieth-century society and by the brutality and irrationality of war. Yet he also believed that war had historically played an important role in the development of human society. Military life possessed an undeniably romantic quality, and war represented the ultimate human test. Those who served in the military, those who survived the test, became infused with manly qualities that laid the groundwork for national greatness. By focusing people's attention on nature rather than on aggression against each other, James hoped to turn the energies of the nation's youth to constructive ends without sacrificing the martial virtues that accompanied military service.[2]

A dozen years after William James penned his essay, the Izaak Walton League made its dramatic appearance on the national conservation scene. Like James, the league acted upon the belief that life in the United States had become insipid, lacking the excitement and physical challenges that had made Americans a virile race. In common with Theodore Roosevelt's seekers of the strenuous life, they recoiled from overcivilization and looked to nature as an antidote to the softness, the boredom, and the complacency of modern civilization.[3]

In a number of ways, however, the league advocated a different outlook on nature than the one espoused by James and Roosevelt. Waltonians thought in terms of scarcity rather than abundance and of recreation rather than production. They believed that contact with unspoiled nature had traditionally formed the finest qualities of the American character. Based on this view of nature, the league put tremendous effort into turning aside the national assault on nature and preserving the remaining fragments of this country's important natural heritage. During a House hearing on the Upper Mississippi River Wildlife and Fish Refuge Act, Missouri con-

2. William James, "The Moral Equivalent of War," in *Essays on Faith and Morals*, pp. 311–28.

3. For a recently published, comprehensive analysis of antimodernism, see T. J. Jackson Lears, *No Place of Grace: Antimodernism and the Transformation of American Culture, 1880–1920.*

gressman Harry Hawes testified, "It is primarily a bill to save a piece of outdoors for ourselves and for our boys. We are going to make mollycoddles of our kids if they don't know how to use a fishing rod and a gun. We are going to lose the best American traditions if we do not have a place for the boys to play."[4]

Waltonians' interest in nature thus provided an opportunity for protest against the vapidness of modern life, but it also served as a mechanism of accommodation to the rigors of an industrial capitalist society. "Ikes" objected loudly to the waste, the greed, and the excesses of unregulated private enterprise. At the same time, men who had the opportunity to camp and fish and relax in the out-of-doors were more contented and labored more efficiently upon their return to work.

Between the completion of the Keokuk hydroelectric dam in 1913 and the founding of the league in 1922, significant changes took place in attitudes toward the use and development of the upper river. For a few years on either side of 1913, discontent manifested itself in the service area of Keokuk dam and even made itself heard in Washington, D.C. Residents of the upper river valley complained about the quality of life in Keokuk, the obstruction of navigation, the lack of new factories, and the price of power. Some protesters resented the loss of decision-making authority to Stone & Webster, the Boston-based company that financed, constructed, and operated the big hydroelectric project. This dissent took place within the context of a one-way relationship that stressed conquering the river and forcing it to accede to the demands of an expanding industrial civilization. In 1913, people regularly participated in and enjoyed a number of noncommercial uses of the river. No identifiable, organized constituency existed, however, for the protection or preservation of assets such as sport fishing, beautiful scenery, or a favorite swimming hole.

By the early 1920s, many residents of the upper river valley had come to believe that these noncommercial benefits could be lost forever, as a result of pollution, siltation, navigational improvements, and wetlands drainage. The sense of crisis created by this realization resulted in a reordering of priorities and in an interest in working out a new relationship with the river that included obligations as well as demands. The Izaak Walton League appealed to

4. U.S. Congress, House, Committee on Agriculture, *Mississippi River Wild Life and Fish Refuge: Hearings on H.R. 4088, a Bill to Establish the Upper Mississippi River Wild Life and Fish Refuge*, p. 15.

people, particularly in the Midwest, who were concerned about the consequences of man-induced environmental change. Ding Darling, a native Iowan, cartoonist, and conservationist, remembered that he and a small group of fellow sportsmen "had watched the Prairie Chicken disappear, the flight of migratory waterfowl dwindle . . . pollution, siltation and complete disregard of fishing laws." He recalled that the league's refuge campaign gave them "the first encouraging hint of how to proceed."[5]

The league provided leadership, institutional structure, and clearly defined issues to people who were worried about degradation of water quality and aquatic habitat, loss of fishing and hunting opportunities, and the destruction of aesthetic and other sensual qualities of the river. Thus, in a manner similar to Rachel Carson's *Silent Spring* several decades later, the league owed much of its early success to the fact that it validated and gave focus to attitudes that had already begun to take shape.

The Meteoric Conservation Career of Will Dilg

The founding of the league and the establishment of the refuge were closely intertwined with the meteoric conservation career of a Chicago advertising man named Will Dilg. Frustratingly little information exists about the man. He was born in Milwaukee, Wisconsin, in 1867 and died in March 1927 after a long, painful battle with cancer of the throat. Most photographs taken in the mid-1920s show him neatly dressed in a business suit, indistinguishable from thousands of other urban professionals. His dark hair, carefully combed and parted down the middle, topped a forehead broadened by an obviously receding hairline. Dilg had a gaunt face, which set off angular features and intense, penetrating eyes. His eyes are the one feature that hints at the passionate and charismatic personality that attracted thousands of men to the league.[6]

Dilg was fifty-four and unknown in conservation circles when he and fifty-three other men met for lunch at the Chicago Athletic Club in January 1922. At that meeting, they formed a new, national conservation organization and named it in honor of Izaak Walton, a

5. Ding Darling to R. G. Townsend, 7 March 1959, quoted in David L. Lendt, *Ding: The Life of Jay Norwood Darling*, pp. 37–38.
6. Henry Clepper, ed., *Leaders of American Conservation*, pp. 94–95. For limited biographical material and pictures of Will Dilg, see William T. Hornaday, "The Upper Mississippi Wildlife Refuge: Will H. Dilg's Monument," and Merton S. Heiss, "Will Dilg and the Early Days."

Will Dilg, founder of the Izaak Walton League of America.

seventeenth-century English writer and angler. Izaak Walton's book *The Compleat Angler*, published in 1653, had become a "bible" for many American sport fishermen.

The new organization experienced phenomenal growth, increasing from 54 members in January 1922, to over 100,000 in 1924, and to more than 175,000 in 1928. In 1928, the league boasted three thousand chapters in forty states. By way of comparison, in 1924 three older conservation groups, the Sierra Club, the American Game Protective Association, and the National Association of Audubon Societies, each had a membership of 7,000 or less. The league established its headquarters in Chicago, making it the first national conservation organization to be based in a city other than New York or Washington, D.C. Unlike the other two national wildlife-protection groups, the American Game Protective Association and the Audubon Association, the league enjoyed its greatest strength in the Midwest rather than in the East.[7]

The fifty-four men who organized the league were united by their love of outdoor recreation, especially fishing, and by their fear that the outdoors they so enjoyed was rapidly becoming a thing of the past. Most of them were businessmen and professionals. Twelve worked in advertising or sales, the largest single occupational group represented. Many of these men gave freely of their time. In addition, monetary contributions made by some of the founders and other early members kept the league from wrecking on the financial shoals toward which Dilg always seemed to be headed. George C. Scott enrolled as the first life member of the league, and at Dilg's request he served as chairman of the executive committee from fall 1923 until April 1925. Scott, vice-president of American Steel Foundries, appealed to friends in Chicago and a number of other cities and raised over $70,000 during his eighteen months on the executive committee. Scott's personal cash contributions amounted to about $10,000. Another member

7. Membership figures may be found in *Mississippi River Wild Life and Fish Refuge: Hearings*, p. 3; "Original 'Fifty-Four' Hold 6th Reunion," *OA* 6 (April 1928):39. Comparative membership figures are reported in Stephen Fox, *John Muir and His Legacy: The American Conservation Movement*, p. 162. Membership comparisons for this period are uncertain at best. For example, on p. 6 of *Mississippi River Wild Life and Fish Refuge: Hearings*, T. Gilbert Pearson claimed an Audubon Association membership of 380,000. It seems likely that he included members of state affiliates in this figure. An article published in 1973 in *Audubon* gives the Audubon Association's 1934 membership as 3,500 (Carl W. Buchheister and Frank Graham Jr., "From the Swamps and Back: A Concise and Candid History of the Audubon Movement," p. 26).

of the executive committee, William V. Kelley, president of the Miehle Printing Press, donated colored covers for eight issues of *Outdoor America*, at a cost of about $3,000.[8]

Will Dilg, nonetheless, was the driving force behind the organization. He ran the league as if it were his property and in the process marked it indelibly with the stamp of his powerful but erratic personality. Dilg's reputation as a conservationist reached its zenith after the refuge victory in 1924. Less than two years later, in April 1926, the membership voted him out of office at the league's annual convention. Dilg's fall from power resulted from a number of factors. He had always been a visionary who had resorted to hyperbole when the facts did not suit his goals. After passage of the refuge act, perhaps as a result of the heady, instant success and his progressively worsening cancer, Dilg began to come apart. He became increasingly messianic and arbitrary in his dealings with others.[9]

Dilg's chronic mismanagement of the league's funds opened a hemorrhage in the organization's already feeble treasury. As president, Dilg refused to accept a salary, and he insisted in public speeches that he worked without pay. Yet, during his tenure as head of the league, Dilg's personal expense account averaged about $1,000 per month. He proved either unwilling or unable to live within the constraints of a budget. Early in 1925, the executive committee cautioned him to adhere to a budget because the league was over $50,000 in the red. Dilg replied that he knew nothing about budgets and had no interest in such things. After the league's third annual convention in May 1925, the executive committee recognized that Dilg was quite ill and appropriated $2,500 so that he could take a vacation. Before he left on his paid vacation, Dilg incurred large bills at two camping equipment stores. Even though he had been asked not to do so, he charged these outfitting expenses to the league. Thus by the spring of 1926, many of the organization's leaders had reluctantly come to view him as a liability. Dilg lost his job, a sick and angry man, and those who

8. Typed, six-page league history written between April 1926 and March 1927, author unknown, located in the files of the Izaak Walton League of America, Suite 806, 1800 N. Kent St., Arlington, Va., 22209 (hereafter cited as IWLA files). George E. Scott to Donald Hough, 3 August 1927, IWLA files; Rush C. Butler to Professor B. Shimek, 21 June 1927, IWLA files; "Original 'Fifty-Four' Hold 6th Reunion," p. 39.

9. Six-page league history; T. Gilbert Pearson, *Adventures in Bird Protection*, pp. 361–62.

followed dedicated themselves to running the league's affairs in a more professional, businesslike manner.[10]

Despite his seemingly self-destructive impulses, Dilg presided over the creation of the largest amateur conservation organization that had existed in the nation up until that time. Under his direction, the league grew from a local club to a militant, national organization. Dilg himself was responsible for much of this growth. He was a bold, charismatic leader who believed devoutly in his conservation cause and who sought converts with the zeal of a great evangelist. William T. Hornaday, long-time director of the New York Zoological Society and champion of wildlife protection, described Dilg as "a conservation John the Baptist, preaching in the Wilderness."[11]

Will Dilg's success with the Izaak Walton League cannot be separated from the cultural milieu in which it evolved. A slightly jaundiced but extremely useful look at that culture is offered in Sinclair Lewis's novel *Babbitt*. George F. Babbitt sold real estate in the medium-sized, fictional city of Zenith, Ohio. In one sense, Babbitt personified the American dream. He owned his own car and a home in a prosperous suburb where he lived surrounded by standardized material comfort. Yet, at forty-six, he was overweight, restless, and vaguely dissatisfied with his life. George slept alone under a khaki blanket he had purchased for a camping trip he had never taken. For him, the blanket suggested freedom and heroism. "It symbolized gorgeous loafing, gorgeous cursing, virile flannel shirts."[12]

Babbitt prized manliness in a society that limited the expression of his manhood to talk, boosterism, and membership in fraternal organizations. In an after-dinner speech given to the Zenith Chamber of Commerce, he explained that a real man was "a God-fearing, hustling, successful, two-fisted Regular Guy" who belonged to "any one of a score of organizations of good, jolly, kidding, laughing, sweating, upstanding, lend-a-handing Royal Good Fellows."[13]

Thousands of real George Babbitts lived in cities and towns throughout the Midwest. Advertiser Will Dilg was one of them. He packaged the league to resemble the fraternal groups and ser-

10. Six-page league history.
11. Hornaday, "The Upper Mississippi Wild Life Refuge," p. 3.
12. Sinclair Lewis, *Babbitt*, pp. 7–8.
13. Ibid., p. 155.

vice clubs to which his prospective members belonged. In 1923, the league hired the former office manager of the Kiwanis national headquarters as its executive secretary.[14] The Izaak Walton League of America gave George Babbitt and his friends a chance to perform a community service by boosting nature. It also provided them with the opportunity to fish and loaf and curse and wear flannel shirts. Dilg addressed the members as "brother," infused them with a sense of purpose, and injected excitement into their lives. A persuasive speaker, energetic organizer, and master of publicity, Dilg spoke the "he-man" language of the booster. He successfully created an atmosphere of masculine camaraderie that thousands of men could not resist. In July 1923, Dilg wrote "The Drainage Crime of a Century," in which he sought to mobilize a constituency for the refuge by appealing to a common fraternal bond: "Boys, oh boys, oh boys, how I wish I possessed the genius to properly describe this wonderful Winneshiek country and the paradise it is for the fisherman and hunter. God never made anything more beautiful. He made it, my brothers, for men like you and me."[15]

Outdoor America

Dilg decided that the league needed a magazine, and he convinced a reluctant board of directors to follow him. Under Dilg's editorship, *Outdoor America* appeared in August 1922. The new journal aimed for a diverse audience by providing a blend of articles on conservation, fishing, bird lore, camping, hunting, and other subjects that attracted the attention of outdoor enthusiasts. Topics of interest to men and boys provided a common denominator for most of the selections published in *Outdoor America*. Examples from the magazine's first edition include "Dedicated to Sam: A Boy's First Dog," "Game Rifles: Original Handling of an Old Subject," and "Sea Angling: A Ten Hour Swordfish Battle," by Zane Grey.[16]

Despite his masculine emphasis, Dilg recognized the importance of the female vote. During its first year of publication, *Outdoor America* carried a section called "The Outdoor Woman,"

14. The information on Kiwanis is cited in Fox, *John Muir and His Legacy*, p. 162.

15. Will Dilg, "The Drainage Crime of a Century," pp. 601, 623.

16. Thomas Ambrose, "Early History of the I.W.L.A.," undated, three-page typescript, IWLA files; letter from Fred N. Peet, undated, two-page typescript on the founding of the league, IWLA files.

edited by Dilg's wife, Marguerite Ives. Thereafter, the magazine continued to print articles by female writers, many of them addressed directly to women. As part of his refuge campaign, Dilg used *Outdoor America* to mobilize women for the cause. Marguerite Ives, for example, wrote "An Appeal to the Outdoor Woman for a Great New National Preserve," in which she pointedly argued, "If you should happen to ask John about this and immersed in the paper, he answers carelessly, 'Oh, don't bother your little head about that—it's nothing that need concern you,' don't be put off—it *does* concern you, American women."[17]

In order to lure readers to his magazine and into the league, Dilg persuaded many well-known writers to donate their talents to *Outdoor America.* In a letter to Hal G. Evarts, a regular contributor to the *Saturday Evening Post,* Dilg pointed out, "Each great American who declares himself for us now adds to our national prestige and our convert-drawing ability." Dilg then invited Evarts to become a "great American" when he added, "What a splendid thing an editorial by you would be for the magazine and the cause it espouses." Flattery got him everywhere. Dilg's magazine printed articles by Evarts, Emerson Hough, Hamlin Garland, and Theodore Dreiser. Outdoor adventure stories by Zane Grey also appeared on a regular basis. *Outdoor America* ran selections by Secretary of Commerce Herbert Hoover as well as by wildlife conservationists William T. Hornaday and Aldo Leopold. James Henshall, a wildlife conservationist, respected authority on fish, and author of many popular books on fishing, edited the magazine's pollution section from August 1922 until his death in the spring of 1925.[18]

Outdoor America played a key role in the league's successful attempt to muster people into its conservation crusade. An examination of the first issue of *Outdoor America* reveals the league's ap-

17. Marguerite Ives, "An Appeal to the Outdoor Women for a Great New National Preserve," p. 97.
18. Dilg's letter to Evarts is quoted in Fox, *John Muir and His Legacy,* p. 160. Hal G. Evarts, "Allies Now—the $ and Sentiment," *OA* 3 (February 1925): 5; contributions by Emerson Hough, Zane Grey, and James Henshall all appear in the first issue of *OA,* August 1922. Zane Grey served on the league's national board of directors. Harry Hawes included Hamlin Garland in a list of contributors to *OA* in "Conserving the Outdoors for Health and Profit," p. 52; Theodore Dreiser, "The Tippecanoe River," *OA* 2 (March 1924): 24–25; Herbert Hoover, "Alaska Salmon Protection," *OA* 2 (December 1923): 196–98, and "An Opportunity," *OA* 3 (January 1925): 16; William T. Hornaday, "Beware of a Gameless Continent," *OA* 2 (November 1923): 144; Aldo Leopold, "Quail Protection," *OA* 3 (November 1924): 42.

peal to the public. Although their subjects varied, most of the authors who wrote for the first issue proclaimed a similar message: a serious crisis confronted American sportsmen. Retreating before the advance of commercial progress, under attack from within by unprincipled hunters and fishermen, the out-of-doors had been reduced to a mere fraction of its former greatness. Soon even the remaining remnants would be gone, and along with them the fishing and hunting opportunities that these authors regarded as their heritage and their children's legacy.

Writers in *Outdoor America* rarely noted another type of technical and social change that also contributed to the decimation of fish and wildlife. Led by advocates of the strenuous life, such as Theodore Roosevelt, turn-of-the-century Americans began to seek the out-of-doors as an antidote to an increasingly flaccid urban, industrial society. Shortened work weeks, regular vacations, and transportation improvements made it easier for the growing legion of sportsmen to reach the fields and streams. The railroad, the private automobile, a gradually improving system of rural roads, and the outboard motor provided hunters and fishermen with ready access to diminishing quantities of fish and wildlife. Thus, by their collective weight, a growing army of "nature lovers" helped to crush the remaining opportunities for outdoor experiences.[19]

As with all other issues published during Dilg's term as editor, the first number of *Outdoor America* bore his imprint. Dilg solicited articles and in some cases suggested the title and the message. The author of an article entitled "My Own Little River (In Memoriam)" explained that he had been asked to write a story about "a stream suddenly polluted." Swayed by Dilg's temperament, *Outdoor America* called for a national conservation crusade to prevent the extinction of the out-of-doors. "The hour has struck," thundered E. C. Kemper, "for the Outdoor God's chosen people—the fishermen if you please—to stand up as one man." In a powerfully written article, strategically placed on the front cover, Emerson Hough threw down the gauntlet and declared, "It is time to call a halt." According to Hough, federal resource agencies and existing conservation organizations had proved unable to stop the destruc-

19. This process of technical, social, and environmental change is discussed from the perspective of the fishery in C. F. Culler, "The Future of the Upper Mississippi Fisheries," *Minnesota Waltonian* 5 (October 1934): 7, 15, entry 162, Record Group 22, Records of the Fish and Wildlife Service, National Archives Building, Washington, D.C. (hereafter cited as RG 22, NA).

tion. And, he accused, not one in ten American sportsmen "have practiced the creed which hypocritically they profess. Claiming self denial, we practice self indulgence." Hough promised that the league offered a fresh start, new hope, and the last chance to save the out-of-doors.[20]

Emerson Hough's reputation attracted readers. Placing his article on the cover of *Outdoor America's* first edition was a stroke of advertising genius. Hough was a living symbol of the kind of values to which the league hoped to appeal. He was a prolific writer of outdoor and western novels. Between 1900 and the early 1920s, he wrote twenty-five novels, two of which were made into successful films. Hough was an avid hunter and fisherman, an amateur conservationist, and for several years he served as an editor of *Field and Stream*. During World War I, he headed up a sportsmen's campaign to save the elk herd in Yellowstone Park when its range was threatened by the encroachment of domestic sheep. In 1922, Hough accepted an appointment to the editorial staff of *Outdoor America*, a position he held until shortly before his death in April 1923.[21]

The first issue of *Outdoor America* eulogized the vanishing opportunities for outdoor experiences, especially fishing, as aquatic habitat fell prey to the consequences of progress. Pollution, declared the subtitle of James Henshall's column, is "The Most Important Problem the I.W.L.A. Will Have to Solve." Several authors looked back with nostalgia at the fishing holes they had enjoyed as boys. The beauty, the challenge, the excitement of those places had made them better men. Yet, by the early 1920s, only the ravaged remains of those remembered streams still existed. Robert H. Davis captured the profound sense of loss many of the writers expressed in a poem entitled "The Rape of the River." On a pilgrimage to a favorite boyhood stream, he found that "Forest and stream in grief had died, / By the vandals crucified." Davis's stream "was now putrid, and loathsome—and

20. Lionel F. Phillips, "My Own Little River (In Memoriam)"; E. C. Kemper, "The Crusade"; Emerson Hough, "Time to Call a Halt"; Will Dilg, "A Message to Out-Door Americans."

21. Although popular, Emerson Hough was not a "great" writer. His reputation faded quickly after his death. Interested readers might consult the following sources: Pauline Grahame, "A Novelist of the Unsung," *Palimpsest* 11 (February 1930): 67–77; *The National Cyclopedia of American Biography* (New York: James T. White & Co., 1926), 19:60; *The Encyclopedia Americana, International Edition* (New York: Americana Corporation, 1973), p. 456.

stinking." It had been destroyed because the owners of a sawmill disposed of their sawdust in the water. Dilg fully expected readers to identify with Davis's distress and be moved to action. To that end, he promised to reprint "The Rape of the River" every six months.[22]

Collectively, then, the various writers mourned a vanishing outdoor America. Between the lines they cried for their lost youth and for a time, not so long ago, when the nation seemed more innocent, business less greedy, and progress less rapacious. In a verse entitled "The Carefree Trail," Orrin A. DeMass contrasted the commercial world and its emphasis on profit with the peaceful riverbanks of his boyhood. A champion of nature, he longed for a chance to flee from the city to a place "Away from the beaten paths of men / Far from the haunts of greed and strife." Not many of De-Mass's readers really wanted to give up their careers in the city, but they understood what the poem meant. It spoke to their dissatisfactions, it acknowledged their wish for a rest, and it indulged their need to dream.

Many of the authors looked to the future with considerable apprehension. In so doing, they sounded a theme that would appear repeatedly in the pages of *Outdoor America*. If the nation's sportsmen turned their backs on the league, American boys would be denied important, character-building contacts with nature. Waltonians made room for women in their magazine, depended upon their energy, and courted their votes. They often thought, however, in terms of saving the out-of-doors for their sons. In an editorial that challenged "It's Up to You Mr. Sportsman," Will Dilg warned, "Already the boy born today is foredoomed to have no fishing at all, unless his parents can take him to far and remote places."[23] Romer Grey, ten-year-old son of Zane Grey, even contributed a two-paragraph article. Undoubtedly coached, young Grey appealed to fathers to join the league for the sake of their sons:

> My Dad takes me places where there are a few fish left. And so I have fun. But I wonder what the lots of boys do who are not so lucky as I am. They ought to have places to fish. It was fishing and hunting that made the pioneers of early days such men. I say the Daddies who love to fish should somehow get together and fix it so their boys could also learn to love to fish.[24]

22. Robert H. Davis, "The Rape of the River"; James A. Henshall, "Pollution."
23. [Will Dilg], "It's Up to You Mr. Sportsman."
24. "From Romer Zane Grey: Veritably a Chip off the Old Block."

In an effort to create esprit de corps, perhaps with a dash of arrogance, the men who genuflected before Izaak Walton liked to view themselves as a favored people of God. Yet, except for this bit of group chauvinism, many Waltonians found little solace in traditional Christian explanations of the relationship between people and nature. Historian Lynn White analyzes the environmental implications of this conventional interpretation of Christianity in his seminal essay "The Historical Roots of Our Ecologic Crisis." White argues that according to Christian theology God created mankind in his own image, separate from and superior to the rest of the natural world. Christianity not only established a division between people and the natural world but also maintained that it was God's will that human beings exploit nature for their own ends.[25] From this perspective, Christianity denied any moral obligation to nature and served as a justification for the kind of environmental degradation that so concerned members of the league.

Several writers in *Outdoor America* rejected the interpretations of Christianity that undergirded the secular gospel of progress. They insisted that God dwelt in the out-of-doors and that people who used nature should do so as his guests. For lawyer E. C. Kemper of Washington, D.C., the love that fishermen had for lakes and streams was "nothing else than the worship of God in its simplest, truest form." Sounding very much like John Muir, he castigated people who ravaged nature in the name of commercial gain. "Here in the East," he said, "we see the pollution of our streams with the tacit approval of State Legislatures, whose members think in the terms of the Almighty Dollar rather than in the terms of Almighty God."[26] Will Dilg clearly saw a religious dimension to the league's conservation crusade. He exhorted his followers with the suggestion that Waltonians marched behind God's holy banner and earned his special blessing for their efforts to protect the out-of-doors. "My brothers," Dilg said, "all the polluters of streams and the fish and game hogs and the market hunters oppose us, but just think how the Supreme Creator of the Universe, who put those fish in our streams, and gave us our wild fowl and our four footed little brothers in the forests MUST LOVE THE IZAAK WALTON LEAGUE OF AMERICA."[27]

25. Lynn White, Jr., "The Historical Roots of Our Ecologic Crisis," *Science*, 155 (10 March 1967): 1203–7.

26. Kemper, "The Crusade"; see also Marguerite Ives, "The Out-Door Woman," p. 17.

27. Dilg, "A Message to Outdoor Americans," p. 32.

Outdoor America's first edition was supported by advertisers who displayed products and services to people interested in outdoor recreation. Various companies touted their sporting goods and fishing equipment, including a "Bass-Enticer" lure endorsed by Will Dilg. For the motorist, the Adams Trailer Corporation offered a folding "motorbungalo," while the Canadian National Railways promoted ideal vacations complete with "real fishing and hunting in virgin streams and unspoiled big game country." From a historical perspective, these advertisements reflect a fundamental change from production to consumption then taking place in American society. Advertisers in *Outdoor America* targeted their appeals at potential customers who viewed nature as consumers rather than as producers. They aimed their ads at people who wanted to enjoy life, who had the leisure time to travel, and who could afford to spend money on outdoor equipment.[28]

By August 1922, the league had already spawned chapters throughout the Midwest. A section of *Outdoor America* called "News of the Chapters" presented brief reports on the activities of ten chapters, including five in Illinois, Iowa, and Wisconsin. These summaries reveal that sportsmen had begun to act on the same kinds of conservation concerns expressed elsewhere in the magazine. Several chapters reported stream-stocking projects, but the articles also made it clear that Waltonians saw themselves as a political force capable of correcting the causes of poor fishing. The Ikes of Osage, Iowa, established a "crime stoppers" group "to act immediately and see that the [game] laws are rigidly enforced." The Louisville, Kentucky, chapter vowed to work for passage of state legislation to stop pollution and end unsportsmanlike practices such as dynamiting fish. In Toledo, Ohio, Waltonians dedicated themselves to getting an antipollution bill through the state General Assembly. The Toledo correspondent stressed that the social significance of pollution extended far beyond its impact on sport fishing. He hoped that *Outdoor America* would "do much to educate the people to . . . appreciate that pollution does not primarily relate to sport, but rather to public health."[29]

Writers in *Outdoor America's* first issue attempted to persuade people that protection of the out-of-doors required militant, collective action by the nation's sportsmen. The struggle to establish

28. Will Dilg's endorsement may be found on p. 34, and the Canadian National Railways ad is on p. 32.
29. "News of the Chapters," *OA* 1 (August 1922): 28–30.

the Upper Mississippi River Wildlife and Fish Refuge, which took place during 1923 and 1924, offered the first real test of the league's ability to function as a national conservation organization. Themes developed in the first number of *Outdoor America* helped establish the frame of reference within which the refuge contest took place. The refuge issue itself provides a convenient reference point from which to measure changes in attitudes toward the upper river that had taken place in the decade after the completion of Keokuk dam.

Winneshiek Bottoms: Opportunity Knocks

Many of the attitudes toward nature expressed in *Outdoor America* long predated the refuge struggle. In nineteenth-century America, Romanticism offered a view of nature as a source of religious experience and spiritual regeneration. Henry David Thoreau shared the Romantic concern that industrial development and urbanization had isolated people from direct contact with nature. As a naturalist, he attempted to redress the balance by acquiring detailed knowledge of nature through regular, intimate contact with the natural world. Romantic landscape painters, such as Thomas Cole and Asher Durand, immortalized the beauty of the Hudson River valley. After the 1825 completion of the Erie Canal, the Hudson became one of the busiest commercial highways in the country. Both artists and others in the Hudson School elected to mute the impact of development and to depict the beauty of humanized landscapes and the aesthetic appeal of undeveloped nature. The paintings of the Hudson School testified to the artists' belief in the social value of the beauty in nature.[30]

In 1864, George Perkins Marsh published *Man and Nature*, one of the most important works on the subject of people and their environment written in the nineteenth century. Based upon a study of the Old World, Marsh argued that people had played a significant, and frequently destructive, role in the physical modification of the earth. He contended, "Man has too long forgotten that the earth was given to him for usufruct alone, not for consumption, still less for profligate waste." The earth, he warned, was fast be-

---

30. Donald Worster, *Nature's Economy*, chaps. 3–5; John K. Howat et al., *The Hudson River and Its Painters*. See also Neil Harris, *The Artist in American Society: The Formative Years, 1790–1860*, chaps. 7–8, and Roderick Nash, *Wilderness and the American Mind*, chap. 3.

coming an unfit place for people to live. He predicted that a continuation of past practices could ruin the productivity of the land and possibly result in unfavorable climatic changes. Such an unfortunate series of events, Marsh continued, could be followed by a breakdown of the human institutions that depended upon nature and "perhaps even extinction of the species."[31]

When he wrote *Man and Nature*, Marsh could still point to vast areas of North America "where the industry and the folly of man have as yet produced little appreciable change."[32] By the early twentieth century, many of Marsh's American descendants felt isolated from nature and threatened by the consequences of man-induced changes in the environment. Champions of the Upper Mississippi River Wildlife and Fish Refuge did not create preservationist sentiment in an unwilling population. Instead, when they shook their fists at the worshipers of materialism and spoke of obligation to the land, beauty, recreation, and closeness to God, they preached to a congregation already prepared to believe.

In its early years, the league sought converts by dispatching organizers from Chicago to proselytize among midwestern sportsmen. In 1922, Will Dilg traveled thousands of miles promoting the league and working for the passage of state conservation legislation. Late in the summer of that year, he put his formidable missionary skills to work in towns along the upper Mississippi River. Merton S. Heiss, who claimed to have been the league's first field representative, accompanied Dilg to the upper river, and many years later he relived parts of their trip in *Outdoor America*. Heiss served as Dilg's advance man. He arranged publicity, located places for Dilg to speak, and generally built "up his appearance as though it were to be the last trip of Barnum and Bailey's circus." According to Heiss, Dilg gave his best performances before large crowds that contained some opposition. He added, "A little heckling made things ideal from his standpoint." Dilg and Heiss made a good team, and together they organized numerous chapters along the upper river.[33]

Dilg's journey with Heiss also had a significance that transcended the chapters they helped create. On that trip, Dilg first envisioned the possibility of a federal wildlife and fish refuge along the upper

31. George Perkins Marsh, *Man and Nature*, pp. 36, 43.
32. Ibid., p. 49.
33. Heiss, "Will Dilg and the Early Days," pp. 4–5.

river. Pleased with their progress, the two men treated themselves to some smallmouth bass fishing in the river. As they fished from one of the riprap dams that jutted into the water, Dilg suddenly exclaimed, "We can do it, we can make this whole cockeyed territory into a fish and game refuge." Having made up his mind, Dilg put away his tackle and "was restless every second of the time until he could get on a train and go back to Chicago and start making history." Dilg was no stranger to the area he picked as the league's first national project and the country's first wildlife and fish refuge. He had previously fished the upper river, and he kept a boat in storage at Wabasha, Minnesota. In 1921, he even claimed that in nineteen out of the previous twenty years he had spent at least sixty days of each fishing season on the upper river.[34]

In 1923, a proposal to drain just under 30,000 acres of overflow land known as the Winneshiek Bottoms provided Dilg with the opening that he needed. The Winneshiek ran for roughly thirty miles along the river, comprising about 13,000 acres south of Lansing, Iowa, on the Wisconsin shore and approximately 15,000 acres north of Lansing on the Iowa side. Only the southern portion of the bottoms faced immediate drainage. Over one-half of the landowners had signed a petition favoring drainage, and an Army engineer had examined the site and recommended that the land be drained. Despite the wishes of the landowners, local sentiment ran against the project. Opponents of drainage charged that two individuals held 75 percent of the land and that these men had only recently purchased their property "with the drainage project in view." The Winneshiek was a favorite fishing and hunting spot for area sportsmen, who protested through organizations such as the La Crosse, Wisconsin, Rod and Gun Club, the McGregor, Iowa, Rod and Gun Club, and the McGregor chapter of the Izaak Walton League.[35]

The McGregor chapter collected four hundred dollars and filed suit in the Wisconsin Supreme Court to stop the drainage. It also contacted the league's Chicago headquarters and asked Will Dilg to conduct an investigation of the proposed project. Dilg agreed to

34. Ibid., p. 5; Dilg, "The Drainage Crime of a Century," p. 600; Will Dilg, "The Cork-Bodied Black-Bass Bug," pp. 162–63.
35. Harry C. Oberholser, "The Winneshiek Bottoms Drainage Project"; the charge that two individuals owned 75 percent of the land is made in Dr. A. T. Rasmussen, "The Passing of the Winneshiek," p. 32.

come if the McGregor Waltonians could find an expert on farmland to accompany him to the site. After they secured the services of Dr. A. L. Bakke, a plant physiologist at the Iowa Experimental Station, Dilg traveled to Iowa for a hectic, three-day tour of the Winneshiek.[36]

After his visit to the Winneshiek, Dilg published articles by himself and Bakke in the July 1923 number of *Outdoor America* to launch his national refuge campaign. Printed at the end of the magazine, Bakke's piece focused on the Winneshiek and systematically condemned the drainage project on economic and moral grounds. He contended that the cost of drainage would be prohibitive and would only result in the creation of unproductive farmland. Bakke further warned that, based on experience with a project near Muscatine, Iowa, the reclaimed land would still be subject to flooding. He argued, "The territory in question . . . gives every evidence of being of more value in its present status." Bakke based this assertion on the area's ability to produce fish, waterfowl, and furbearing animals. He also pointed out that the bottoms served as a holding area for floodwaters and thus protected downstream communities and farms. Bakke concluded that the drainage of the Winneshiek would "erase forever the recreational features and natural beauty of this section, which we are now the mere custodians of and have no moral right to destroy or mar."[37]

Dilg's article, which began on the front cover, emotionally capitalized on the Winneshiek issue as a springboard to a much grander plan. He took advantage of the Winneshiek crisis and attendant antidrainage sentiment to rally support for the refuge he had conceived of in the summer of 1922. By 1923, several hundred thousand acres of land along the upper Mississippi had been drained for agriculture. Many of these undertakings had not delivered the expected social and economic benefits. By the mid-1920s, unwise drainage projects had a reputation for creating marginal farmland, poor farmers, and wealthy speculators. Notable failures at Lake Keokuk, Muscatine, and the mouth of the Trempealeau River in Wisconsin had soured the farming community on drainage. Professional resource managers in the Bureau of Fisheries and the Bureau of Biological Survey condemned indiscriminate

36. Dilg, "The Drainage Crime of a Century," p. 601.
37. A. L. Bakke, "Report of the Winneshiek Drainage Project."

drainage because it destroyed valuable habitat for fish, wildfowl, and furbearing animals. Conservationists and sportsmen who lived along the upper river disapproved of drainage because it reduced populations of fish and wildlife, destroyed recreational opportunities, and ruined the aesthetic appeal of the river.[38]

The headline above Dilg's article cried out, "The Drainage Crime of a Century Is About to Be Committed and You Can Stop It. Will You Do It?" He then warned of an unspecified drainage threat to the entire area from Rock Island, Illinois, to Lake Pepin, supported only by the evidence of the proposed Winneshiek project. Indeed, at congressional hearings in February 1924, the president of the league's Winona, Minnesota, chapter testified that he knew of only one other serious drainage proposal, and it was "on the verge of defeat and dissolution." Dilg suggested that the federal government purchase all the riverbottom lands between Rock Island and Lake Pepin, a distance of about three hundred miles. He urged his "brothers" to write to President Harding and ask him to endorse the federal purchase of overflow lands along the upper river. For those too busy to write, Dilg provided a form letter that needed only to be clipped, signed, and mailed.[39]

The league petitioned Congress in 1923 to preserve about three hundred miles of overflow lands along the upper river by creating the Upper Mississippi River Wildlife and Fish Refuge. The original draft of the refuge act was written by Judge Jacob M. Dickinson, secretary of war under President Taft and ex-president of the American Bar Association. At Will Dilg's request, Rep. Harry Hawes of Missouri and Sen. Medill McCormick of Illinois agreed to sponsor the legislation in Congress. The refuge act authorized

38. Dr. L. H. Pammel, "Speaking of Drainage!"; Dr. E. W. Nelson, Chief U.S. Bureau of Biological Survey, "Unwise Drainage," *Bulletin of the American Game Protective Association* 13 (January 1924): 8–9, entry 146, RG 22, NA. Testimony on drainage along the upper Mississippi may be found in *Mississippi River Wild Life and Fish Refuge: Hearings*, pp. 27–28, 34–35, 57–58, 67–68, 72–74, 77–79, 83–84. Estimates of drained land are hard to find. Testimony at a 1932 congressional hearing indicated 392,000 acres had been drained along the upper river. Most of this was accomplished during the first quarter of the twentieth century. U.S. Congress, House, *Mississippi River Between Mouth of Missouri River and Minneapolis: Hearings on the Subject of the Improvement of the Mississippi River Between the Mouth of the Missouri River and Minneapolis*, 72d Cong., 1st sess., p. 77.

39. Dilg, "The Drainage Crime of a Century"; *Mississippi River Wild Life and Fish Refuge: Hearings*, p. 69.

the secretary of agriculture to acquire overflow lands between Rock Island, Illinois, and Wabasha, Minnesota, at the foot of Lake Pepin.[40]

The act divided administration of the refuge, giving control over wildlife to the Bureau of Biological Survey and granting authority to manage fish life to the Bureau of Fisheries. In large part, this arrangement grew out of jealousy between the Department of Agriculture and the Department of Commerce, the respective parent agencies of the Bureau of Biological Survey and the Bureau of Fisheries. Authorized employees of the Departments of Agriculture and Commerce had police powers within the refuge to enforce fish and game laws.[41]

Congress made one important change in the refuge legislation drafted by Judge Dickinson. At the routine suggestion of the chief of the U.S. Army Corps of Engineers, Congress amended the bill to ensure the primacy of navigation. The amendment stated in part that the refuge act prohibited "any interference with the operations of the War Department in carrying out any project now or hereafter adopted for the improvement of said river."[42] In taking this action, Congress protected the interests of the corps and incorporated into the statute the potential for the destruction of the refuge.

Victory: The Upper Mississippi River Wildlife and Fish Refuge

Backed by the league, Congress did indeed prevent Will Dilg's "Drainage Crime of a Century." "Victory!" proclaimed a headline in the July 1924 number of *Outdoor America*. The barely controlled euphoria was occasioned by an event that had taken place in Washington, D.C., on 7 June 1924. On that day, President Cal-

40. Information on Judge Dickinson may be found in Rush C. Butler to Professor B. Shimek, 21 June 1927; Harry B. Hawes, "Conserving the Outdoors for Health and Profit," p. 52; and "Senator McCormick Undertakes Gigantic Conservation Task for League," *OA* 2 (December 1923): 224–25, 241.

41. The text of the refuge bill as drafted by Judge Dickinson may be found in *Mississippi River Wild Life and Fish Refuge: Hearings*, pp. 1–3. Jealousy between the Department of Commerce and the Department of Agriculture is discussed on p. 14.

42. U.S. Congress, House, *Upper Mississippi River Wild Life and Fish Refuge*, pp. 1–2.

vin Coolidge signed the bill that created the Upper Mississippi River Wildlife and Fish Refuge. Congress approved $1.5 million for the purchase of land between Rock Island, Illinois, and Wabasha, Minnesota. By 1929, the federal government had purchased over 100,000 acres for the refuge, which eventually encompassed more than 195,000 acres. Although federal wildlife refuges were not a new phenomenon, this refuge represented a departure from past practice in terms of the amount of money appropriated, the size of the area considered for acquisition, and the general mandate to protect birds, fish, and other wildlife.[43]

After affixing his name to the refuge act and posing for photographers, President Coolidge presented the pen he had just used to a representative of the Izaak Walton League of America. (In 1981, a citation that included a picture of the "refuge victory pen" hung in a prominent location at the league's national headquarters at Arlington, Virginia.) The president's action publicly recognized the indispensable role that the young conservation organization had played in the passage of the refuge legislation. The league had provided a large, enthusiastic constituency and had piloted the legislation through Congress. By his action, President Coolidge also acknowledged that the league had become a force to be reckoned with on the national conservation scene. In his "Victory" article, Dilg boldly announced, "We have assumed the solemn responsibility of leadership and it is our duty to hold aloft the banner of county, state and National Conservation—to point out *and to lead the way.*"[44]

Increased membership was one method through which Dilg intended the league to lead the way. His "Victory" article urged Waltonians to enroll anyone "who ever has loved this America of ours" and to "tell them that this league *pays dividends to its members.*" Apparently the league did benefit considerably from the sense of mission associated with the refuge issue and the momentum generated by its victory in Congress. *Outdoor America* began its campaign to forge a constituency for the refuge in July 1923, and con-

43. Will Dilg, "Victory!" Information on the size of the refuge may be found in U.S. Congress, Senate, *Upper Mississippi River Wild Life and Fish Refuge*, pp. 1–2; Raymond H. Merritt, *Creativity, Conflict & Controversy: A History of the St. Paul District U.S. Army Corps of Engineers*, Ira N. Gabrielson, *Wildlife Refuges*, pp. 8, 23 (see also chap. 1); Henry A. Schneider, "Upper Mississippi River National Wildlife and Fish Refuge," p. 8.
44. Dilg, "Victory!" p. 38.

gressional debate on the league's proposal occurred during the first six months of 1924. In February 1924, 52 new chapters joined the Izaak Walton fold, followed by 118 in March, and 124 in April.[45]

Several important factors contributed to the success of the league's refuge campaign. Will Dilg's personality and leadership ability played a significant role in the victory. T. Gilbert Pearson, who served as president of the Audubon Association from 1922 to 1934, devoted several pages in his autobiography to Dilg and the league. While the two men apparently had little liking for each other, Pearson nonetheless described Dilg as a leader who "possessed an unusual ability to fire men and women with enthusiasm for conservation work." Dilg was the kind of person who refused to believe he could fail and who refused to accept no for an answer. He had almost no experience with Washington politics. Yet he moved confidently ahead even after a knowledgeable correspondent informed him that his chances were "not quite so thick as tissue paper." Harry Hawes, the House sponsor of the refuge bill, recalled that at first he had "viewed prospective success with trepidation. . . . But the compelling personality of Dilg secured my consent."[46]

Hawes was not the only Washington politician who found he could not resist Will Dilg. In September 1923, Dilg secured an appointment with President Coolidge and at that meeting persuaded the president to sign the refuge bill if the league got it through Congress. As Dilg left the executive office, the president's secretary pointed out that Coolidge had just granted him a forty-minute interview—a sure sign that Dilg "must have interested the President immensely." With confidence born of zealousness, Dilg commented, "I think I did interest President Coolidge immensely. I had something to say and I put it plainly to the President."[47]

Dilg had a flair for the dramatic. He created a sense of urgency and then convinced people that their individual efforts could help transform an impending disaster into a conservation victory. Dilg frequently reminded his readers, "'*Let George Do It*' won't do this time, you have got to do it yourself OR IT WON'T BE DONE." Dilg flattered people, he bullied them, he pleaded with them, and

45. Ibid.; membership figures are cited in Fox, *John Muir and His Legacy*, p. 162.

46. Pearson, *Adventures in Bird Protection*, p. 362; J. H. McFarland to W. H. Dilg, 7 January 1924, quoted in Fox, *John Muir and His Legacy*, p. 168. Harry B. Hawes, *My Friend the Black Bass: With Strategy, Mechanics and Fair Play*, p. 275.

47. [Will Dilg], "Forty Minutes with President Coolidge."

he personalized his appeals for assistance. Many Waltonians probably responded as much to Dilg as they did to the refuge issue. In one of many letters to the membership, Dilg stated, "It is up to every mother's son of us to move Heaven and earth" to persuade Congress to approve the league's bill. He added, "I am anxious to receive *a personal letter* from you on this matter so that we can keep tab of matters here at headquarters."[48]

Because of the nature of the issue, refuge proponents were able to pull together a broad coalition of supporters. Sportsmen's clubs responded to the league's call and rallied to the refuge cause. Dilg negotiated a short-lived alliance with the American Game Protective Association. The secretary of the Alabama Fishermen's and Hunter's Association wrote to the president and requested that he do what he could to prevent the drainage of the Winneshiek. "I ask this," the secretary said, "for myself and 3,300 members of this Association and our boys who represents [*sic*] our country's TO-MORROW." Situated next to the proposed refuge site, the La-Crosse, Wisconsin, Rod and Gun Club formally affiliated with the league.[49]

Dilg and other league officials eagerly sought the support of newly enfranchised women. *Outdoor America* addressed itself to unorganized women, and Dilg solicited the sanction of the General Federation of Women's Clubs. The federation's endorsement significantly reinforced the league's claim of popular approval for the refuge bill. Thus, a headline in the November 1923 issue of *Outdoor America* proudly announced, "Two Million Women in Defense of the League's Proposed National Preserve." Mrs. Francis E. Whitley, conservation and resources chair, sent a request for assistance to each official in the federation. She reported an enthusiastic response from women who in most cases had little interest in hunting or fishing.[50] In his "Victory" article, Will Dilg gratefully acknowledged "the *fighting* ability of our women," and he thanked

48. Dilg, "The Drainage Crime of a Century," p. 623; Hawes, *My Friend the Black Bass*, p. 277; Will Dilg to brother Waltonian, 1923, IWLA files.

49. For a one-sided account of the brief alliance between the league and the American Game Protective Association, see Will Dilg, "It Is Impossible to Please Everybody." See also Hornaday, "The Upper Mississippi Wild Life Refuge," p. 15. The secretary of the Alabama Fishermen's and Hunters Association is quoted in "What Our Members Are Saying and Doing About the Winneshiek," p. 38. Rasmussen discusses the La Crosse Rod and Gun Club in "The Passing of the Winneshiek," p. 32.

50. A Message from Mrs. Francis E. Whitley, *OA* 2 (February 1924): 353; Will Dilg to Madam President, 10 December 1923, IWLA files.

League cartoon acknowledging the role of women in preserving the Upper Mississippi River, from *Outdoor America* 2 (November 1923):160.

them for their indispensable support: "They knew our bill was right; that we were only asking for something which our children and children's children might enjoy—a part of the great out-of-doors. They—the mothers, knew the value of outdoor recreation to the future generations."[51]

At hearings before the House Committee on Agriculture in February 1924, the league assembled an array of witnesses who represented people from all over the country. The president of the Winona chapter of the league arrived at the hearing with three

51. Dilg, "Victory!" p. 38.

hundred letters, which he claimed demonstrated support for the refuge from 125,000 citizens of Minnesota. His endorsements included churches, fraternal and service organizations, manufacturers, retailers, banks, and the Winona County Farm Bureau Association. The secretary of the Ecological Society of America spoke for the twenty-eight groups affiliated with the Council on National Parks, Forests, and Wild Life. Listed among the member associations were the Sierra Club, the Boone and Crockett Club, the American Automobile Association, the Appalachian Mountain Club, and the National Geographic Society. T. Gilbert Pearson testified in favor of the refuge, as did officers of the American Game Protective Association and the Potomac Anglers' Association of Washington, D.C. Francis E. Whitley submitted a resolution passed by the board of directors of the General Federation of Women's Clubs, and she spoke at length in support of the refuge. Even a group of repentant drainage promoters from Lansing, Iowa, forwarded a letter to the committee in which they approved the refuge proposal.[52]

During 1924 and 1925, the Izaak Walton League and the American Game Protective Association each agreed to support refuge bills favored by the other organization. By July 1925, their efforts at cooperation had disintegrated into a bitter, personal conflict between Will Dilg and John B. Burnham, president of the American Game Protective Association. But it was during their brief alliance that the Upper Mississippi River Wildlife and Fish Refuge came up for debate before Congress.[53] Considerable controversy surrounded the association-backed legislation, and proponents of a refuge along the upper river worked hard to ensure that Congress considered the two refuge proposals separately. The league's decision to steer an independent course greatly facilitated congressional approval of the Upper Mississippi River Wildlife and Fish Refuge.

The American Game Protective Association's refuge legislation had its origin in the Bureau of Biological Survey. By the early 1920s, Dr. E. W. Nelson, chief of the bureau, had become ex-

52. *Mississippi River Wild Life and Fish Refuge: Hearings*, pp. 5–12, 23–27, 56, 80, 87–93.
53. For Dilg's perspective, see Dilg, "It Is Impossible to Please Everybody," pp. 20–26. For a viewpoint more sympathetic to the American Game Protective Association, see Pearson, *Adventures in Bird Protection*, chap. 17. Before the alliance dissolved, John B. Burnham published his "Our Game" on the public-shooting-grounds bill.

tremely concerned about the threat to waterfowl posed by wetlands drainage. Nelson wanted the U.S. Government to purchase
waterfowl habitat and to designate these preserves as public shooting grounds. He had a bill drawn up that embodied his ideas, and
he asked the American Game Protective Association to sponsor the
legislation in Congress. A number of other organizations, including the Audubon Association, endorsed the bill also. First introduced in March 1921, nearly two years before the Upper Mississippi Wildlife and Fish Refuge Act, the bill had three main
provisions: it established a migratory bird refuge commission to
oversee land acquisition, it required hunters to purchase a federal
license in order to shoot migratory birds in the preserves, and it
stipulated that the license fees be used for land procurement, law
enforcement, and administration.[54]

Opposition to the shooting-grounds bill appeared almost immediately and reached such intensity that it took until 1929 for Congress to pass a modified version of the legislation. Serious objections to the association's proposal centered on two issues that
became pivotal during a May 1926 Senate debate on the bill. Opponents argued that the American Game Protective Association
acted as a front for the makers of guns and ammunition. They contended that the association and its backers were interested not in
conservation but in the profits to be made from selling shells and
other products to hunters. Speaking before the Senate, William
King of Utah charged that the association "was born of a conspir-
acy concerned only with the sordid purpose of making profits out
of the slaughter of the wild life of the country." King presented
evidence that in each of two years during the early 1920s gun and
powder manufacturers had subscribed more than $20,000 to the
American Game Protective Association.[55]

Will Dilg and other spokesmen for the league recognized that
charges such as these could destroy opportunities for the passage
of conservation legislation. From the first, they had emphasized
that the Izaak Walton League had no financial support from any
commercial interests. In his lead editorial in the first edition of

54. Pearson, *Adventures in Bird Protection*, pp. 289–92, 361; Nelson, "Unwise
Drainage," pp. 8–9, 11.
55. Pearson, *Adventures in Bird Protection*, pp. 292–93, Hawes, *My Friend the
Black Bass*, p. 225; U.S. Congress, Senate, "Migratory Bird Refuges," 69th Cong.,
1st sess., 24 May 1926, *Congressional Record* 67, pp. 9906–8; see also 9909–17.
Stephen Fox discusses the public-shooting-grounds controversy in *John Muir and
His Legacy*, pp. 163–69.

Outdoor America, Emerson Hough had charged, "Of the alleged protective leagues there is not one which does not have commercial or personal gain . . . as its real basis." For his part, Will Dilg promised that the league was "totally undefiled by some hidden commercial purpose." Supporters of the Upper Mississippi River Wildlife and Fish Refuge continued to stress that point during the 1923–1924 refuge campaign. In congressional testimony, Will Dilg emphatically stated, "The league has no commercial basis."[56]

Adversaries of the shooting-grounds bill, particularly from the South and West, also charged that it gave powers to the national government that belonged to the states. States' rights advocates, such as Utah's Senator King, focused on the necessity for a federal license, which the Upper Mississippi Wildlife and Fish Refuge Act did not require. In 1926, Senator King told his colleagues, "The bill before us contains a provision which . . . to me is more obnoxious than any other, and that is the Federal license provision." Opponents objected on principle to government licensing of hunters, and they also feared the increase in federal influence that could result from the expenditure of the license fees. Under the proposed shooting-grounds bill, the Bureau of Biological Survey could use the license money to hire more federal employees. Foes of the bill worried about increased federal bureaucracy, more regulations, and a concomitant loss of police power by the states. In addition, people sensitized by prohibition found the prospect of more federal agents roaming the woods particularly onerous. It is interesting to note that during the May 1926 Senate debate both sides claimed the support of Will Dilg and the league. That they did so is an indication of the prestige that the league had acquired as a result of its refuge victory.[57]

The First Modern Environmental Campaign

Dilg and the league waged a campaign that in many ways anticipated the increasingly sophisticated efforts of environmental groups in the post–World War II period. Thus, an analysis of the refuge campaign invites comparison with an earlier, better-known struggle to preserve land from development. During the late nine-

56. Hough, "Time to Call a Halt"; Dilg, "It's Up to You Mr. Sportsman," p. 20; *Mississippi River Wild Life and Fish Refuge: Hearings*, p. 3.

57. Pearson, *Adventures in Bird Protection*, pp. 292–93; "Migratory Bird Refuges," p. 9918; see also 9892–99, 9911, 9916–22.

teenth century, San Francisco began to outgrow existing developed supplies of fresh water. In the mountains about 150 miles to
the east, glaciation and the Tuolumne River had created the steep-
sided, ruggedly beautiful Hetch Hetchy Valley. In 1890, Congress
established Yosemite National Park and included Hetch Hetchy
within the borders of the new preserve. Eleven years later, in
1901, San Francisco, which had long cast thirsty glances at Hetch
Hetchy, applied to the federal government for permission to use
the valley as the site for a reservoir. Although the city suffered an
initial setback, Secretary of the Interior James Garfield approved
San Francisco's application in May 1908. President Woodrow
Wilson completed the process in December 1913 when he signed
a bill that granted Hetch Hetchy Valley to San Francisco.[58]

Between 1907 and 1913, a nationwide conflict took place over
whether Hetch Hetchy should remain wild or be developed to
provide water for San Francisco. Conservationists entered the fray
on both sides, a fact that highlighted fundamental differences over
the meaning of conservation. Preservationists represented by John
Muir, president of a divided Sierra Club, argued that wild areas
provided a necessary sanctuary from the growing tensions of an increasingly materialistic culture. Wilderness, the unmarred creation of God, also offered an unequalled opportunity for prayer and
restoration of the soul. From Muir's perspective, the effort to protect Hetch Hetchy from the ravages of unrestrained commercialism was merely one skirmish in "the universal battle between right
and wrong." On the other hand, utilitarian conservationists, typified by Gifford Pinchot, bowed before the altar of use. Pinchot declared, "The fundamental principle of the whole conservation policy is that of use." He insisted that the value of flooding Hetch
Hetchy to meet the domestic needs of San Francisco far outweighed
"the delight of the few men and women" who would occasionally
hike into the remote valley.[59]

John Muir and the other defenders of Hetch Hetchy emphasized the beauty of wild places, the need for public playgrounds,
and the spiritual significance of wilderness. Hetch Hetchy's cham-

58. For more details on the history of the Hetch Hetchy controversy, see Nash,
Wilderness and the American Mind, chap. 10; Holway R. Jones, *John Muir and the
Sierra Club: The Battle for Yosemite*, chaps. 4–6; John Ise, *National Park Policy: A
Critical History*, chap. 2, esp. pp. 85–96.

59. John Muir, "The Tuolumne Yosemite in Danger," p. 488; U.S. Congress,
House, *Hetch Hetchy Grant to San Francisco*, pp. 26–27.

pions also wrapped themselves in a mantle of righteousness. Muir, who saw the struggle as a contest between good and evil, referred to his opposition as "Satan and Company," "temple destroyers," and "devotees of ravaging commercialism." "Instead of lifting their eyes to the God of the mountains," he cried, they "lift them to the Almighty Dollar." This moral dichotomy between wilderness and development found widespread acceptance among people opposed to granting Hetch Hetchy to San Francisco.[60]

In their quest for victory, Muir and his allies pinned almost all their hopes on public education. They very successfully used pamphlets, circulars, and newspaper and magazine articles to arouse public opinion and focus it on Congress. By the fall of 1913, they had organized such an effective national protest that one key senator, Reed Smoot of Utah, estimated he received five thousand letters from people who wanted Hetch Hetchy to remain wild.[61]

Despite public support, hard work, and a strong sense of mission, the friends of Hetch Hetchy lost because of political inexperience. They ran a campaign that was intended to influence Congress from New York City and San Francisco and found themselves outlobbied in Washington, D.C. By focusing almost entirely on the benefits of wild places, the preservationists gave away the economic, technical, and utilitarian issues to their opponents. Finally, by emphasizing the rectitude of their position and the depravity of commercialism, those who wished to save Hetch Hetchy lost the votes of congressmen who did not see the problem in terms of good versus evil. In *Wilderness and the American Mind*, Roderick Nash points out that many congressmen who voted to give Hetch Hetchy to San Francisco believed they were making a choice "between two goods." While the majority of congressmen placed the material needs of San Francisco first, "they still proclaimed their love of unspoiled nature."[62]

Important similarities existed between the Hetch Hetchy struggle and the movement to establish the Upper Mississippi River Wildlife and Fish Refuge. Will Dilg and the other architects of the successful refuge campaign used many of the same tactics and arguments employed by the champions of Hetch Hetchy. Both

60. John Muir, *The Yosemite*, pp. 261–62 (see also chap. 15); Jones, *John Muir and the Sierra Club*, pp. 158–60, 163–64, 168.

61. Smoot's estimate of the mail that he received from the champions of Hetch Hetchy is mentioned in Nash, *Wilderness and the American Mind*, p. 176.

62. Ibid., p. 181.

groups emphasized public education, the personal values of wild places, and the moral turpitude of their opponents. Waltonians wanted Congress to purchase several hundred thousand acres in order to protect them from agricultural drainage and preserve the habitat of fish and wildlife. In common with the friends of Hetch Hetchy, they asked Congress to reverse the traditional assumption that all wild land should be conquered and civilized in the name of progress and material prosperity.

Will Dilg and the league conducted a vigorous public-relations campaign in order to generate interest in the refuge. Between July 1923 and July 1924, *Outdoor America* published nearly two dozen refuge-related articles. Most of these stories exhorted Waltonians to participate in the campaign by writing to the president and their congressional representatives. Bold-faced statements at the bottoms of pages reminded readers that "Fish and game cannot vote" and asked "Have you written the President about the Winneshiek?" *Outdoor America* reached thousands of league members—newly organized and eager to protect the out-of-doors.

Dilg worked hard to influence the media he did not directly control. In November 1923, the league held a banquet in honor of Sen. Medill McCormick, who had agreed to introduce the refuge bill in the Senate. Dilg promoted the gathering as "the largest sportsmen's banquet ever held in America," and he intended it to be a media event. Remember, he said in a letter to the membership, "a big crowd means that news of our banquet will be sent forth by the Associated Press and a small crowd means just the opposite." National magazines such as *The Saturday Evening Post* and *Outlook* also printed articles on the refuge bill. An *Outlook* piece asked, "When is conservation not conservation?" and answered, "When it attempts to make poor farms out of good fishing and hunting territory." The story quoted extensively from the articles by Dilg and A. L. Bakke in the July 1923 issue of *Outdoor America*.[63]

Writer after writer in *Outdoor America* asserted that scarcity had conferred considerable social value on the nation's remaining undeveloped land. Donald Hough, a league director, argued that enough of nature had already been conquered to guarantee the development of the country. Now, he said, "we are beginning to de-

63. Will Dilg to brother Waltonian, 30 October 1923, IWLA files; "Destroying a National Asset"; "Saving Swamp Life."

Have you written the President about the Winneshiek?

85

"When a Feller Needs a Friend," from *Outdoor America* 2 (October 1923):85.

stroy that part which can serve us only by living." Proponents contended that a preserve on the upper river would protect a place of great natural beauty that offered unsurpassed hunting and fishing opportunities. Visitors to the refuge would find a place to relax and to seek the close communion with God that could only be found in unspoiled natural surroundings. "There," declared Harry Hawes, "we go to church and worship God by conversing with the things He made."[64]

64. Donald Hough, "A National Preserve for the Mississippi Valley," cover; Hawes, "Conserving the Outdoors for Health and Profit," p. 37.

In company with other refuge advocates, Hawes and Hough urged people to seize this fleeting chance to save the land along the upper river for themselves and their children. Their emphasis on posterity pervaded pro-refuge literature. Concern over future generations often focused on the fate of boys forced to grow up in a country that could no longer provide them contact with nature. Hough urged his readers to write to the president "because you realize the importance of preserving for ourselves and for our sons some of those things which have played such [an] important part in the formation of the character of this nation."[65]

Friends of the refuge also saw a clear moral dimension to their struggle. Many contributors to *Outdoor America* wanted their readers to become morally outraged so that they would be moved to action. "Think of *your boy and the coming generations of boys* who are being SOLD OUT," Will Dilg wrote.[66] Waltonians exhibited little reticence when it came to labeling drainage promoters as greedy, selfish, shortsighted men. They portrayed the refuge as a place that would provide benefits, many of which money could not buy, to the majority of Americans. Drainage, on the other hand, would destroy a place only God could make in order to enrich a minority. Francis Whitley spoke for most active refuge enthusiasts when she asked: "Shall the good of all be sacrificed to the pecuniary profit of a few? Shall the lovers of nature allow one after another of the elements of beauty and use to be stripped away by a short sighted policy which sacrifices future good for immediate gain?"[67]

Significant differences distinguished Hetch Hetchy Valley from the upper Mississippi River. The portion of the upper river included within the proposed refuge flowed through parts of four states and was accessible to millions of midwesterners by automobile or train. Far more people used the upper Mississippi than journeyed to remote Hetch Hetchy Valley, and many of them were becoming increasingly sensitive to the value of outdoor recreational opportunities. As a result of these factors, a large number of congressmen and senators received direct pressure from their own constituents to preserve the overflow lands along the upper river. Unlike Hetch Hetchy, the Upper Mississippi River Wildlife and Fish Refuge did not conflict with any other, obvious public

65. Hough, "A National Preserve for the Mississippi Valley," p. 29.
66. Dilg, "The Drainage Crime of a Century," p. 600.
67. A Message from Mrs. Francis E. Whitley, p. 353.

Have you written the President about the Winneshiek? 25

"Help Save the Winneshiek Bottoms," from *Outdoor America* 1 (August 1923):25.

good. Drainage for agricultural purposes already had a bad reputation for failure, and Congress amended the refuge act to guarantee the priority of navigation.

Advocates of the Upper Mississippi River Wildlife and Fish Refuge combined the organized grass-roots pressure used by the proponents of Hetch Hetchy with expert testimony and direct lobbying of Congress. In so doing, they assembled all the elements of the first modern environmental campaign. Beginning with A. L. Bakke's article in July 1923, the league effectively used the services of experts to support the refuge on technical and economic grounds. The hearings before the House Committee on Agriculture in February 1924 represented a tour de force of specialists in fish and wildlife management, soil science, forestry, plant physiology, biology, and botany. These men represented the Ecological Society of America, the Bureau of Biological Survey, the Bureau of Fisheries, the soil section of the Iowa Experiment Station, the University of Iowa and Iowa State College, the Illinois Soil Survey, the Illinois and Minnesota state departments of forestry, and the Massachusetts Fish and Game Protective Association.[68]

B. Shimek, professor of botany at the University of Iowa, presented a comprehensive statement at the refuge hearing, and his testimony provides a good example of the kinds of arguments offered by the league's expert witnesses. Shimek prefaced his remarks by reciting impressive credentials: a degree in civil engineering, experience with smaller drainage projects, two years as an instructor of zoology at the University of Nebraska, several years as a field assistant for the Iowa Geological Survey, and nearly thirty-four years as a plant ecologist at the University of Iowa. Shimek informed the committee that the lands in question had more value in their natural condition than they would if drained. He explained that these overflow lands provided recreational opportunities, mitigated downstream floods, controlled the amount of silt that entered the river, and contained valuable habitat for fish, freshwater mussels, furbearing animals, and waterfowl. Shimek further pointed out that if properly managed the forests could prevent erosion and still yield a valuable harvest of hardwood lumber. Finally, he told the congressmen that a refuge could aid scientific research in areas such as plant succession, soil development, and bird migration.[69]

In another decided improvement on the techniques of the Hetch Hetchy preservationists, Will Dilg moved his headquarters to Washington, D.C., during the 1923–1924 session of Congress.

68. *Mississippi River Wild Life and Fish Refuge: Hearings*, Barrington Moore, Secretary, Ecological Society of America, pp. 26–27; Dr. E. W. Nelson, Chief of the Biological Survey, pp. 27–33; H. C. Oberholser, Biological Survey, pp. 34–41; Henry O'Malley, Commissioner, Bureau of Fisheries, pp. 41–46; G. C. Leach, Bureau of Fisheries, pp. 46–56; C. F. Culler, Bureau of Fisheries, pp. 57–61; W. G. Baker, Soil Section, Iowa Experimental Station, 67–70, 72–76; R. S. Smith, Chief, Illinois Soil Survey, pp. 76–77; C. J. Telford, Illinois State Forest Service, pp. 77–79; A. A. Holmes, County Conservation Warden, pp. 79–80; A. L. Bakke, Plant Physiologist, Iowa State College, pp. 80–83; W. T. Cox, State Forester of Minnesota, pp. 84–85; Dr. George Wilton Field, Consulting Biologist, Sharon, Mass., pp. 85–87; B. Shimek, Professor of Botany, University of Iowa, pp. 96–100.

69. *Mississippi River Wild Life and Fish Refuge: Hearings*, pp. 96–100.

Along with other refuge supporters and a staff of assistants, he occupied an entire suite of rooms at the New Willard Hotel. With typewriters clacking, messengers scurrying in and out, and callers coming and going, Dilg sat at the epicenter of one of the most expensive and effective conservation campaigns that Washington observers had ever seen. T. Gilbert Pearson estimated that the league financed its campaign on a "scale heretofore unknown in conservation circles."[70]

Dilg went to Washington and spent money in unprecedented amounts in order to put direct pressure on Congress and to lobby anyone else who might be able to affect the fate of the refuge bill. He met twice with President Coolidge and more than once with Secretary of Commerce Hoover. Despite Dilg's commanding presence, the Washington campaign was not a one-man show. George E. Scott, president of the league's executive committee, had several interviews with President Coolidge's secretary. Scott also enlisted the assistance of the chairman of the National Republican Committee and persuaded a friend to speak with the director of the budget. Several years after the refuge struggle, William T. Hornaday remembered that Dilg and Scott were "antithetical types" who cooperated "in a single undertaking. Without the one, the other would have failed. Both had the same thought, the same vision, and contributed in their joint efforts the elements that make for success."[71]

In 1913, when Congress gave Hetch Hetchy to San Francisco and Stone & Webster completed Keokuk dam, most the residents of the upper river valley placed a higher value on the river's commercial potential than they did on its amenities. Nonetheless, the river played an important role in people's lives that was only tangentially related to commercial development. Dominated by men and boys, a sizable segment of the local population fished and swam in the river and hunted and camped along its shores. Steamboat excursions formed an important part of the warm-weather social life in river towns. An ad in the *Hannibal Morning Journal* for a river excursion promised, "There is no prettier river upon this mundane sphere than that magnificent body of water that flows by your very door step." In the summertime, picnickers spread their blankets and watched pleasure boaters pass by on the river. In

70. Pearson, *Adventures in Bird Protection*, p. 360.
71. Hornaday, "The Upper Mississippi Wild Life Refuge," p. 15.

March 1913, the *Hannibal Morning Journal* reported, "In and around Quincy over two hundred launches and speed boats are owned by sportsmen and business men who find recreation, after their working hours or on holidays, in spending several hours on the water."[72]

Between 1913 and the early 1920s, significant increases in drainage, siltation, and pollution threatened activities that people had long enjoyed and in the process enhanced their value considerably. At the same time, existing institutions provided neither the values to help people cope with the new circumstances nor the mechanisms to allow them to translate their concerns into action. It was this situation that permitted the Izaak Walton League to spread so rapidly throughout the Midwest. The league emerged from the refuge struggle with national credibility and a motivated, organized following ready to continue the conservation crusade.

In securing establishment of the wildlife and fish refuge, the league acquired a rallying point, something specific to protect. In the 1920s, pollution from the Twin Cities began to endanger the water quality in the refuge. This risk of contamination motivated league members to lead a fifteen-year-long campaign to clean up the river below Minneapolis and St. Paul. After Will Dilg's departure in 1926, the league's national leadership declared water pollution control to be the organization's highest priority. In so doing, they focused the energy of a confident, expanding membership on the problem of water quality and sought to rationalize the scattered efforts that individual chapters had carried on since 1922. During the 1930s and 1940s, Waltonians joined the Bureau of Fisheries and other concerned organizations in working for passage of national water-pollution-control legislation.

72. "Palatial Steamer Dubuque of the Streckfus Line," advertisement, *Hannibal* (Mo.) *Morning News*, 9 April 1912, p. 3; "Rivermen Are Stirred by Spring Weather . . . ," reprinted from *Quincy* (Ill.) *Journal*, in *Hannibal* (Mo.) *Morning News*, 14 March 1913, p. 5.

5 Pollution of the Upper Mississippi River

The great Father of Waters enters the metropolitan area of Minneapolis and St. Paul fairly pure, but, like many a country youth, contaminated by city life, he leaves it unspeakably vile. Here for the first time he encounters the befouling influence of large, modern sewer systems. —Judson L. Wicks, 1930[1]

Beginning in the late nineteenth century, a growing number of specialized interests exerted mounting pressure on the upper Mississippi River. By the early 1920s, the conflicting nature of many river use and development practices ran head-on into the river's finite ability to meet the demands of an expanding urban, industrial society. Groups such as the Minnesota Board of Health, the Izaak Walton League, and the U.S. Bureau of Fisheries began to express concern that pollution threatened the river's ability to provide for a range of clean-water needs. Response to this deterioration of the river environment precipitated a protracted debate over pollution control that both reflected and intensified conflicts in a fragmenting, interest-group-oriented society.

Ever since the settlement of Jamestown, Americans have had to confront the question of what to do with the wastes generated by their own biological functions and their burgeoning economic system. Shortly after the Civil War, however, changes already underway began to accelerate and in the process greatly exacerbated the problems of waste disposal. Shopkeepers, craftsmen, and other small-scale entrepreneurs gave way before a system of mass production and distribution based upon increased use of coal, a union of science and technology, a managerial revolution, and improved transportation and communications. Particularly in the Northeast and the upper Midwest, manufacturing moved to the city, to be joined there by rural migrants and foreign immigrants who added their own wastes to the contaminants discharged from the facto-

---

1. Judson L. Wicks, "Pollution of the Upper Mississippi River," p. 286.

ries.[2] When people and manufacturing had been scattered in rural areas, natural processes had usually proved equal to the task of dissipating and degrading wastes. In the new urban environment, the volume and concentration of various pollutants overwhelmed the recuperative powers of nature and severely taxed the existing mechanisms for waste disposal. Cities became smoke-shrouded, sooty, foul-smelling, unpleasant, and unhealthy places in which to live.

Until the 1880s, sewage disposal was largely a private responsibility attended to by contractors who periodically emptied privy vaults and cesspools. In the latter decades of the nineteenth century, an increasing amount of sewage and a growing understanding of the connections between sewage, germs, and disease led cities to begin to look for other methods of disposal. The most common solution consisted of publicly funded construction of sanitary sewers, in order to channel human wastes into waterways and away from the cities. Rivers and tidewaters also became receptacles for expanding quantities of industrial effluents, garbage, and other solid wastes.[3]

From one perspective, sewers may be viewed as a reform—a technical solution to urban social problems posed by accumulations of waste. Like many other reforms, this one soon developed its own professionals, sanitary engineers who staffed city health departments, state boards of health, and the U.S. Public Health Service. From a somewhat different perspective, waterway dumping transformed a local waste problem into a regional water pollution crisis. Waterborne pollution crossed political boundaries, conflicted with numerous other water uses, and elicited a mounting public protest. Water pollution became the subject of a decades-long debate over pollution control that, especially on the national level, became caught up in the cross pressures of an evolving pluralist society. Urban sewers offer an illustration of a technological innovation that developed at a faster rate than either public attitudes or institutions. Indeed, much of twentieth-century pollution-related history may be understood in terms of public response

2. For a further analysis of these themes, see Alfred D. Chandler, Jr., *The Visible Hand: The Managerial Revolution in American Business*, and David F. Noble, *America By Design: Science, Technology, and the Rise of Corporate Capitalism*.

3. Martin V. Melosi, ed., *Pollution and Reform in American Cities, 1870–1930*, pp. 14, 106–7. See also Joel A. Tarr, "The Separate vs. Combined Sewer Problem: A Case Study in Urban Technology Design Choice," *Journal of Urban History* 5 (May 1979):308–39.

and institutional adjustment to the unintended consequences of sewer technology.

The upper Mississippi River provides an opportunity for a microcosmic analysis of the developing water pollution situation. During the last third of the nineteenth century, cities and towns all along the upper Mississippi constructed sanitary sewers, with their outfalls in the river. By the 1920s and 1930s, sizable segments of the Mississippi had become degraded by domestic sewage, especially below the largest cities of Minneapolis/St. Paul and St. Louis. Federal and state laws lacked the authority to force a cleanup of the river. This absence of effective legislation created a classic illustration of the tragedy of the commons. Without uniform regulation, generalized river pollution discouraged unilateral installation of expensive sewage treatment facilities. Commenting on this phenomenon in 1935, the National Resources Committee noted, "The isolated effort of a community to reduce its pollution may generally result . . . in a cost which it alone must bear, while many of the benefits are diffused among other communities without cost to them."[4]

National Water Pollution Legislation: The Least Common Denominator

On 3 March 1899, Congress passed the Rivers and Harbors Act, giving the Corps of Engineers carefully circumscribed authority to regulate the pollution of navigable waters. By approving this seminal act, Congress acknowledged the increasing seriousness of water pollution but limited federal authority to instances that obstructed navigation. Section thirteen of the 1899 statute made it unlawful to discharge refuse matter into navigable streams or their tributaries but exempted anything that flowed from streets or sewers in a liquid form. Section thirteen also made it illegal to deposit any material on the banks of waterways that might wash into the water and thereby interfere with navigation. Half a century later, in 1948, Congress passed the first weak national water-pollution-control act. An examination of the struggle over national water pollution legislation leads to the conclusion that the act of 1948

4. National Resources Committee, Water Resources Section, *Report on Water Pollution* (July 1935), p. 7, entry 269, Record Group 22, Records of the Fish and Wildlife Service, National Archives Building, Washington, D.C. (hereafter cited as RG 22, NA). Garrett Hardin, "The Tragedy of the Commons," pp. 250–64.

represented the least common denominator in the contradictory demands of the interests involved.[5]

In the early 1920s, the first successful broad-based movement for a federal pollution law coalesced around opposition to oil pollution. Although the American oil industry had its beginning in 1859, serious oil pollution is a twentieth-century phenomenon directly correlated with a growing demand for petroleum as a motor fuel and as a lubricant. By 1920, oil pollution had become a nationwide problem as petroleum flowed into waterways from oil fields, pipelines, storage facilities, refineries, and oil-burning ships that routinely flushed their fuel tanks into the water. In 1922, for example, the U.S. game warden at St. Louis received numerous complaints about a Standard Oil refinery near Kansas City that discharged oil into the Missouri River. He reported that the refinery's effluent "covered the entire river for miles with oil and black substances." Worried about commercial fishermen who had been put out of work and about the fate of migratory ducks, the warden pointed out that he had no recourse but to refer complaints to Missouri officials.[6]

Oil fouled both inland and coastal waters, but effective opposition came first from the northeastern seaboard. At a conference in August 1922, the League of Atlantic Seaboard Municipalities resolved itself into the National Coast Anti-Pollution League. Organizers set out to create a politically powerful constituency capable of pressuring cities, states, and the federal government into passing antipollution laws. The group's statement of purpose drafted in 1922 spoke boldly of fostering "the enactment of and enforcement of adequate remedies and legislation to prevent the pollution of navigable and inland waters."[7]

5. An analysis of the Rivers and Harbors Act of 1899 may be found in Albert E. Cowdrey, "Pioneering Environmental Law: The Army Corps of Engineers and the Refuse Act." State pollution laws are discussed in "Laws Relating to Stream Pollution," Abstract and Tabulation by Harold D. Padgett, 30 March 1935, entry 269, RG 22, NA; U.S. Congress, Senate, Committee on Commerce, *Stream Pollution: Hearings on S. 3958 a Bill to Prevent the Pollution of the Navigable Waters of the United States . . . S. 3959 a Bill to Amend Section 13 of the Act of March 3, 1899, . . . and Section 3 of the Oil Pollution Act, 1924 S. 4342 and S. 4627 Bills to Create a Division of Stream Pollution Control in the Bureau of the Public Health Service . . .* , pp. 144–45; National Resources Committee, *Drainage Basin Problems and Programs: 1937 Revision*, p. 130.

6. Harry Barmeier, U.S. Game Warden, to Chief of Biological Survey, 22 August 1922, entry 162, United States Agriculture Department, Bureau of Biological Survey, RG 22, NA.

7. Sedley H. Phinney, Secretary National Coast Anti-Pollution League, to Dear Sir, 11 October 1922, entry 162, RG 22, NA.

By the league's second conference in October 1923, the organization had narrowed its goals to preventing oil pollution of navigable waters. This action seems to have stemmed from a desire to advance a limited, attainable objective acceptable to an array of supporters that included numerous state and local officials, public health officers, port authorities, fish and game commissions, representatives of the shellfish and fishing industries, hotel and resort owners, chambers of commerce, yacht clubs, ship owners, fire insurance underwriters, and women's organizations.[8]

The Anti-Pollution League's greatest triumph came when Congress passed the Oil Pollution Act of 1924. Enacted along restrictive lines favored by Secretary of Commerce Herbert Hoover, the 1924 law gave the Army Corps of Engineers authority to prohibit the discharge of oil from vessels into tidal waters. The ordinance further directed the corps to study the effect of pollution on navigation and commerce and report its findings to Congress.[9]

Congress intended the Rivers and Harbors Act of 1899 and the Oil Pollution Act of 1924 to remedy specific problems in navigable waters. As a result, these statutes did little to ameliorate generalized, nationwide water pollution. There is also evidence to suggest that, during the 1920s, the Corps of Engineers adopted a strict construction of the 1899 act. As complaints became more numerous, the office of the chief of engineers developed a standard reply: pollution was a state and local problem unless it physically obstructed navigation.[10]

The engineers' recalcitrance may be partially explained by two factors that threatened the agency's hegemony over navigable waters. First, federal agencies interested in fish or wildlife and private organizations concerned about the availability and quality of outdoor experiences began to insist that the pollution problem be

8. "The National Coast Anti-Pollution League, Second Annual Conference, Haddon Hall, Atlantic City, N.J., October 1, 2, 3, 1923," entry 162, RG 22, NA.

9. For Herbert Hoover's viewpoint, see U.S. Congress, House, Committee on Rivers and Harbors, *Hearings on the Subject of the Pollution of Navigable Waters, Part 2*, pp. 91–94. For a detailed discussion of the Oil Pollution Act of 1924, see Joseph Pratt, "The Corps of Engineers and the Oil Pollution Act of 1924." An overview of the oil pollution problem in the early 1920s is contained in *Oil Pollution of Navigable Waters: Report to the Secretary of State by the Interdepartmental Committee*. The report of the investigation required by the 1924 act is contained in U.S. Congress, House, *Pollution Affecting Navigation or Commerce on Navigable Waters*.

10. The use of a strict construction of the 1899 act as a defense of corps interests is more fully developed in the section of this chapter that deals with the nine-foot channel.

addressed before the corps impounded free-flowing rivers. Second, in the 1930s, the federal government experienced a renaissance of interest in multiple-purpose river-basin development. The corps had been one of the leading opponents of the first multiple-purpose movement that ended with the passage of the 1920 Water Power Act. The engineers continued their tradition of opposition when neo-multiple-purpose advocates contended that wise use demanded the coordination of projects for flood control, navigation, irrigation, soil conservation, water supply, hydroelectric power, pollution abatement, and, as far as possible, recreation and fish and wildlife habitat.[11]

The first sustained effort to enact federal water pollution legislation began in 1933, boosted by the passage of the National Industrial Recovery Act. In September 1933, Sen. Augustine Lonergan of Connecticut wrote to the chief of engineers, the sergeant general of the Public Health Service, and the administrator of the Public Works Administration, calling for a coordinated, two-pronged assault on the evil of water pollution. He proposed direct federal action to eliminate pollution of interstate rivers and the establishment of a national fund from which the states and the Public Health Service could draw money to clean up intrastate streams. Lonergan's plan took into account the concerns of states' rights advocates, the anxieties of state agencies that feared federal encroachment, and the close working relationship between state public health departments and the U.S. Public Health Service.[12]

Senator Lonergan sought to allay misgivings about the constitutionality of direct federal involvement in pollution control by pointing to the broad emergency powers of the National Industrial Recovery Act. Specifically, the senator singled out section 202 of the act (relating to public works), which authorized the administrator of the Public Works Department to prepare a program for

11. An analysis of the response by the corps to the Progressive-era multiple-purpose movement may be found in Samuel P. Hays, *Conservation and the Gospel of Efficiency: The Progressive Conservation Movement, 1890–1920*, pp. 108–9, 206–18, 230–40.

12. Augustine Lonergan to Major General Lytle Brown, Chief of Engineers, 30 September 1933, entry 109, U.S. War Department Army Corps of Engineers, Record Group 77, Records of the Office of the Chief of Engineers, National Archives, Suitland, Maryland (hereafter cited as RG 77, Suitland); Lonergan to Dr. Hugh S. Cumming, Sergeant General, Public Health Service, 30 September 1933, entry 109, RG 77, Suitland; Lonergan to Hon. Harold Ickes, Administrator of Public Works, 30 September 1933, entry 109, RG 77, Suitland.

the conservation and development of natural resources that included the control, use, and purification of waters.[13]

On 6 December 1934, more than one year after Senator Lonergan sent his initial inquiries, he and Secretary of War George H. Dern cosponsored a conference on water pollution. During the summer of 1934, Grover C. Ladner, honorary president of the Philadelphia chapter of the Izaak Walton League, had spoken to the directors of the Pennsylvania division of the league about the need for national pollution-control legislation. Ladner's plan called for uniform enforcement with federal authority organized by principal watersheds. His ideas greatly impressed Dr. M. D'Arcy Magee of Washington, D.C., the national vice-president of the Izaak Walton League. Magee lobbied Senator Lonergan, who had already written his letters calling for federal pollution legislation, and initiated a chain of events that culminated with the convening of the Dern-Lonergan conference in December 1934.[14]

Testimony at the Dern-Lonergan conference came from over twenty experts, who represented the Public Health Service, the Bureau of Fisheries, the Bureau of Biological Survey, the Corps of Engineers, the Smithsonian Institution, the Izaak Walton League, the city of Philadelphia, and the states of Connecticut, New Hampshire, and Virginia. At the conclusion of the conference, Senator Lonergan appointed a subcommittee to draft legislative proposals. Unable to agree on the role that the federal government should play in pollution control, the subcommittee submitted a majority and a minority report. The majority report, signed by representatives of the Public Health Service, National Resources Board, and Bureau of Fisheries, favored a plan that left authority over pollution abatement with the states. Under the majority plan, federal participation would be limited to conducting research, disseminating information, encouraging the formation of interstate compacts, and providing financial assistance. The minority report, prepared by Grover C. Ladner and M. D'Arcy Magee, closely paralleled Ladner's original plan and called for national supremacy over pollution control and a strong federal agency with powers of investigation and enforcement.[15]

13. Lonergan to Cumming and Lonergan to Ickes, 30 September 1933.
14. "A National Plan for Water Purification: Pollution Parley Seeks United Action"; Kenneth A. Reid, "We Believe in Clean Streams But—," p. 6.
15. A report of the Dern-Lonergan conference, including the majority and minority reports, is located in U.S. Congress, Senate, *Stream Pollution and Stream*

In 1936, two sets of legislation introduced into the 74th Congress followed recommendations made in the majority and minority reports. Bills sponsored by Senator Lonergan and Sen. Alben W. Barkley of Kentucky are representative of the many variants. Senator Lonergan's proposal followed recommendations made in the minority report of the Dern-Lonergan conference. In order to overcome the objections of congressmen who opposed creation of a new agency, Lonergan suggested assigning pollution abatement to the National Resources Committee, composed of the secretaries from the Departments of Interior, War, Treasury, Agriculture, Commerce, and Labor, the Federal Emergency Relief administrator, and three additional members appointed by the president. Lonergan's bill encouraged the National Resources Committee to cooperate with the states but also gave it the power to control pollution and to stimulate state and local action by financing construction of water treatment facilities.[16] Senator Barkley's bill, which drew its inspiration from the majority report, left the authority over pollution control with the states. The federal role, to be vested in a new Division of Stream Pollution in the Public Health Service, was limited to assisting the states through activities such as investigation, preparation of a master plan, and financial aid.[17] Although both bills failed in the 74th Congress, they established the pattern for water pollution legislation introduced into Congress during the next dozen years.

The divisions that appeared during deliberations over the Lonergan and Barkley bills persisted in subsequent Congresses and repeatedly stalemated attempts to enact pollution legislation. The Izaak Walton League strongly endorsed the Lonergan bill. League officials urged the membership to write letters in support of Lonergan's proposal, and they lobbied for its passage in Congress. The league's officers also denounced the Barkley bill for its continued

Purification. A summary of the conference and its legislative aftermath in 1936 may be found in Elmer Higgins, "Legislation Proposed in the 74th Congress for the Abatement of Water Pollution," pp. 5–8. Considerable information on the Lonergan initiative, the conference, and the majority and minority reports is located in entry 109, RG 77, Suitland.

16. Higgins, "Legislation Proposed in the 74th Congress," pp. 6–8. The most significant of the pollution bills debated in the 74th Congress were Senator Lonergan's S. 3958 and Senator Barkley's S. 4627. The text of these bills is printed in *Stream Pollution: Hearings*.

17. Higgins, "Legislation Proposed in the 74th Congress," p. 9.

reliance on a combination of ineffective state legislation and a federal role largely restricted to investigation and advice.[18]

Guarded endorsement for the Lonergan bill came from the U.S. Commerce Department, parent agency of the Bureau of Fisheries. The Commerce Department's ambivalence no doubt stemmed from its close association with many polluting industries and from its access to the information contained in the Bureau of Fisheries' pioneering investigations of water pollution. As their studies progressed, scientists from the bureau had concluded that standards adequate to protect public health would not necessarily maintain the biological productivity of rivers and streams.[19] This emphasis on water quality and aquatic life put the bureau at odds with the Public Health Service, which stressed human health, and the Corps of Engineers, which insisted on the supremacy of navigation.

Opposition to Senator Lonergan's bill and support for the Barkley bill came from chambers of commerce, industries, trade associations, state health departments, the Army Corps of Engineers, and the Public Health Service. At Senate hearings, numerous representatives of industries, trade associations, and chambers of commerce testified against the Lonergan bill. It is hard to avoid the conclusion that many of these witnesses preferred ineffective state ordinances and fragmented jurisdiction to a centralized, enforceable federal law. State health departments, which commonly administered state laws concerning water quality, insisted on the principle of states' rights and correctly concluded that the Lonergan bill represented a threat to their sovereignty.[20]

The Corps of Engineers and the Public Health Service both based their objections to Lonergan's bill on three points: that existing federal legislation was equal to the task of pollution control, that coercive federal laws would interfere with voluntary abatement programs, and that the Natural Resources Committee was not the appropriate agency to take charge of pollution. President

18. "Lonergan Bill Strikes at Pollution"; "A National Emergency," editorial, *Outdoor America* 1 (March 1936):3 (hereafter cited as *OA*); Reid, "We Believe in Clean Streams, But—." Extensive testimony by representatives of the league may be found in *Stream Pollution: Hearings*.
19. Higgins, "Legislation Proposed in the 74th Congress," p. 7. M. M. Ellis's testimony before Congress is printed in *Stream Pollution: Hearings*, pp. 121–25.
20. Positions taken by proponents of the Barkley bill are summarized in "National Legislation on Stream Pollution." More extensive remarks by these same interests may be found in *Stream Pollution: Hearings*.

Roosevelt shared the position adopted by these two agencies.[21] Between the lines, both the corps and the health service opposed strong federal pollution legislation because it threatened their water-related spheres of influence. The Public Health Service valued its constituency relationship with state health departments, while Corps of Engineers officials viewed effective federal pollution laws, particularly when administered by another agency, as a threat to the primacy of navigation.

World War II interrupted attempts to enact national water pollution legislation. Nonetheless, several wartime developments heightened the sense of urgency that attended postwar efforts to pass a federal pollution law. In 1939, a presidential reorganization removed the Bureau of Fisheries from the Department of Commerce and the Bureau of Biological Survey from the Department of Agriculture and placed them in the Department of Interior. The following year they became the primary building blocks of a new agency, the Fish and Wildlife Service, located in the Department of Interior. M. M. Ellis's water pollution research unit accompanied the Bureau of Fisheries on its move.

Almost from the first, Ellis's reports warned that the incorporation of wartime technological developments into the civilian economy would greatly increase the level of contamination in the nation's waters. Ellis sounded one of the earliest alarms about the potential threat to fish and wildlife posed by the widespread, private manufacture and use of new synthetic compounds, such as plastics and DDT. In 1944, he began path-breaking studies on the effect of DDT on fish life. With the end of hostilities, Ellis voiced concern about a continuation of the disregard for pollution that had characterized the war emergency, and he called for immediate, nationwide "restraint on and elimination of stream pollution."[22]

In 1945, the 79th Congress became the battlefield between champions of states' rights and federal supremacy in the area of

21. Higgins, "Legislation Proposed in the 74th Congress," pp. 7–8. Testimony by representatives of the Treasury Department and War Department is printed in *Stream Pollution: Hearings*, pp. 98–102. Franklin Roosevelt's position is stated in U.S. Congress, House, *Stream Pollution by Federal Agencies, with Recommendations*, p. 2.

22. Two early assessments of the impact of World War II on water quality may be found in "Memorandum for Secretary Ickes," from Chas. E. Jackson, Acting Director, Fish and Wildlife Service, 15 February 1941, entry 269, RG 22, NA; and "Memorandum for Mr. Day," from Elmer Higgins, Chief, Division of Fishery Biology, 24 March 1942, entry 269, RG 22, NA. Information on DDT may be found in

pollution control. Advocates of a strong federal role lined up in support of legislation introduced by Rep. Karl E. Mundt of South Dakota, while proponents of state sovereignty endorsed a bill placed before the House by Rep. Brent Spence of Kentucky. Mundt's bill may be characterized as a descendant of Augustine Lonergan's 1936 antipollution measure, while Spence's proposal belonged to the lineage established by Senator Barkley. Support for Mundt's legislation came from the Izaak Walton League, the Fish and Wildlife Service, and the National Park Service. Spence's bill received its greatest backing from state public health officials and the U.S. Public Health Service.[23]

In an attempt to overcome chronic inertia, the Izaak Walton League helped to persuade the House Rivers and Harbors Committee to report a bill that combined elements of both Mundt's and Spence's legislation. This compromise measure gathered a broad base of support, including the first Public Health Service endorsement of a law that granted some enforcement power to the federal government. The failure of all pollution bills in the 79th Congress demonstrated that no legislation would pass that did not win the approval of state health departments and of interstate compacts.[24]

A breakthrough finally came in November 1946 when the Conference of State Sanitary Engineers directed its Committee on National Water Policy to draft suitable federal pollution legislation. In fulfilling this charge, the committee chairman held a meeting in New York City to which he invited representatives of other organizations, including the Public Health Service, the Fish and Wildlife Service, and the Izaak Walton League. Recognizing that any federal legislation would have to be predicated on a compromise, the

---

entry 269, NA, and in the *Annual Report of the Director of the Fish and Wildlife Service to the Secretary of the Interior, 1945–46*. Ellis's concerns about wartime disregard for pollution may be found in M. M. Ellis, Sr. Aquatic Physiologist, to Mr. Paul E. Thompson, Acting Chief Division of Fisheries Biology, 3 July 1946, entry 269, RG 22, NA.

23. For the positions of various Interior Department Agencies, see "Memorandum for Mr. Brophy . . ." et al., on the subject of pollution legislation, 2 January 1947, entry 269, RG 22, NA. See also "National Pollution Control Bill Introduced," January 1945, files of the Izaak Walton League of America, Suite 806, 1800 N. Kent St., Arlington, Va., 22209 (hereafter cited as IWLA files); and Kenneth A. Reid, "Reports of Special Committees: Pollution Study." Testimony from hearings on the Mundt (H.R. 519) and Spence (H.R. 4070) bills is printed in U.S. Congress, House, Committee on Rivers and Harbors, *Pollution of Navigable Waters: Hearings on H.R. 519, H.R. 587 and H.R. 4070; Bills for the Control of Water Pollution*.

24. Reid, "Reports of Special Committees: Pollution Study," pp. 427–28.

delegates at this gathering agreed to support a rewritten version of the Spence bill that seemed to grant each of the interests its minimum requirements. Introduced in 1947, the new bill provided for federal technical and financial aid to the states, under the direction of the Public Health Service. It acknowledged the primary authority of the states but held federal power in reserve in case the states failed to act. Although the conference participants spoke confidently of a quick victory in Congress, passage of a much attenuated version did not take place until 1948.[25]

The Water Pollution Act of 1948 proved to be a weak and ultimately ineffective statute. It limited the federal role to study, technical assistance, and financial aid by requiring a state's consent before the Public Health Service could exercise any authority in that state. Approval of this act can be accounted for by the continued opposition to federal control by industries and municipalities and by the desire on the part of many frustrated congressmen to get something on the books. Kenneth A. Reid, executive director of the Izaak Walton League, devoted several years to the passage of a national pollution-control law. In 1949, he spoke for many disappointed proponents of a strong federal act when he predicted "that 5 years hence, we will be forced to admit that the present bill was a failure. But we will not only have lost 5 years—we will have gained another costly bureau which will continue indefinitely feeding at the public trough."[26]

Because Congress was unable to pass effective legislation, state and local officials retained a fragmented jurisdiction over pollution control. Beginning hesitantly after the turn of the century and gathering force during the 1920s and 1930s, sentiment developed in many river communities for a cleanup of the upper Mississippi River. This regional effort shared important similarities with the national struggle. It also exhibited significant differences. Both movements were driven by a sense of urgency rooted in the belief that pollution had reached crisis proportions. Many of the key in-

25. A discussion of the compromise may be found in "Memorandum from Arthur D. Weston," Chief Sanitary Engineer, Mass. Dept. of Public Health, 25 November 1946, entry 269, RG 22, NA; Vlado A. Getting, Secretary-Treasurer, The Association of State and Territorial Health Officers, to Members of the Association of State and Territorial Health Officers, 26 November 1946, entry 269, RG 22, NA; Kenneth A. Reid, Executive Director, Izaak Walton League, to Mr. Arthur D. Weston, 9 December 1946, entry 269, RG 22, NA; Arthur D. Weston to Honorable Karl E. Mundt, 29 January 1947, entry 269, RG 22, NA; Kenneth A. Reid, "A Report on the Pollution Front."

26. Edward Schneberger, "Reports of Special Committees: Committee on Pollution Study."

terests at the national level, such as the Izaak Walton League, the Corps of Engineers, the Public Health Service, and the Bureau of Fisheries, also participated in the debate over upgrading the quality of the Mississippi River. At the same time, in the absence of uniform legislation, the contest along the upper river took place city by city so that success or failure depended upon local circumstances.

Dirty Water

In about 1906, the heroine of Sinclair Lewis's novel *Mainstreet* stood atop a hill that afforded her a view of the Mississippi River as well as the factories and skyscrapers of Minneapolis/St. Paul. The hilltop offered a pleasant retreat from classes at Blodgett College, a beautiful natural setting in which to dream and act out "the eternal aching comedy of expectant youth." Had she walked down to the shores of the Mississippi, Carol Milford's meditation would likely have been interrupted by the stench of raw sewage. By 1906, the same process of development that had created the Twin Cities had already turned the river below that metropolitan area into an open sewer.[27]

During the last three decades of the nineteenth century, the population of Minneapolis doubled four times, expanding from slightly over 13,000 in 1870 to about 200,000 in 1900. In the same time period, St. Paul grew from 20,000 to 163,000. This geometric progression in the population was accompanied by an exponential increase in waste. Confronted with a waste crisis, the cities turned to the Mississippi River as a cheap, convenient way to carry away garbage and sewage. It was in this period that the Twin Cities began to construct sanitary sewer systems. In 1884, for example, the Minneapolis Board of Trade observed that in response to rapid urban growth the most populous areas of the city had already been "provided with capacious and well-constructed sewers, built on one comprehensive system and emptying into the Mississippi river below the city." The board of trade reported that the sewer system was rapidly being extended throughout the remainder of the city.[28]

27. Sinclair Lewis, *Mainstreet*, p. 7.
28. Ninth Census of the U.S., 1870, pp. 178, 180; Twelfth Census of the U.S., 1900, pp. 219, 225; Minneapolis Board of Trade, *History and Growth of Minneapolis, Minnesota*, p. 54.

Even at this early date, the Father of Waters occasionally gagged on its diet of urban waste. By the late 1880s, Minneapolis dumped about five hundred tons of garbage per day into the Mississippi, while St. Paul contributed even more. In 1888, the Corps of Engineers removed a bar that had formed next to the St. Paul waterfront. Upon examination, this shoal proved to be composed almost entirely of rotting garbage. The engineers acted after private citizens became so disgusted by the odor that they obtained a court order enjoining the Twin Cities from disposing of their garbage in the river.[29]

By the turn of the century, industrial pollution also contributed significantly to the degradation of water quality downriver from the Twin Cities. Between 1903 and 1905, the U.S. Geological Survey conducted a study of Minnesota's surface waters in cooperation with the Minnesota Board of Health. This investigation revealed that in 1903 sawmills in Minneapolis produced about 328 million board feet of lumber. Sawdust and bark from these and other mills along the upper Mississippi regularly ended up in the river. This material formed deposits that obstructed the flow of the river and fouled the water as it decayed. Neither the states nor the Corps of Engineers effectively regulated the dumping of sawmill refuse, which continued until the end of the white-pine industry. At the Twin Cities, a pulp mill, coal gas works, several large breweries, packinghouses, and stockyards also added to the pollution load of the river. According to the Geological Survey report, contamination from the packing industry consisted, "mainly, of foul, bloody, wash water, yard drainage, and putrescent scraps of animal matter." Based upon their findings, the Geological Survey and the Minnesota Board of Health concluded, "The river is grossly polluted . . . it would be decidedly dangerous for domestic consumption without purification."[30]

At the lower end of the upper river, St. Louis grew from a population of about 78,000 in 1850 to over 575,000 in 1900, doubling nearly three times in fifty years.[31] In common with their counter-

29. Roald Tweet, *A History of the Rock Island District Corps of Engineers,* p. 53.

30. R. B. Dole and F. F. Wesbrook, "The Quality of Surface Waters in Minnesota," *Water-Supply and Irrigation Paper No. 193,* U.S. Geological Survey, pp. 40–44, 98–99, 106. For further information on pollution of the upper river prior to 1915, see Raymond H. Merritt, *Creativity, Conflict & Controversy: A History of the St. Paul District U.S. Army Corps of Engineers,* pp. 138, 176–79.

31. Ninth Census of the U.S., 1870, p. 194; Twelfth Census of the U.S., 1900, p. 247.

parts in the Twin Cities, St. Louis officials used the Mississippi to carry away a mounting volume of waste. Like Minneapolis, St. Louis drew its drinking water from the same river into which it regularly dumped its garbage, street sweepings, and sewage.

By 1913, the river at St. Louis had degraded to the point where it began to receive considerable attention in the *Post-Dispatch*. A letter to the editor, signed "A Boatman," complained about organic material thrown into the river by the city street department. The boatman went on to chide the city for electing to dispose of its garbage in the river simply because that proved to be the cheapest option available. In a similar vein, a *Post-Dispatch* editorial attacked the city for neglecting its responsibility to care for the health of its citizens. The paper pointed to an increase of typhoid fever in South St. Louis caused by contaminated river water. Finally, in a satirical editorial, the *Post-Dispatch* warned that throwing the city's garbage into the river could have one of two outcomes. Either the sheer mass of garbage would block the river or the catfish would eat the garbage, multiply, and increase in size to the point where they obstructed river traffic.[32]

By the early twentieth century, other cities and towns along the upper river had also begun to experience water pollution problems. At a June 1912 meeting of commercial clubs in Hannibal, Missouri, Maj. Montgomery Meigs of the Army Corps of Engineers spoke about the federal government's efforts to keep the Mississippi free of garbage and other refuse. The following summer, in 1913, residents of Keokuk, Iowa, faced an immediate crisis. As the city grew, a local tributary of the Mississippi became choked with sewage. People living next to this stream demanded that something be done to prevent all that waste from being carried in the open past their homes. The *Keokuk Daily Gate City* reported that at times accumulations of sewage stopped the flow of the creek until enough water backed up to burst through the foul obstruction.[33]

During the early twentieth century, ice harvested from the Mississippi helped cool the drinks and preserve the food of residents of the upper river valley. In the summer of 1913, an ice-making

32. "The Mississippi as Dumping Ground," letter to the editor, *St. Louis Post-Dispatch*, 30 August 1913, p. 4 (hereafter cited as *St. Louis P-D*); "Refouling the River," editorial, *St. Louis P-D*, 27 August 1913, p. 12; "Catfish Dam, Missouri," editorial, *St. Louis P-D*, 6 June 1913, part 2, p. 14.

33. "Mississippi to Be Kept Sanitary," *Keokuk* (Ia.) *Daily Gate City*, 23 June 1912, part II, p. 5 (hereafter cited as *DGC*); "Must Decide on Sewer System," *DGC*, 10 March 1913, p. 5.

factory opened in Keokuk, and its advertisements capitalized on people's unwillingness to trust their health to untreated river water. A typical ad proclaimed that our ice "contains no germs and is free from all dirt and filth that is found in ice that comes from the river."[34]

Despite a steady deterioration of the river and a growing amount of discussion and study, very little was actually accomplished in the way of pollution abatement until the 1930s. As late as 1928 only one river city between Minneapolis and the northern border of Iowa had constructed a sewage treatment plant.[35] Several factors help to explain this phenomenon. In most cases, the river did effectively and cheaply carry away wastes. Waste treatment was quite expensive, while alternatives such as filtering river water to make it potable or developing other sources of domestic supply were technically possible and cheaper. Cost was not the only consideration. Given the lack of uniform pollution laws, municipalities knew that if they constructed a sewage treatment plant they would bear nearly the entire cost while downstream cities would enjoy most of the benefits. Under these circumstances, voters proved quite reluctant to approve funds for pollution abatement projects. Finally, the intense competition for factories among river towns made it extremely unlikely that a single city would disadvantage itself by enacting ordinances controlling industrial pollution.

The Nine-foot Channel Becomes the Great Divide

Development of the river for navigation finally forced the issue of pollution control. Major improvement of navigation on the upper river began in June 1878 when Congress authorized a four-and-a-half-foot-deep low-water channel from St. Louis to St. Paul. About three decades later, in 1907, Congress responded to pressure from river-improvement organizations such as the Lakes-to-the-Gulf Deep Waterway Association and approved a six-foot-deep channel for the upper river. In the case of both projects, the Corps of Engineers attempted to achieve the desired depth by dredging

34. "Hold Your Ice Orders," advertisement, *DGC*, 6 June 1913, p. 2.
35. A map of cities in the Mississippi drainage north of the Iowa border that had sewer systems and sewage treatment in 1928 may be found in *Report of the Investigation of the Pollution of the Mississippi River Minneapolis to La Crosse, Inclusive by the Minnesota State Board of Health in Collaboration with the Minnesota Commissioner of Game and Fish and the Wisconsin State Board of Health*, p. iv.

and by constructing wing dams. These techniques constricted the Mississippi, thus speeding up its current and having little negative influence on the river's ability to transport wastes out of populated areas.

Beginning in 1917, the Corps of Engineers began the construction of a series of locks and dams in order to improve the navigability of the upper Mississippi. Use of this new technology greatly complicated the pollution problem in the upper river. In 1917, the corps completed the Twin Cities lock and dam. Into the five-mile-long pool created by this structure flowed all but one of the sewers in the Minneapolis system and eleven sewers in the St. Paul system. Thirteen years later, in 1930, the engineers finished a second lock and dam at Hastings, Minnesota, located about thirty-seven miles below St. Paul. The reservoir behind Hastings dam extended to the foot of the Twin Cities lock and dam. This new body of quiet water became the resting place for the remainder of the sewage from the Twin Cities and for all of the effluent from sewers located in South St. Paul and Newport, including wastes from several packinghouses and stockyards.[36] Finally, in July 1930, Congress passed a Rivers and Harbors Act that authorized the construction of several locks and dams between Alton, Illinois, and the Twin Cities, in order to create a nine-foot-deep navigation channel. The pools behind these dams threatened to become the septic tanks for wastes from cities and towns all along the upper river.

The Corps of Engineers began to build a constituency for major structural improvement of the upper Mississippi River as early as 1926. In January of that year, the secretary of war appealed to commercial interests to finance the construction of a fleet of towboats and barges so that the government-owned Inland Waterways Corporation could begin operations between the Twin Cities and St. Louis. Given a chance to demonstrate their support for river transportation, several hundred businessmen and shippers organized the Upper Mississippi Barge Line Company. This group raised $670,000, paid for the fleet that had been requested by the secretary of war, and leased it to the Inland Waterways Corporation.[37]

36. An analysis of the impact of the Twin Cities lock and dam and the Hastings lock and dam may be found in *Second Annual Report of the Metropolitan Drainage Commission of Minneapolis and St. Paul on the Subject of Sewage Disposal of Minneapolis, St. Paul, and Contiguous Areas.*
37. The formation of the Upper Mississippi Barge Line Company is discussed in U.S. Congress, House, Committee on Rivers and Harbors, *Mississippi River Be-*

After fulfilling its initial mission, the Upper Mississippi Barge Line Company continued its existence as a lobbying organization. In that capacity, members supported the position of the Corps of Engineers on development of the upper Mississippi River in testimony before the Interstate Commerce Commission, the courts, and the U.S. Congress. At the request of the corps, the Upper Mississippi Barge Line Company advanced $30,000 for surveys of the Hastings dam site and gave $12,000 to the Inland Waterways Corporation to pay for terminal engineers and traffic solicitors. Activities of the Barge Line Company represented only part of the corps efforts to build a constituency on the upper river. Urged to act by the corps, the cities of Burlington and Dubuque, Iowa, Rock Island, Illinois, and St. Paul, Minneapolis, and Stillwater, Minnesota, spent over $2 million for modern river and railroad terminal facilities.[38]

Businessmen and shippers sought to guarantee their investments of time and money by pressuring Congress to fund permanent improvement of the river. Congress responded in 1927 by authorizing the Corps of Engineers to survey the upper Mississippi with a view toward securing a nine-foot depth. In 1930, the engineers issued an interim report and in an unprecedented action Congress authorized the nine-foot channel based upon this preliminary examination. The Corps of Engineers completed its final report in December 1932. After a three-year delay, Congress released all the funds needed to complete the project, which at that time the engineers estimated to be $148,217,000.[39]

The strong show of support from commercial interests in the up-

tween Mouth of Missouri and Minneapolis: Hearings on the Subject of the Improvement of the Mississippi River Between the Mouth of the Missouri River and Minneapolis, 71st Cong., 2d sess., pp. 14–15; 72d Cong., 1st sess., pp. 31–32. Arthur Maass has noted that the Corps of Engineers routinely engaged in constituency building as a means of winning congressional approval for river development projects. See Maass, *Muddy Waters: The Army Engineers and the Nation's Rivers,* p. xi.

38. *Mississippi River Between Mouth of Missouri and Minneapolis: Hearings,* 72d Cong., 1st sess., p. 33.

39. U.S. Congress, House, *Mississippi River, Between Mouth of Missouri River and Minneapolis, Minnesota (Interim Report)*; U.S. Congress, House, *Survey of Mississippi River Between Missouri River and Minneapolis: Part 1—Report.* A discussion of the unprecedented nature of Congress's actions in 1930 may be found in *Mississippi River Between Mouth of Missouri and Minneapolis: Hearings,* 71st Cong., 2d sess., pp. 23–24. A more detailed look at the approval process for the nine-foot channel may be found in Merritt, *Creativity, Conflict & Controversy,* pp. 187–214.

per river valley played an indispensable role in advancing the project toward completion. At congressional hearings in 1930 and 1932 a parade of enthusiastic witnesses offered a logic that Congress found hard to ignore. These men contended that the people of the upper river valley had done as much as they could to help themselves. Now it was time for Congress to reward their faith by approving the nine-foot channel. In a representative statement, the secretary of the Dubuque, Iowa, Chamber of Commerce explained that in 1926 his city had built municipal terminal facilities valued at $400,000 at the request of federal authorities. He then expressed great concern that "it will be impossible for the city of Dubuque to make this investment a profitable one until such time as the United States Government completes the 9-foot channel on the upper Mississippi River."[40]

The proposed construction of the nine-foot channel in an already heavily polluted river touched off an intense debate over river use and development. This controversy reflected and reinforced divisions among river-related interests that had taken place since the 1913 completion of Keokuk dam. In 1913, commercial development of the river had reigned supreme. Seventeen years later the nine-foot channel received strong support from several newspapers and organizations such as the Upper Mississippi Barge Line Company, the Minneapolis Real Estate Board, the Mississippi Valley Association, and the Mississippi and St. Croix River Improvement Commission. Unlike Keokuk dam, however, the nine-foot channel faced challenges from within the Corps of Engineers and from groups concerned about public health, fish and wildlife, recreation, and aesthetics.

Some of the earliest criticism of the nine-foot channel project came from Maj. Charles L. Hall, district engineer at Rock Island, Illinois. During late 1928 and early 1929, Major Hall submitted two reports that condemned the nine-foot channel on the grounds that it could not be economically justified. In an address before the

40. *Mississippi River Between Mouth of Missouri and Minneapolis: Hearings*, 72d Cong., 1st sess., p. 30. Between the early twentieth century and the 1930s, the arguments favoring river improvement remained remarkably consistent. Readers wishing more information on this subject might wish to consult the following sources: Emory R. Johnson, *Ocean and Inland Water Transportation*, chaps. 24–29; Herbert Quick, *American Inland Waterways: Their Relation to Railway Transportation and to the National Welfare; Their Creation, Restoration, and Maintenance*; Harold G. Moulton, *Waterways Versus Railways*; Charles Van Hise, *The Conservation of Natural Resources in the United States*, pp. 162–85.

School of Wildlife at McGregor, Iowa, the major expanded the scope of his criticism and in so doing reinforced a mounting chorus of protests by people who believed that damming the river would seriously aggravate the pollution problem. Major Hall warned his audience at the School of Wildlife that channelizing the river would complicate sewage disposal, radically alter the flora and fauna of the river, and drive some species of fish and wildlife into extinction. Howls of protest from project supporters followed the publication of Hall's remarks. The *Minneapolis Journal* could not "see why Major Hall should worry about *flora* and *fauna* at all. His duties are neither floral nor faunal, but engineering." Two months after his McGregor speech, the Corps of Engineers without comment dismissed Major Hall from his position on a special board of engineers assigned to survey the upper river.[41]

Major Hall's removal by no means ended the conflict. Conservationists and sportsmen attacked the project for its neglect of values other than navigation. Early in October 1929, the "Voice of the Outdoors," a regular feature of the *Winona* (Minnesota) *Republican-Herald*, predicted, "The nine-foot slackened river would become a giant sewer, a death trap for fish and a menace to public health." The author recommended that, if the government went ahead with its plans, it should also contribute liberally toward the cost of sewage treatment facilities. Joined by an outdoor column in the *La Crosse* (Wisconsin) *Tribune*, the "Voice of the Outdoors" pressed its assault on the nine-foot channel for several years.[42]

These outdoor features circulated among a readership that considered the Upper Mississippi River Wildlife and Fish Refuge to be sacrosanct. Many of these readers were sportsmen who had participated in the 1924 refuge campaign. The refuge had a personal meaning for them as a symbol of their victory, as a recreational asset, and as a legacy for their children. A letter from a Wisconsin man to President Roosevelt typified this point of view. The writer asked Roosevelt to block a wasteful expenditure of public funds

41. *The Minneapolis Journal*, editorial, "Pre-Judging the Nine-Foot Channel," 23 August 1929, p. 12; *St. Paul Pioneer Press*, "Hall Removed as Member of Channel Board," 26 October 1929, entry 162, RG 22, NA. See also Merritt, *Creativity, Conflict & Controversy*, pp. 187–206. Additional information on the School of Wildlife at McGregor may be found in Patrick J. Brunet, "The Corps of Engineers and Navigation Improvement of the Channel of Upper Mississippi River to 1939," pp. 146–49.

42. "Voice of the Outdoors," *Winona Republican-Herald*, 9 October 1929, entry 162, RG 22, NA.

that would bring "the utter destruction of the 90,000 acre Wild Life Reserve in the Winneshiek Bottoms."[43]

At the national level, the Izaak Walton League dedicated itself to ensuring that the corps designed the project to minimize damage to the refuge. By adopting this position, the league's national officials broke with many local conservationists who insisted that the nine-foot channel should not be constructed. A member of the league's executive board informed the commissioner of the Bureau of Fisheries that the local people were "over-sensitive about the building of the channel. They are apparently too close to the subject to have the best of judgement." Not satisfied that the engineers would protect values other than navigation, the league initiated a successful drive to include the Bureau of Fisheries and the Bureau of Biological Survey in the planning process. Henry Baldwin Ward, national president of the Izaak Walton League, explained to President Hoover, "This question can not be decided without representation of biological interests." On 7 March 1931, the Wisconsin, Illinois, Iowa, and Minnesota divisions of the league held their own hearing on the nine-foot channel at Winona, Minnesota. Members of the league heard testimony from fellow Waltonians, the Corps of Engineers, the Bureau of Biological Survey, and the Bureau of Fisheries. Thereafter, the league adopted an official position on the project at its annual Chicago convention.[44]

Written as a series of five resolutions, the league's position amounted to an alternative program for development of the river. Frank M. Warren, an executive board member, forwarded the resolutions to the secretary of war. Warren argued in a cover letter, "The proponents of the nine-foot channel have considered only the commercial aspect of the river and in so doing have brought about this present complicated situation." He insisted that full development of the river's commercial potential required that "all other values—e.g., scenic, recreational, health, etc.—must be cared for." Immediate control of water pollution headed the league's recommendations. The organization's national officials were convinced that the federal government should not pay to clean up a

43. George W. Allen to President Franklin D. Roosevelt, 16 May 1933, entry 162, RG 22, NA.

44. Frank M. Warren, Executive Board, Izaak Walton League, to Mr. Henry O'Malley, Commissioner, Bureau of Fisheries, 12 March 1931, entry 269, RG 22, NA; Henry Baldwin Ward to President Herbert Hoover, 6 December 1929, entry 162, RG 22, NA; "U.S. Experts Forecast Effect of Channel Dams," *Winona Republican-Herald*, 7 March 1931, entry 146, RG 22, NA.

Inoculation

Eighty-five per cent of our streams are polluted. Little boys when they swim in them lose their eye-sight, get sores in their ears, sores on their bodies and pollution is taking its yearly toll of human life—and to a larger extent than the people know. When will our people wake up?

"Inoculation," from *Outdoor America* 2 (December 1923):204.

mess created by Minneapolis/St. Paul and other river cities. Instead, they opted for pressuring cities and states into taking appropriate action. The league's program further called for erosion control to minimize silting, stabilized water levels in the pools to permit the greatest productivity of fish and wildlife, location of the dams so that the refuge would not be used as a reservoir, and the installation of suitable fishways around the locks and dams.[45]

Both the Bureau of Fisheries and the Bureau of Biological Survey viewed the proposed nine-foot channel from a professional management perspective. Despite this and other areas of agreement, large enough differences separated the two bureaus that they agreed to submit separate reports to the Corps of Engineers. The agencies based their recommendations to the corps on studies of the lake created by Keokuk dam. F. M. Uhler, the investigator for the Bureau of Biological Survey, reported that the refuge could become a much more productive wildlife area provided that a series of relatively low dams maintained stable, shallow water levels over the newly flooded land. M. M. Ellis, the representative of the Bureau of Fisheries, concurred on the need for fixed levels in the navigation pools. In addition, based upon his evolving interest in aquatic environment, Ellis urged that the government acquire the overflow lands as fish refuges so that they would not be drained by private developers. He further pointed out that maintenance or restoration of a quality fishery in the upper river depended upon the control of erosion silt and pollution.[46]

Criticism of the corps for its intention to dam the upper river was not limited to sportsmen, conservationists, and professional resource managers. In March 1931, W. H. Hunt, a state senator from Wisconsin, informed the chief of engineers that sewage-laden water from the Mississippi had repeatedly backed up the St. Croix River to Prescott, Wisconsin, where it created an almost unbearable stench. Residents of Prescott blamed their plight on the Hastings lock and dam, completed in the Mississippi in November 1930. In June 1932, Sen. John J. Blane of Wisconsin forwarded a letter to the Corps of Engineers in which a constituent worried that sewage from the Twin Cities would turn the new navigation reservoirs into septic tanks.[47] Dissatisfied with the reply he re-

45. Frank M. Warren to Patrick J. Hurley, 6 May 1931, Resolutions appended, entry 111, U.S. War Department Army Corps of Engineers, RG 77, Suitland.

46. A recommendation for separate reports is contained in "Memorandum for Mr. Henderson," from W. L. McAtee, In Charge Food Habits Research, 13 February 1931, entry 162, RG 22, NA. F. M. Uhler, "Report on an Investigation of the Lake Keokuk Section of the Mississippi River . . . July 7 to 19, 1930," entry 162, RG 22, NA; Ellis, "A Survey of Conditions Affecting Fisheries in the Upper Mississippi River." Ellis's report was also printed in somewhat different form as Appendix C of *Survey of Mississippi River Between Missouri River and Minneapolis*.

47. W. H. Hunt to Brigadier General G. R. Pillsbury, Acting Chief of Engineers, 19 March 1931, entry 111, RG 77, Suitland; John J. Blane to Major General Lytle Brown, Chief of Engineers, 27 June 1932, entry 111, RG 77, Suitland.

M. M. Ellis inspecting bottom samples near Oquawka, Illinois, 1931.

ceived from the engineers, Senator Blane retorted, "It would be a part of wisdom to have such situation corrected before it is too late. It is not sufficient to say that there is no authority and law for the Federal Government to exercise jurisdiction." [48]

The intensity and scope of the conflict over the nine-foot channel had a significant impact on the way the project took shape. By including the Bureau of Fisheries and the Bureau of Biological Survey in the planning, the Corps of Engineers agreed to consider noncommercial qualities of the river. Although leaving no doubt as to his priorities, the secretary of war did make it clear that the corps "would welcome the opportunity of discussing plans for preservation of wild life as an incidental to improvement of the river in the interests of navigation." [49]

Pressure from the Bureau of Fisheries, the Bureau of Biological Survey, the Izaak Walton League, and local conservationists resulted in two important modifications to the project's original design. First, the Corps of Engineers abandoned its intention of draining the navigation pools during the winter. In the interests of fish and wildlife, the final specifications called for stable, shallow water levels in the overflow areas. This victory, however, proved to be far from permanent; during World War II, the corps precipitated a renewed controversy by drawing down many of the pools in the winter as an aid to navigation on the lower river. Second, the government purchased a considerable amount of the newly flooded land along the shores of the navigation reservoirs as fish and wildlife refuges. [50]

In addition to intensifying the pollution problem at Minneapolis/St. Paul, the dams also drew the Corps of Engineers into a local debate over the control of water pollution. The corps became the target of severe criticism and the focus of demands that the federal government help finance sewage treatment facilities for the Twin Cities. The corps strongly resisted any threats to the swift comple-

48. Blane to Brown, 5 July 1932, entry 111, RG 77, Suitland.
49. F. Trubee Davison, Acting Secretary of War, to the Secretary of Agriculture, 19 April 1930, entry 162, RG 22, NA.
50. On the subject of drawdowns, see Edward W. Baily, Acting Chief, Division of Fishery Biology, to M. M. Ellis, 21 January 1944, entry 269, RG 22, NA. Considerable information on drawdowns is also located in the IWLA files. For the reports of two surveys on the suitability of newly flooded areas between Rock Island and Alton for fish and wildlife refuges, see Robert H. Smith, Division of Wildlife Refuges, "Report of Reconnaissance Survey . . . ," 14 November 1940, entry 269, RG 22, NA; Eugene W. Surber, "A Reconnaissance of the Mississippi River Bottoms . . . ," November 1940, entry 269, RG 22, NA.

tion of the nine-foot channel and to the supremacy of navigation over other uses of the river. Thus, suggestions that pollution control should precede the construction of the locks and dams or that the federal government should accept financial responsibility for pollution abatement received a cold reception from the Corps of Engineers.

In May 1931, Rep. W. I. Nolan of Minnesota recommended that the War Department share the cost of a waste treatment plant for the Twin Cities. Representative Nolan based his argument on the fact that the government's dams would make it impossible for the river to continue to carry sewage away from the metropolitan area. In response to Nolan's proposal, the chief of engineers clearly explained his priorities on the subject of pollution control. Gen. Lytle Brown asserted, "The cities are the cause of their own trouble, and the United States can do anything in the bed of the river that it wants to do for navigation, no other authority than the Almighty having anything to say."[51]

Although rarely as blunt as General Brown, when challenged on the issue of pollution the corps tenaciously protected its interests by retreating into a strict construction of the Rivers and Harbors Act of 1899. In August 1930, the U.S. district attorney for Minnesota recommended to the attorney general that the secretary of war take immediate action "to prevent all further discharge of sewage into the Mississippi River." The U.S. attorney forecast both direct and indirect damage to navigation if the sewage from Minneapolis, St. Paul, and South St. Paul continued to flow unabated into the river. In particular, he contended that sewage solids would accumulate in the channel and impede river traffic, while disagreeable sewage odors would discourage the use of the river for commercial purposes.[52]

Evidence to back up the district attorney's contentions came from a report by Lt. Col. Wildurr Welling, the St. Paul district engineer. Based upon soundings taken behind the Twin City lock and dam, Colonel Welling predicted, "The pool is being filled in, and if the discharge of untreated sewage . . . continues it will be only a

---

51. W. I. Nolan to Patrick J. Hurley, Secretary of War, 4 May 1931, entry 111, RG 77, Suitland; Lytle Brown, Chief of Engineers, to Walter H. Newton, Secretary to the President, 8 May 1931, entry 111, RG 77, Suitland.

52. Lewis L. Drill, United States Attorney, to The Attorney General, 5 August 1930, entry 111, RG 77, Suitland.

matter of time before the deposits will become a physical obstruction to navigation." Colonel Welling also expressed concern about
damage to machinery and threats to the health of river users, especially the crews of boats.[53]

In his reply to the U.S. attorney, Patrick J. Hurley, the secretary
of war, argued that if sewage merely constituted a nuisance in
terms of either health or sanitation its control came within the police powers of the states. He then interpreted the Rivers and Harbors Act of 1899 to the effect that the corps could take no action
unless sewage actually hindered navigation. In the event that sewage deposits did impair river transportation, the corps could in-
voke the 1899 law and require that the offending obstructions be
removed.[54] Secretary Hurley proved unwilling, however, to suggest that the engineers address the problem at its source by order-
ing the primary treatment necessary to separate solids from the
sewage before it entered the river.

The Twin Cities and St. Louis

Severe pollution of the upper river represented the combined
consequences of two single-purpose technologies: sewers developed to eliminate local accumulations of waste, and locks and dams
designed to improve navigation. During the 1920s and 1930s,
technologies existed for the treatment or alternative disposal of
nearly all the pollutants that ended up in the river. Sewage and
organic wastes from packinghouses accounted for most of the degradation below the Twin Cities. Treatment methods for these wastes
had been developed in the United States during the late nineteenth and early twentieth centuries. In the mid-1920s, when
Minneapolis/St. Paul began to study the possibility of constructing
waste treatment facilities, the cities had several processes from
which to choose. At St. Louis, sewage and domestic garbage formed
a major segment of the pollution load added to the river. Once
again, the city had options other than river dumping. During a
portion of the 1930s, St. Louis had elected to sell its garbage to
hog farmers. In the absence of technical obstacles, a comparison of
the responses of the Twin Cities and St. Louis to river pollution

53. Wildurr Welling to Drill, 1 August 1930, entry 111, RG 77, Suitland.
54. Secretary of War to Mr. Attorney General, 4 October 1930, entry 111, RG
77, Suitland.

must consider a variety of environmental, social, and economic factors.[55]

For several years after the Twin Cities installed sanitary sewers, the river did the job imposed on it and carried sewage out of the metropolitan area. Gradually, however, the level of contamination within the cities began to climb. By 1907, the Minneapolis water supply, which came unfiltered from the river, had been condemned by health officials. Three years later, Minneapolis joined St. Paul in chlorinating its municipal water supply. Despite the threat to public health, sensory evidence of pollution in Minneapolis/St. Paul did not become apparent until some years after the Corps of Engineers completed the Twin Cities lock and dam in 1917. For the first seven years of the dam's existence, the corps opened the dam in the winter and flushed out accumulated sewage sludge. In 1924, however, the corps contracted to sell the hydroelectricity generated at the dam to a Ford Motor Company assembly plant. Thereafter the dam remained closed year-round, and pollution became a significant local nuisance. Scum floated on the water, and in warm weather gases generated in sludge deposits rose to the surface and created an obnoxious odor.[56]

Rank conditions caused by the closure of the Twin Cities lock and dam stimulated a fifteen-year-long campaign to clean up the river at Minneapolis/St. Paul. Completion of the Hastings dam in November 1930 and proposed construction of the nine-foot channel provided additional, powerful incentives to conquer inertia. In July 1923, the Minnesota State Board of Health asked the city councils of Minneapolis and St. Paul to initiate the steps necessary to clean up the river. Two years later, a renewed appeal from the Board of Health and the increasing accumulation of sewage behind the Twin Cities lock and dam prompted the city governments to action. Each council voted to appropriate $2,500 to fund a study of the river adjacent to the metropolitan area. At this point, in response to public pressure, the legislatures of Minnesota and Wisconsin formed a joint interim committee to gather information

55. A general discussion of waste water treatment may be found in Ellis L. Armstrong, ed., *History of Public Works in the United States, 1776–1976*, pp. 404–9.

56. Dole and Wesbrook, "The Quality of Surface Waters in Minnesota," p. 63. St. Paul did not obtain its drinking water from the river. Minnesota State Board of Health, *Stream Pollution in Minnesota; Special Report*, p. 140; *Report of the Metropolitan Drainage Commission*, p. 1.

about the quality of the river. In January 1926, this committee conducted a hearing in St. Paul at which witnesses urged treatment of the cities' sewage in order to protect public health, eliminate threats to fish life, and preserve recreational opportunities.[57]

At the conclusion of its hearing, the joint interim committee asked the U.S. Public Health Service and the U.S. Bureau of Fisheries to investigate the condition of the Mississippi River. When issued in 1927, the reports of these agencies confirmed what people already knew—wastes from the Twin Cities had grossly polluted a large segment of the upper river downstream from Minneapolis/ St. Paul. The investigator for the Bureau of Fisheries concluded that during the month of August the river for more than forty-five miles below St. Paul lacked "a sufficient supply of dissolved oxygen to sustain fish life of any sort."[58] The Public Health Service advised the cities to begin planning for proper sewage disposal and argued that even "assuming no detriment to the public health, the river is unsightly in appearance, odors are noticeable at certain points, property values are affected and parks and playgrounds lose their attractiveness due to the condition of the river in their immediate vicinity. With increasing loads on the river, objections will occur more frequently and be of longer duration."[59]

After reviewing these investigations, during its 1927 session the Minnesota legislature created the Metropolitan Drainage Commission and empowered it to analyze and recommend ways to improve the condition of the river. This new state agency functioned for six years and, after examining numerous alternatives, suggested a combined sewage system for the Twin Cities, with a single treatment plant located just downriver from St. Paul. Before work could begin, the Minnesota legislature had to approve the creation of a Twin Cities sanitary district—a municipal corporation empowered to finance, construct, and operate a sewage system. At

57. George J. Schroepfer, "Minneapolis-Saint Paul Sewage Disposal Project," p. 85; *Report of the Metropolitan Drainage Commission*, p. 1; "Survey of River Pollution Problem Assured by Pledges of Balance of Sum Necessary," *Saint Paul Pioneer Press*, 24 January 1926, entry 111, RG 77, Suitland.

58. A. H. Wiebe, "Preliminary Report Concerning the Biological Survey of the Upper Mississippi River with Special Reference to Pollution," p. 323, contained in Wisconsin State Board of Health, *Stream Pollution in Wisconsin*.

59. H. R. Crohurst, "Preliminary Report of the Investigation of the Pollution of the Mississippi River in the Vicinity of Minneapolis and St. Paul," p. 321, contained in Wisconsin State Board of Health, *Stream Pollution in Wisconsin*.

the statehouse in St. Paul, the stench from the nearby Hastings pool assisted the lobbyists in securing passage of an enabling act in 1933.[60]

The multi-million-dollar price of such an extensive facility posed a final, major obstacle to construction. The federal government helped the cities to surmount this hurdle when the Public Works Administration approved a grant that covered 30 percent of the cost. The availability of this money resulted from the intersection of three factors: the Depression, Franklin Roosevelt's New Deal, and his administration's interest in conservation. After creation of the Public Works Administration in 1933, federal assistance stimulated a significant increase in the construction of municipal sewage treatment facilities. Ground breaking for the project in the Twin Cities took place in July 1934, and in May 1938 Minneapolis/St. Paul dedicated a $15.7 million sewage treatment plant.[61] A quarter-century later, in 1963, the U.S. Fish and Wildlife Service pronounced the effort a success:

> Elimination of gross pollution and constant upgrading of water quality were . . . achieved for many years following completion of a jointly owned sewage treatment facility serving both Minneapolis and St. Paul. . . . Species of game fish returned in catchable numbers to the Mississippi River flowing through that urban area.[62]

Two organizations, the Izaak Walton League of America and the U.S. Bureau of Fisheries, provided consistent and complementary support for sewage treatment at Minneapolis/St. Paul. After Will Dilg's ouster, the league underwent an internal reorganization in 1926, and at that time a new national leadership declared water pollution to be the group's highest priority. During the 1930s and 1940s, the national officers and staff consciously became more pro-

60. Schroepfer, "Minneapolis-Saint Paul Disposal Project," pp. 85–86; *Report of the Metropolitan Drainage Commission*, pp. 2–7.

61. Between 1932 and 1937, the federal government assisted with the construction of 720 sewage treatment plants in incorporated areas. Upon completion, these facilities served about 14.2 million people. In the same period, 115 plants, with a tributary population of 788,000, were constructed without federal assistance. See Special Advisory Committee on Water Pollution, "Second Report on Water Pollution," National Resources Committee (February 1937), p. 22, entry 269, RG 22, NA; National Resources Committee, *Drainage Basin Problems and Programs, 1937 Revision*, pp. 126–31; "Twin Cities Dedicate Sewage Treatment Plant," p. 12.

62. "Memorandum to Regional Directors . . .," from Chief, Division of Sport Fisheries, 10 June 1963, p. 20, entry 246, General Correspondence 1921–69, U.S. Department of Interior, Fish and Wildlife Service, Division of Wildlife Refuges, RG 22, NA.

fessional, while membership gradually declined and the league lost much of the evangelical zeal that had characterized its early years. Nonetheless, during this same period, the Izaak Walton League of America was the most important citizens' conservation organization working for enactment of national water-pollution-control legislation.

Within this framework of concern over water quality, the Izaak Walton League stood in the forefront of the fifteen-year campaign to clean up the Mississippi below the Twin Cities. Led by Judson L. Wicks, president of the Minnesota division of the league, Waltonians rallied public support and put pressure on city and state officials. Early in 1926, the joint interim committee appointed the presidents of all the Izaak Walton League chapters in Minnesota and Wisconsin as its public education committee. In 1931, the Minnesota division called a meeting that included representatives from the Metropolitan Drainage Commission, the Bureau of Fisheries, and seventeen Mississippi River towns. The delegates scolded the Twin Cities for failing to begin construction of a treatment plant, and they passed resolutions urging the Minnesota legislature to "enact laws which would compel immediate solution of the problem." Two years later, in 1933, the Minnesota division proved instrumental in the creation of the Twin Cities sanitary district by marshaling public opinion and by directly lobbying state representatives.[63]

During the 1920s and 1930s, the position of the Bureau of Fisheries on water quality evolved along with the developing pollution situation at Minneapolis/St. Paul. For the first three decades of the twentieth century, one of the bureau's primary activities in the Midwest was stocking the upper Mississippi River drainage with freshwater mussels. By the late 1920s, pollution, siltation, wetlands drainage, and navigational improvements had rendered much of the upper Mississippi drainage unfit for commercially useful mussels. In response to this significant habitat degradation, scientists from the bureau began to evolve an incipient ecological perspective. The agency did not abandon programs aimed at producing marketable species or controlling the conditions of their

63. "Survey of River Pollution Problem Assured by Pledges"; Suitland; "Report on Minneapolis Pollution Meeting," A. H. Wiebe, Assistant Aquatic Biologist, to Chief Division of Inquiry, 16 June 1928, entry 121, RG 22, NA; "Waltonians Ask State Action On Mississippi Contamination"; Judson L. Wicks, "Clean the Mississippi."

propagation. Rather, scientists such as M. M. Ellis shifted their emphasis from the propagation of useful species to the enhancement of water quality necessary to support a diversity of aquatic life.[64]

The Bureau of Fisheries strongly advocated construction of a municipal sewage treatment system by Minneapolis and St. Paul. Fisheries experts considered the Twin Cities the key to the clean-up and habitat revitalization of a large segment of the upper river. It seemed unlikely that any downriver city located in Minnesota or Wisconsin would pay for treatment facilities as long as the Twin Cities continued to discharge raw sewage into the Mississippi. Lacking any enforcement power, the agency had to limit its efforts to scientific investigation and expert advice. Employees of the bureau testified at numerous public meetings and in so doing professionally reinforced the popular appeals of the Izaak Walton League. Subsequent events validated the bureau's emphasis on Minneapolis/St. Paul. After the Twin Cities committed themselves to the construction of a treatment plant, several smaller cities as far downstream as La Crosse, Wisconsin, signed contracts for facilities of their own.[65]

In 1934, the same year the Twin Cities began construction of their sewage works, St. Louis officials asked the Army Corps of Engineers for permission to dispose of all the city's domestic garbage in the Mississippi River. During the early 1930s, St. Louis had transported its garbage across the Mississippi and sold it to hog farmers in Illinois. With its hog farm contract about to expire in February 1935, the city opted to purchase garbage grinders that would reduce its average daily output of 253 tons of garbage to pieces of one inch or less. These particles could then be flushed into the sewers and conveyed to the Mississippi River. For the sake of efficiency and in order not to overload any single sewer, the Department of Streets and Sewers proposed to scatter several grinding plants throughout the city.[66]

64. Examples of this incipient ecological perspective may be found in Robert E. Coker, "Keokuk Dam and the Fisheries of the Upper Mississippi River," *Bulletin of the U.S. Bureau of Fisheries, vol. 45, 1929*; M. M. Ellis, "A Survey of Conditions Affecting Fisheries in the Upper Mississippi River," *U.S. Bureau of Fisheries, Fishery Circular Number 5*.

65. In "The Future of the Upper Mississippi Fisheries," *Minnesota Waltonian* 5 (October 1934):7, entry 162, RG 22, NA; C. F. Culler notes that several smaller cities had closed contracts for treatment plants.

66. Frank J. McDevitt, "Supplementary Report on the Grinding of Garbage and Disposal of Same through Sewers into the Mississippi River," p. 2, 8 December 1934, entry 269, RG 22, NA. I have used the figure provided by the city. The Bu-

The chief protagonists in the St. Louis garbage controversy were the U.S. Bureau of Fisheries and the St. Louis Department of Streets and Sewers. At the request of the St. Louis district engineer of the Army Corps of Engineers, M. M. Ellis undertook a study of the garbage disposal plan proposed by St. Louis. During September 1934, Ellis examined conditions in the 190-mile section of the river between St. Louis and Cairo, Illinois. He also analyzed samples from a pilot garbage plant run by the city. Ellis's conclusions condemned the St. Louis plan. He discovered that the pollution load already added to the river at St. Louis significantly depleted the water of its dissolved oxygen content in two extensive zones between St. Louis and Cairo. Even the addition of a tremendous volume of water from the Ohio River at Cairo did not restore the oxygen in the Mississippi to the levels found above St. Louis. Ellis predicted that during warm weather the added oxygen demand of St. Louis's garbage would create adverse to critical conditions for aquatic life at several points below the city. He added that this situation could only get worse as the population grew and produced more sewage and garbage.[67]

Based upon his analysis, Ellis drew additional conclusions that transcended the immediate impact on aquatic life downstream from St. Louis. He reminded his superior in Washington, "We are faced with a situation involving much more than the saving of the Fisheries below St. Louis which everyone knows are at present of very little consequence." Ellis feared that the solution to its garbage problem proposed by St. Louis would set an unwelcome precedent. Indeed, Ellis viewed the city's proposal as a way to avoid more expensive and more effective methods of garbage disposal.[68]

Acting on information supplied by Ellis, the commissioner of the U.S. Bureau of Fisheries and the secretary of commerce both recommended that St. Louis find an alternative to discharging its garbage into the river. Commissioner Frank T. Bell informed the

---

reau of Fisheries argued that the average daily output of garbage in St. Louis was 600 tons.

67. Ellis based his calculations on an average daily output of 600 tons of garbage. M. M. Ellis, "A Study of the Mississippi River from Chain of Rocks, St. Louis, Missouri, to Cairo, Illinois, with Special Reference to the Proposed Introduction of Ground Garbage into the River by the City of St. Louis," U.S. Fish and Wildlife Service, *Special Scientific Report Number 8*. See also Ellis to Elmer Higgins, In Charge, Division of Scientific Inquiry, 17 October 1934, entry 269, RG 22, NA; "Bureau Studies New Pollution Menace on the Mississippi River," Fisheries Service Bulletin, November 1934, entry 269, RG 22, NA.

68. Ellis to Higgins, 17 October 1934.

St. Louis director of streets and sewers that the controversy reinforced the importance of appropriate sewage treatment for cities
located on inland waters. Bell contended, "With adequate sewage
disposal works the city sewers can be utilized safely and economically in the disposal of ground garbage without detriment to the
fisheries." Officials of the bureau also argued that aesthetic considerations and potential threats to public health should influence the
corps to deny St. Louis's request.[69]

Frank J. McDevitt, director of streets and sewers, was the point
man in the city's campaign to win corps approval for its garbage-
grinding proposal. Drawing on his own analysis, McDevitt maintained that the addition of St. Louis's garbage to the river would
not bring about the unfavorable conditions for aquatic life cited in
Ellis's report. McDevitt further contended that in terms of investment in equipment and operating costs river dumping was the
most economical alternative for the city. He pointed out that
nearly every large city on the river discharged its sewage into the
water and concluded that it would be unfair to single out St. Louis
and force it to pay for treatment facilities. McDevitt did concede
that at some future date the city's pollution might endanger fish
life. Even in this event, he expressed doubt as to whether or not
the problem would be important enough to increase the tax bur-
den to pay for a disposal plant. McDevitt also noted that the Rivers
and Harbors Act of 1899 exempted material discharged from sewers
in a liquid state. He no doubt hoped that consistency would require the Corps of Engineers to interpret the act so as to grant the
city its request.[70]

The interpretation by the corps of the Rivers and Harbors Act
fulfilled McDevitt's expectation. The fact that the St. Louis district
engineer asked Ellis to conduct a survey indicated his sensitivity to
the potential costs associated with the St. Louis garbage disposal
plan. Nonetheless, at the end of 1934, the Corps of Engineers is-

69. Frank T. Bell, Commissioner, to Mr. Frank McDevitt, Director of Streets
and Sewers, 18 January 1935, entry 269, RG 22, NA; Daniel C. Roper, Secretary of
Commerce, to Hon. Bernard F. Dickman, Mayor, 12 November 1934, entry 269,
RG 22, NA. A good summary of the bureau's position may be found in Charles E.
Jackson, Acting Commissioner, to Chief of Engineers, 25 October 1934, entry 269,
RG 22, NA.
70. McDevitt, "Supplementary Report on the Grinding of Garbage," pp. 5–7, 9.
McDevitt made his calculations based up "average adverse conditions of garbage
and river flow." Ellis challenged his use of average figures. Good summaries of
McDevitt's position are contained in McDevitt to Hon. John J. Cochran, 2 October,
11 December 1934, entry 269, RG 22, NA.

sued a controversial decision that allowed the city to proceed provided the garbage did not impede navigation. The district engineer advised the city of St. Louis, "No objection will be interposed to the disposal of diluted garbage . . . so long as the navigable capacity of the Mississippi River is not adversely affected thereby."[71]

An explanation of why the Twin Cities and St. Louis developed such divergent water pollution policies must consider a number of factors. Although differences existed, neither Minnesota nor Missouri had state laws that could force an unwilling city to install sewage treatment facilities. On the federal level, both the Twin Cities and St. Louis suffered the same handicap imposed by a national law that had been interpreted to exclude the effluents from sewers. Both also had equal access to Public Works Administration grants for water purification projects. Minneapolis and St. Paul did have the advantage of an active, organized conservation constituency, while St. Louis lacked a strong conservation lobby of the type represented by the Izaak Walton League in Minnesota and Wisconsin. In 1934, for example, when St. Louis applied for permission to flush its garbage into the river, a local Waltonian met with employees of the Department of Streets and Sewers. At this interview the league's representative satisfied himself that the introduction of garbage into the river would not endanger aquatic life.[72]

In the final analysis, the one outstanding difference between St. Louis and Minneapolis/St. Paul remains the construction of navigation dams in the upper river. Although they did not cause the pollution problem, the dams aggravated the situation and focused attention on the deteriorating quality of the river. The active interest in pollution control in the Twin Cities can be dated from 1925, after the Corps of Engineers began year-round closure of the Twin Cities lock and dam. River dumping ceased to be an acceptable alternative when sewage backed up into the metropolitan area and residents began to pay the social and environmental costs of pollutants that had formerly been washed away by the river. The Twin Cities found it possible to finance a treatment facility, overcome

71. The quote from the St. Louis District Engineer is contained in James L. Green, Military Assistant, to Dr. Edward H. Brune, 4 March 1937, entry 111, RG 77, Suitland.

72. Comments on the St. Louis Izaak Walton League representative may be found in Seth Gordon, President, American Game Association, to Frank T. Bell, U.S. Commissioner of Fisheries, 14 December 1934, entry 269, RG 22, NA. Gordon opposed the St. Louis plan. The Missouri and Minnesota pollution laws are discussed in Harold D. Padgett, "Laws Relating to Stream Pollution."

inadequate legislation, and smooth over differences among river-related interests when the dams once again made pollution a local problem. At St. Louis, a much larger river continued to flow unimpeded to the Gulf of Mexico. For St. Louis officials, the Mississippi remained a cheap, expedient means of carrying wastes out of the city.

During the 1920s and 1930s, St. Louis represented the typical response to water pollution. Generalized water pollution control required uniform legislation enacted regionally by drainage basin or nationally for the entire country. In the absence of such legislation, sanitary sewers usually proved to be the cheapest, most convenient means of disposal. Like St. Louis, individual cities situated on polluted rivers could see little to be gained from acting alone to finance and construct treatment facilities. From this perspective, the lengthy and successful attempt by the Twin Cities to clean up the river may be seen as the convergence of a number of anomalous circumstances, including the construction of the locks and dams, the persistence of the Izaak Walton League, and the professional concerns of scientists in the Bureau of Fisheries. Most important of all was the fact that Minneapolis/St. Paul straddled the river at the head of navigation, where the Mississippi entered the urban area in a relatively pure condition. Thus, money spent on sewage treatment had an immediate local impact and also had the effect of encouraging cities downstream from the Twin Cities to sign contracts for plants of their own.

Conclusion

Down the great Valley, twenty-five hundred miles from Minnesota,
Carrying every rivulet and brook, creek and rill,
Carrying all the rivers that run down two-thirds the continent—
The Mississippi runs to the Gulf.—Pare Lorentz, *The River*

In 1817 and again in 1926, an explorer and a scientist surveyed the Mississippi near the mouth of the St. Croix. The explorer, Maj. Stephen Long, marveled at the clarity of the water upriver from the St. Croix. A prophet of progress, Long included clean water as one of many resources that the upper Mississippi region offered to an expanding American nation. The scientist, A. H. Wiebe, studied the Mississippi below the Twin Cities in order to determine whether pollution from that rapidly growing metropolitan area was a factor in destroying aquatic life in the river. At the mouth the St. Croix, about fifty miles downstream from Minneapolis, Wiebe described the river as grossly polluted, a witches' caldron stirred by gases generated in the decomposing organic wastes that blanketed the riverbottom. Rising gases lifted large masses of rotting solids that broke the surface and then sank back into the murky water.[1]

The interaction between people and the river was a dynamic phenomenon that cannot be separated from the society that gave it life. Keokuk dam resulted from the confluence of a decades-old dream with the end of white-pine prosperity and the growth of an integrated electric power industry. The pearl-button industry had its origins in a favorable tariff schedule, the expansion of the ready-made clothing industry, and the persistence of John Boepple. The water pollution that killed the button industry was a product of urbanization, industrialization, and a widely held belief that the river could serve as a waste dump and still fulfill the clean-water

1. Stephen H. Long, *Voyage in a Six-Oared Skiff to the Falls of Saint Anthony in 1817*, pp. 28, 30; A. H. Wiebe, "Biological Survey of the Upper Mississippi, With Special Reference to Pollution," *Bulletin of the U.S. Bureau of Fisheries, vol. 43, Part II, 1927*, pp. 141, 149–50.

needs of society. The Upper Mississippi River Wildlife and Fish Refuge represented the work of the Izaak Walton League, an organization that developed in response to the destruction of aquatic environments.

Degradation of the environment of the upper Mississippi River was a part of the process that created a modern urban industrial nation. Yet this process of modernization was not an autonomous one. Instead, it represented the accumulated results of individuals' decisions and was at least partially informed by these individuals' attitudes toward nature. The men who founded the Keokuk and Hamilton Waterpower Company chose to build a dam across the river, to hire Hugh L. Cooper as chief engineer, and to transfer their franchise to Stone & Webster. These men turned to the Des Moines rapids as a way to revitalize the regional economy after the demise of the white-pine industry. They acted on the belief that the highest use of the rapids was to develop their potential energy for industrial power.

During the late nineteenth and early twentieth centuries, residents of the upper Mississippi region transformed the river and its valley to meet perceived economic and social needs. In so doing, they created a human artifact that bore witness to a dynamic and historic interaction between culture and environment. Initially the environment presented a range of options, only some of which were capitalized on by people who emphasized economic development and progress. Selection of some options opened new ones, closed others, and oftentimes produced unanticipated consequences.

Although many projects for using and developing the river performed exactly as their promoters wanted them to, they also gave rise to significant unanticipated consequences. Keokuk dam improved navigation over the Des Moines rapids and eventually generated several hundred thousand electrical horsepower. The Minneapolis sewer system did a very good job of conveying wastes out of the city. Yet, in spite of their successes, these activities had a range of unexpected social and environmental impacts. Most citizens of the "Power Zone" who backed the Keokuk project did not wish to surrender decisions that affected employment and energy to Stone & Webster and The North American Company. Nor, for that matter, did the voters of Minneapolis who approved municipal bonds for the construction of sewers intend to convert the Mississippi into a cesspool.

The unanticipated consequences of various river use and development practices proved to be one of the most important factors in bringing about changes in attitudes and actions toward the river. The national debate over damming California's Hetch Hetchy valley that occurred between 1907 and 1913 received little attention along the upper Mississippi River. Residents of the "Power Zone" closed ranks in enthusiastic support of the economic and social benefits of Keokuk dam. Many of those who boosted the undertaking acted on the belief that improvement of the Mississippi for power and navigation would not rule out the chance to enjoy its recreational potential. A decade later, growing concern over degradation of the river environment stimulated two important groups to take action. Scientists in the Bureau of Fisheries began to emphasize maintenance of the river's biological productivity, while outdoor recreationists increasingly insisted on protecting the river's amenities. These changes in attitudes became incorporated in two new institutions, the bureau's Cooperative Research Laboratory at the University of Missouri and the Izaak Walton League of America.

When the Izaak Walton League and the Bureau of Fisheries became involved in water quality issues, they learned a lesson that modern environmentalists often claim as their own. Technical innovation frequently proceeds at too fast a rate to allow society to anticipate its consequences or evolve institutions to mitigate their impact. DDT and nuclear fallout dramatized this problem in the post–World War II period. Yet, during the 1920s and 1930s, sanitary sewers, locks and dams, and other technologies presented the same kind of difficulty. Individuals in both organizations concluded that a regional problem like water pollution required uniform regulation, and they joined forces to lobby for an effective federal water-pollution-control act. The nation, however, had yet to develop either the will or the institutions to deal with pollution problems at the federal level. Thus, the league and the bureau were forced to seek such mechanisms for amelioration as they could find at local and state levels.

In the period covered by this study, several notable changes took place in the relationship between people and the river. The general direction was toward a proliferation of interests and a mounting conflict over the river's finite ability to meet the often contradictory demands of society. During the late nineteenth and early twentieth centuries, not everyone shared the same perceptions of the upper river. Nonetheless, published commentaries on the drainage of overflow lands, the mussel fishery, and the Keokuk hydroelectric project indicate considerable accord. Most people agreed that the river's resource potential should be utilized in order to foster the social benefits associated with economic growth.

During the 1920s, cracks appeared in the surface of this agreement and then widened as people confronted each other over a range of activities that ten or fifteen years earlier would have received almost unanimous endorsement. At the June 1921 conference on interior waters held at Fairport, Iowa, one of the delegates succinctly stated the major problem faced by water resource managers:

> The most important barrier to progress lies in this matter of reconciling these interests. How, for instance, may we force a common interest with the angler, the manufacturer, the conservationist and the city which uses the stream to carry off pollution. The promoter of construction work. The farmer who sees fit to drain the swamp. The lumber men who believe forests were meant for them. I see no harm in submitting the question to them.[2]

In the years after the Fairport conference, growing controversy among user groups characterized the relationship between people and the river. This discord had its roots in three interrelated responses to environmental degradation. Represented by the Izaak Walton League, a new constituency emerged in the early 1920s for the preservation of the recreational and aesthetic qualities of the river. By involving themselves in conservation politics, Waltonians precipitated controversy over river-related issues where little had previously existed. During the late 1920s, professional resource managers in the Bureau of Fisheries shifted their emphasis from propagating useful species to enhancing the river's ability to support aquatic life. Although the bureau lacked regulatory authority, the expert testimony of scientists such as M. M. Ellis injected an ecological element into the growing public debate over use and development of the river. Finally, proponents of projects such as the nine-foot-deep channel and the use of the river to dispose of St.

2. Statement of Dr. Ray C. Osborn, professor of zoology and entomology, Ohio State University, typed transcript of "Conservation Conference for Resources of Interior Waters, Held at United States Fisheries Biological Station, Fairport, Iowa, 8–10 June 1921," p. 94, entry 121, Record Group 22, Records of the Fish and Wildlife Service, National Archives Building, Washington, D.C. (hereafter cited as RG 22, NA).

Louis's garbage found their proposals under attack. They organized in defense of their plans and in so doing introduced further turmoil into a political arena that had formerly been characterized by a relative harmony of interests.

Several characteristics of the river contributed to the trend toward fragmentation and controversy. The upper Mississippi River plays a central role in the lives of people who live along its shores. From Minneapolis to the mouth of the Missouri, the Mississippi flows for about seven hundred miles through five states and past hundreds of cities and towns. Along its great length an increasingly urban industrial population exerted a range of contradictory demands that precipitated confrontations among various user groups. The river often transformed local problems into regional ones and brought the consequences of otherwise discrete activities into contact with each other. In most cases people regarded the river as a "common property" resource, a situation that created a dilemma for river users. On the one hand, free access presented numerous opportunities. On the other hand, discerning individuals or communities who recognized the consequences of exploiting a common resource found themselves trapped in a situation that made remedial action extremely difficult in the absence of uniform regulation.

Conservation is a term that came into widespread use in the first decade of the twentieth century. Thereafter, conservation became an ever-present theme in public discussions of the Mississippi River. Yet conservation did not mean the same thing to everyone, and its various shades of meaning reflected differences among river-related interests. When Keokuk dam became caught up in the national debate over water-resource legislation, conservation terminology reinforced the arguments of both sides in the dispute. Proponents of free, perpetual concessions defined conservation in terms of use or prevention of waste. Advocates of user fees and limited-duration, recoverable leases turned to a multiple-purpose view of conservation to support their program. When Robert Coker published his first study of Lake Cooper in 1913, his analysis revealed a third perspective emphasizing the scientific management of useful species, a viewpoint that caused him to express reservations about the impact of Keokuk dam on the fishery.

Historians have generally portrayed the 1920s as a conservation wasteland, barren of the excitement and significance associated with the conservation crusades of Theodore Roosevelt Progressives and the agencies of Franklin Roosevelt's New Deal. Those who have found evidence of conservation activity in the 1920s have usually located it in Herbert Hoover's Department of Commerce as a part of that agency's efforts to rationalize production and eliminate waste.[3] These interpretations share a focus on the federal government that has resulted in a truncated picture of conservation during the 1920s and 1930s. Examination of the upper Mississippi region has demonstrated that a vibrant conservation movement developed below the federal level and in many ways anticipated the post–World War II environmental movement.[4]

Beginning during the 1920s, the Izaak Walton League and the Bureau of Fisheries gave institutional expression to two new and complementary interpretations of conservation. Waltonians were self-styled nature lovers. Yet their evangelical zeal sprang as much from fear that their children would be denied outdoor experiences as it did from their own love of unspoiled nature. Under the guidance of the Izaak Walton League, these sentiments coalesced into a popular movement to preserve the remnants of outdoor America in the upper Mississippi River valley. In the late 1920s, scientists in the Bureau of Fisheries developed a theory of conservation that stressed the biological productivity of rivers. This concept was predicated on an awareness of the consequences of river use and development practices and on an understanding of the river as an interdependent system. Together, the league and the bureau, the amateur and the professional, helped redefine the relationship between people and the river to include obligations as well as de-

3. Although he mentions the Bureau of Fisheries only briefly, Ellis Hawley has written some of the best studies on conservation in the 1920s and early 1930s as a means of rationalizing production and eliminating waste. See Ellis W. Hawley, *The Great War and the Search for a Modern Order: A History of the American People and Their Institutions, 1917–1933* and "Herbert Hoover, the Commerce Secretariat, and the Vision of an 'Associative State,' 1921–1928." A regional study that offers a similar interpretation of the Bureau of Fisheries may be found in Richard A. Cooley, *Politics and Conservation: The Decline of the Alaska Salmon.* See also Kendrick A. Clements, "Herbert Hoover and Conservation, 1921–33."

4. Roderick Nash, *Wilderness and the American Mind.* With only a brief look at the careers of Aldo Leopold and Robert Marshall, Nash skips from Hetch Hetchy (1913) to the struggle to save Dinosaur National Monument (1950s). Samuel P. Hays, "The Environmental Movement," p. 219. Hays argues that the modern environmental movement originated in the late 1950s and early 1960s in response to "the massive social and economic changes that took place in American society after World War II." He contends that the postwar environmental movement may be distinguished from the earlier conservation movement by its concern over protecting and enhancing the quality of the environment. He further asserts, "These twin objectives . . . often gave rise to a broader concern for the long-run viability of the physical and biological world upon which sustained human institutions depended."

mands. These two organizations formed an effective conservation lobby that lasted until the late 1940s.

In the decades after World War II, the effectiveness of both the league and the bureau in the area of conservation eroded considerably. Enrollment in the league hit a low of 50,000 in 1975, at a time when the memberships of other national conservation organizations had burgeoned as a result of the popular environmental movement of the late 1960s and early 1970s. The Bureau of Fisheries, transferred in 1940 to the newly established Fish and Wildlife Service in the Department of Interior, also suffered a reversal of fortune. In the spring of 1947, Congress slashed the budget of the Fish and Wildlife Service. Forced to retrench, the service closed the seventeen-year-old pollution investigation unit at Columbia, Missouri. This move drastically reduced federal research directed toward developing water quality standards that could serve as guidelines for maintaining a diversity of aquatic life in rivers and streams. By the early 1960s, the service had forgotten much of the work performed at the facility.[5]

Despite their postwar misfortunes, the league and the bureau pioneered in a direction of travel that has endured. These organizations represented important antecedents of the environmental movement of the 1960s and 1970s. The league provided an institutional focus for popular concerns over threats to the amenities of nature, and it was the first national conservation organization to combine all the elements of modern environmental campaigns. Research conducted by the Bureau of Fisheries developed an understanding of the river as a complex system that included life and the ability to support life, that had to meet a variety of conflicting social needs, and that could not be separated from the land through which it flowed. This point of view anticipated the emphasis on ecology that gained increasing popularity during the 1960s and 1970s.

5. Membership figures may be found in Stephen Fox, *John Muir and His Legacy: The American Conservation Movement*, p. 315. Closing of the Columbia facility is discussed in numerous letters, including Albert M. Day, Director, to Dr. Frederick A. Middlebush, President, University of Missouri, 27 June 1947, entry 269, RG 22, NA.

Bibliography

Manuscript Collections

Izaak Walton League of America. Arlington, Virginia. Files.

Keokuk Public Library. Keokuk, Iowa. Bickel Collection. Binder on "Bridges & Rivers."

National Archives. Washington, D.C. Record Group 22, Records of the Fish and Wildlife Service; Record Group 187, National Resources Planning Board, Central Office Correspondence, 1933–1943.

National Archives. Suitland, Maryland. Record Group 77, Records of the Chief of Engineers.

Western Historical Manuscripts. Ellis Library, University of Missouri–Columbia. Winterton Conway Curtis (1875–1965) Papers, 1892–1962; School of Medicine Records, University of Missouri–Columbia.

Newspapers

Burlington (Iowa) *Hawkeye*, 1910–1913.
Canton (Missouri) *News*, 1913–1915.
Hannibal (Missouri) *Morning Journal*, 1901, 1912–1915.
Keokuk (Iowa) *Daily Gate City*, May-August 1899, 1912–1915.
Minneapolis Journal, 1929.
St. Louis Post-Dispatch, 1913.
St. Louis Republic, 1913.
Winona (Minnesota) *Republican-Herald*, 1929–1930.

Interview

Platner, Dr. Wesley, and Mary McConathy Platner. Columbia, Missouri. June 1983.

U.S. Government Documents

Coker, Robert E. "Water-Power Development in Relation to Fishes and Mussels of the Mississippi." In *U.S. Bureau of Fisheries Annual Report With Appendixes, 1912/13*, pp. 1–29. Washington, D.C.: GPO, 1913.
———. "The Protection of Fresh-Water Mussels." In *U.S. Bureau of*

Fisheries Annual Report With Appendixes, 1911/12, pp. 1–23. Washington, D.C.: GPO, 1914.

―――. "Fresh-Water Mussels and Mussel Industries of the United States." In *Bulletin of the U.S. Bureau of Fisheries, vol. 36, 1917–18,* pp. 11–90. Washington, D.C.: U.S. Government Printing Office, 1921.

―――. "Natural History of Fresh-Water Mussels." In *Bulletin of the U.S. Bureau of Fisheries, vol. 37, 1919–20,* pp. 79–181. Washington, D.C.: GPO, 1922.

―――. "Keokuk Dam and the Fisheries of the Upper Mississippi River." In *Bulletin of the U.S. Bureau of Fisheries, vol. 45, 1929,* pp. 87–139. Washington, D.C.: GPO, 1929.

―――. "Studies of Common Fishes of the Mississippi River at Keokuk." In *Bulletin of the U.S. Bureau of Fisheries, vol. 45, 1929 ,* pp. 141–225. Washington, D.C.: GPO, 1929.

Coker, Robert, et al. "Natural History and Propagation of Fresh-Water Mussels." In *Bulletin of the U.S. Bureau of Fisheries, vol. 37, 1919–20,* pp. 75–182. Washington, D.C.: GPO, 1922.

Curran, John M. "Prices in the Button Industry." *War Industries Board Price Bulletin Number 29.* Washington, D.C.: GPO, 1919.

Dole, R. B., and F. F. Wesbrook. "The Quality of Surface Waters in Minnesota." *Water-Supply and Irrigation Paper No. 193.* U.S. Geological Survey. Washington, D.C.: GPO, 1907.

Ellis, M. M. "A Survey of Conditions Affecting Fisheries in the Upper Mississippi River." *U.S. Bureau of Fisheries, Fishery Circular Number 5.* Washington, D.C.: GPO, September 1931.

―――. "Some Factors Affecting the Replacement of the Commercial Fresh-Water Mussels." *U.S. Bureau of Fisheries, Fishery Circular Number 7.* Washington, D.C.: GPO, December 1931.

―――. "A Study of the Mississippi River from Chain of Rocks, St. Louis, Missouri, to Cairo, Illinois, with Special Reference to the Proposed Introduction of Ground Garbage into the River by the City of St. Louis." U.S. Fish and Wildlife Service. *Special Scientific Report Number 8.* Mimeographed, 1943 (first submitted December 1934).

―――. "Detection and Measurement of Stream Pollution." In *Bulletin of the U.S. Bureau of Fisheries, vol. 48, 1937,* pp. 365–437. Washington, D.C.: GPO, 1937.

Executive Documents. *Annual Reports of the War Department, 1903, Report of the Chief of Engineers, Part 2.* "Report of Maj. C. McD. Townsend, Corps of Engineers, upon Examination of Mississippi River at the Foot of Des Moines Rapids . . . To Determine the Advisability of Constructing a Dam at the Foot of Said Rapids. . . ." 58th Cong., 2d sess., 1903–1904, pp. 1500–1512.

―――. *Message from the President of the United States to the Two Houses of Congress, at the Commencement of the Third Session of the Twenty-fifth Congress.* Executive Document 2, 25th Cong., 3d sess., 1838–1839, pp. 233–35.

————. *Message from the President of the United States to the Two Houses of Congress, at the Commencement of the First Session of the Twenty-sixth Congress.* Executive Document 2, 26th Cong., 1st sess., 1839–1940, pp. 197–99.

"Fresh-Water Mussel Fishery." In *U.S. Bureau of Fisheries Annual Report with Appendixes, 1915/16*, pp. 50–55. Washington, D.C.: GPO, 1916.

Glatsoff, P. S. "Limnological Observations in the Upper Mississippi, 1921." In *Bulletin of the U.S. Bureau of Fisheries, vol. 39, 1923–24*, pp. 347–438. Washington, D.C.: GPO, 1924.

Kunz, George F. "A Brief History of the Gathering of Fresh-Water Pearls in the United States." In *Bulletin of the U.S. Fish Commission for 1897, vol. 17*, pp. 321–30. Washington, D.C.: GPO, 1898.

————. "The Fresh-Water Pearls and Pearl Fisheries of the United States." In *Bulletin of the U.S. Fish Commission for 1897, vol. 17*, pp. 375–426. Washington, D.C.: GPO, 1898.

Lefevre, George, and Winterton C. Curtis. "Studies on the Reproduction and Artificial Propagation of Fresh-Water Mussels." In *Bulletin of the U.S. Bureau of Fisheries, vol. 30, 1910*, pp. 105–97. Washington, D.C.: GPO, 1912.

Leighton, Marshall O. "Pollution of Illinois and Mississippi Rivers by Chicago Sewage: A Digest of the Testimony Taken in the Case of the State of Missouri v. the State of Illinois and the Sanitary District of Chicago." *Water-Supply and Irrigation Paper No. 194.* U.S. Geological Survey. Washington D.C.: GPO, 1907.

Meek, Seth E. "A Report upon the Fishes of Iowa, Based upon Observations and Collections Made During 1889, 1890, and 1891." In *Bulletin of the United States Fish Commission for 1890, vol. 10*, pp. 217–48. Washington, D.C.: GPO, 1892.

National Resources Committee. *Drainage Basin Problems and Programs: 1937 Revision.* Washington, D.C.: GPO, 1938.

Nicollet, J. N. *Report Intended to Illustrate a Map of the Hydrographical Basin of the Upper Mississippi River.* House Doc. No. 52, 28th Cong., 2d sess., 1845.

Oil Pollution of Navigable Waters. Report to the Secretary of State by the Interdepartmental Committee. 13 March 1926. Washington, D.C.: GPO, 1926.

Platner, Wesley S. "Water Quality Studies of the Mississippi River." U.S. Fish and Wildlife Service. *Special Scientific Report Number 30.* 1946.

Simpson, Charles T. "The Pearly Fresh-Water Mussels of the United States: Their Habits, Enemies, and Diseases, with Suggestions for Their Protection." In *Bulletin of the U.S. Fish Commission for 1898, vol. 18*, pp. 2790–88. Washington, D.C.: GPO, 1899.

Smith, Hugh M. "The Mussel Fishery and Pearl-Button Industry of the Mississippi River." In *Bulletin of the U.S. Fish Commission for 1898, vol. 18*, pp. 289–314. Washington, D.C.: GPO, 1899.

————. Fresh-Water Mussels: A Valuable National Resource Without Sufficient Protection. *U.S. Bureau of Fisheries, Economic Circular Number 43.* Washington, D.C.: GPO, 1919.

Surber, Thaddeus. "Notes on the Natural Hosts of Fresh-Water Mussels." In *Bulletin of the U.S. Bureau of Fisheries, vol. 32, 1912,* pp. 101–16. Washington, D.C.: GPO, 1913.

Townsend, C. H. "Statistics of the Fisheries of the Mississippi River and Tributaries." In *U.S. Commission of Fish and Fisheries, Commissioner's Report, 1901,* pp. 659–740. Washington, D.C.: GPO, 1902.

U.S. Congress. House. *Rapids of the Mississippi River.* House Report No. 69, 34th Cong., 1st sess., 1855–1856.

————. *Dam Across the Mississippi River.* House Report No. 3989, 58th Cong., 3d sess., 1904–1905.

————. "Dam Across the Mississippi River." Debate over H.R. 15284. 58th Cong., 3d sess., 27 January 1905. *Congressional Record* 58:1495–96.

————. "Amendment of General Dam Act." Debate over H.R. 16053. Remarks of William C. Adamson. 63d Cong., 2d sess., 30 June 1913. *Congressional Record* 51:11417–18.

————. "Bill to Construct Dams Across Navigable Waters." Debate over H.R. 16053. 63d Cong., 2d sess., 27 April 1913–5 August 1913. *Congressional Record* 51:7350, 7404, 7598, 11068–71, 11401–5, 11413–32, 12283–84, 12328–40, 12406–8, 12568–99, 12657–716, 12748–78, 12892–909, 13016–41, 13237–76, [appendix 767], 13268–69, 13275–76, 13296.

————. *Hetch Hetchy Grant to San Francisco.* House Report No. 41. 63d Cong., 1st sess., 1913.

————. *Upper Mississippi River Wild Life and Fish Refuge.* House Report No. 747. 68th Cong., 1st sess., 14 May 1924.

————. *Pollution Affecting Navigation or Commerce on Navigable Waters.* House Doc. No. 417. 69th Cong., 1st sess., 7 June 1926.

————. *Mississippi River, Between the Mouth of Missouri River and Minneapolis, Minnesota (Interim Report).* House Doc. No. 290, 71st Cong., 2d sess., 15 February 1930.

————. *Survey of Mississippi River Between Missouri River and Minneapolis: Part 1—Report.* House Doc. No. 137, 72d Cong., 1st sess., 9 December 1931.

————. *Stream Pollution by Federal Agencies, with Recommendations.* House Doc. No. 495. 74th Cong., 2d sess., 13 May 1936.

————. *Water Pollution in the United States: Third Report of the Special Advisory Committee on Water Pollution* (National Resources Committee). House Doc. No. 155, 76th Cong., 1st sess., 16 February 1939.

U.S. Congress. House. Committee on Agriculture. *Mississippi River Wild Life and Fish Refuge: Hearings on H.R. 4088, a Bill to Establish the Upper Mississippi River Wild Life and Fish Refuge.* 68th Cong., 1st sess., 11–13 February 1924.

————. *Mississippi River Wild Life and Fish Refuge Amendment: Hearings on H.J. Res. 320, Part 2.* 68th Cong., 2d sess., 22 January 1925.

U.S. Congress. House. Committee on Interstate and Foreign Commerce. *Bridges at Keokuk: Hearings on Bills H.R. 26559 and H.R. 26672.* 62d Cong., 3d sess., 17 January 1913.

U.S. Congress. House. Committee on Rivers and Harbors. *Mississippi River—Impounding of Water Above Keokuk Dam: Hearings on the Subject of House Resolution 468 Directing an Investigation of the Alleged Impounding of Water Above the Dam in the Mississippi River at Keokuk and Its Effects upon the Navigation of the River.* 64th Cong., 2d sess., 14–15 February 1917.

————. *Hearings on the Subject of the Pollution of Navigable Waters, Part 2.* 67th Cong., 2d sess., 7–8 December 1921.

————. *Mississippi River Between Mouth of Missouri and Minneapolis: Hearings on the Subject of the Improvement of the Mississippi River Between the Mouth of the Missouri and Minneapolis.* 71st Cong., 2d sess., 18, 27 March 1930.

————. *Mississippi River Between Mouth of Missouri River and Minneapolis: Hearings on the Subject of the Improvement of the Mississippi River Between the Mouth of the Missouri River and Minneapolis.* 72d Cong., 1st sess., 25–27 January 1932.

————. *Pollution of Navigable Waters: Hearings on H.R. 519, H.R. 587 and H.R. 4070; Bills for the Control of Water Pollution.* 79th Cong., 1st sess., 13–15, 20 November 1945.

U.S. Congress. House. Committee on Rules. *The Keokuk Dam: Hearings on H. Res. 390, a Resolution to Authorize and Direct the Committee on Interstate and Foreign Commerce of the House of Representatives to Make an Investigation as to the Keokuk Dam and Conditions Created by It.* 63d Cong., 2d sess., 7 April 1914.

U.S. Congress. Senate. *Memorial of the General Assembly of Missouri.* Senate Doc. No. 71, 21st Cong., 2d sess., 1830–1831.

————. *Report from the Secretary of War, in Compliance with a Resolution of the Senate of the 25th Instant, in Relation to the Rock River and Des Moines Rapids of the Mississippi River.* Senate Doc. No. 139, 25th Cong., 2d sess., 1837–1838.

————. *Dam Across the Mississippi River.* Senate Report No. 3569, 58th Cong., 3d sess., 1904–1905.

————. "Keokuk Dam Co. and North American Co." Senator Poindexter introduces St. Louis Progressive Party Club resolutions. 63d Cong., 1st sess., 22 November 1913. *Congressional Record* 50:5962.

————. *Upper Mississippi River Wild Life and Fish Refuge.* Senate Report No. 974, 68th Cong., 1st sess., 1924–1925.

————. *Stream Pollution and Stream Purification.* Senate Doc. No. 16, 74th Cong., 1st sess., 30 January 1935.

U.S. Congress. Senate. Committee on Commerce. *Hearings on S. 1558: A*

Bill to Establish the Upper Mississippi River Wild Life and Fish Refuge.
68th Cong., 1st sess., 15 February 1924.

———. *Stream Pollution: Hearings on S. 3958 a Bill to Prevent the Pollution of the Navigable Waters of the United States S. 3959 a Bill to Amend Section 13 of the Act of March 3, 1899, . . . and Section 3 of the Oil Pollution Act, 1924 S. 4342 and S. 4627 Bills to Create a Division of Stream Pollution Control in the Bureau of the Public Health Service. . . .* 74th Cong., 2d sess., 26 February, 23–26 March, and 21 May 1936.

U.S. Department of Commerce. *Census of Manufacturers, 1914, vol. I.* Washington, D.C.: GPO, 1918.

———. *Census of Manufacturers, 1914, vol. II.* Washington, D.C.: GPO, 1919.

———. *Thirteenth Census of the U.S., 1910, Population, vol. II.* Washington, D.C.: GPO, 1913.

———. *Fourteenth Census of the U.S., 1920, Population, vol. I.* Washington, D.C.: GPO, 1921.

———. *Fifteenth Census of the U.S., 1930, Population, vol. III, Part 1.* Washington, D.C.: GPO, 1932.

U.S. Department of Commerce and Labor. Bureau of Corporation. *Report of the Commissioner of Corporations on Water-Power Development in the United States.* 14 March 1912. Washington D.C.: GPO, 1912.

U.S. Department of the Interior. *Eighth Census of the U.S., 1860, Population.* Washington, D.C.: GPO, 1864.

———. *Ninth Census of the U.S., 1870, Statistics of Population.* Washington D.C.: GPO, 1872.

———. *Tenth Census of the U.S., 1880, Statistics of Population.* Washington, D.C.: GPO, 1883.

———. *Twelfth Census of the U.S., 1900, Population, Part 1.* Washington, D.C.: GPO, 1901.

Wiebe, A. H. "Biological Survey of the Upper Mississippi, with Special Reference to Pollution." In *Bulletin of the U.S. Bureau of Fisheries, vol. 43, Part II, 1927,* pp. 137–67. Washington, D.C.: GPO, 1930.

State Government Documents

Bates, C. G., and Zeasman, O. R. "Soil Erosion: A Local and National Problem." *Wisconsin Agricultural Experiment Station Research Bulletin* 99 (August 1930):1–100.

Crohurst, H. R. "Preliminary Report of the Investigation of the Pollution of the Mississippi River in the Vicinity of Minneapolis and St. Paul." In *Stream Pollution in Wisconsin,* pp. 282–321. Minnesota State Board of Health, 1929.

Report of the Investigation of the Pollution of the Mississippi River Minneapolis to LaCrosse, Inclusive by the Minnesota State Board of Health in Collaboration with the Minnesota Commissioner of Game and Fish and the Wisconsin State Board of Health (1928).

Report of the Iowa State Drainage Water-Ways and Conservation Commission. Cedar Rapids, Iowa: Torch Press, 1911.

Report of the Metropolitan Drainage Commission, 1927. In *Second Annual Report of the Metropolitan Drainage Commission of Minneapolis and St. Paul (1928).*

Second Annual Report of the Metropolitan Drainage Commission of Minneapolis and St. Paul on the Subject of Sewage Disposal of Minneapolis, St. Paul, and Contiguous Areas (1928).

Stream Pollution in Minnesota: Special Report. Minnesota State Board of Health, 1929.

Stream Pollution in Wisconsin. Madison: Wisconsin State Board of Health, January 1927.

Thiel, Pamella A. "A Survey of Unionid Mussels in the Upper Mississippi River (Pools 3 Through 11)." *Technical Bulletin No. 124.* Madison: Department of Natural Resources, 1981.

Wiebe, A. H. "Preliminary Report Concerning the Biological Survey of the Upper Mississippi River with Special Reference to Pollution." Contained in *Stream Pollution in Wisconsin*, pp. 322–28. Madison: Wisconsin State Board of Health, January 1927.

Books

Adams, Henry. *The Education of Henry Adams.* Ed. Ernest Samuels, Boston: Houghton Mifflin Co., 1974.

Armstrong, Ellis L., ed. *History of Public Works in the United States, 1776–1976.* Chicago: American Public Works Association, 1976.

Beltrami, J. C. *A Pilgrimage in Europe and America, Leading to the Discovery of the Sources of the Mississippi and Bloody River; with a Description of the Whole Course of the Former, and of the Ohio.* Vol. 2. London: Hunt and Clarke, 1828.

Blair, Walter A. *A Raft Pilot's Log: A History of the Great Rafting Industry on the Upper Mississippi, 1840–1915.* Cleveland: Arthur H. Clark Co., 1930.

Brunet, Patrick J. "The Corps of Engineers and Navigation Improvement on the Channel of Upper Mississippi River to 1939." M.A. thesis, the University of Texas at Austin, 1977. P170

Carlander, Harriet Bell. *A History of Fish and Fishing in the Upper Mississippi River.* Publication sponsored by the Upper Mississippi River Conservation Committee, 1954.

Chambers, Julius. *The Mississippi River and Its Wonderful Valley: Twenty-Seven Hundred and Seventy-Five Miles from Source to Sea.* New York: Knickerbocker Press, 1910.

Chandler, Alfred, Jr. *The Visible Hand: The Managerial Revolution in*

American Business. Cambridge, Mass.: The Belknap Press of Harvard University Press, 1977.

Clepper, Henry, ed. *Leaders of American Conservation*. New York: Ronald Press, 1971.

Coleman, Martha Bray, ed. *The Journals of Joseph N. Nicollet: A Scientist on the Mississippi Headwaters with Notes on Indian Life, 1836–37*. Trans. Andre Fertey. St. Paul: Minnesota Historical Society, 1970.

Cooley, Richard A. *Politics and Conservation: The Decline of the Alaska Salmon*. New York: Harper & Row, 1963.

Coues, Elliott, ed. *The Expeditions of Zebulon Montgomery Pike, to the Headwaters of the Mississippi River, Through Louisiana Territory, and in New Spain, During the Years 1805-6-7*. Vol. 1. 1810. Reprint. New York: F. P. Harper, 1895.

Curtis, Samuel R. *Engineer's Report No. 1, to the Directors of the Navigation and Hydraulic Company of the Mississippi Rapids; December 1, 1849*. Cincinnati: George W. Tagert, 1849.

Enders, Donald L. "The Des Moines Rapids: A History of Its Adverse Effects on Mississippi River Traffic and Its Use as a Source of Water Power to 1860." M.A. thesis, Brigham Young University, 1973.

Fox, Stephen. *John Muir and His Legacy: The American Conservation Movement*. Boston: Little, Brown & Co., 1981.

Freeman, Douglas Southall. *R. E. Lee: A Biography*. vol. 1. New York: Charles Scribner's Sons, 1934.

Fries, Robert F. *Empire in Pine: The Story of Lumbering in Wisconsin, 1830–1900*. Madison: State Historical Society of Wisconsin, 1951.

Gabrielson, Ira N. *Wildlife Refuges*. New York: Macmillan Co., 1943.

Glazier, Willard. *Down the Great River: Embracing an Account of the Discovery of the True Source of the Mississippi, Together with Views, Descriptive and Pictorial, of the Cities, Towns, Villages and Scenery on the Banks of the River, as Seen during a Canoe Voyage of Over Three Thousand Miles from its Head Waters to the Gulf of Mexico*. Philadelphia: Hubbard Brothers, 1891.

Haites, Erik F., et al. *Western River Transportation: The Era of Early Internal Development, 1810–1860*. Baltimore: Johns Hopkins University Press, 1975.

Harris, Neil. *The Artist in American Society: The Formative Years, 1790–1860*. New York: Simon & Schuster, 1966.

Hartsough, Mildred L. *From Canoe to Steel Barge on the Upper Mississippi*. Minneapolis: The University of Minnesota Press for the Upper Mississippi Waterway Association, 1934.

Hawes, Harry B. *My Friend the Black Bass: With Strategy, Mechanics and Fair Play*. New York: Frederick A. Stokes Co., 1930.

Hawley, Ellis W. *The Great War and the Search for a Modern Order: A History of the American People and Their Institutions, 1917–1933*. New York: St. Martin's Press, 1979.

Hays, Samuel P. *Conservation and the Gospel of Efficiency: The Progressive Conservation Movement, 1890–1920.* New York: Atheneum, 1974.

Heilbron, Bertha L. *Making a Motion Picture in 1848: Henry Lewis' Journal of a Canoe Voyage from the Falls of St. Anthony to St. Louis.* St. Paul: Minnesota Historical Society, 1936.

Hidy, Ralph W., et al. *Timber and Men: The Weyerhaeuser Story.* New York: Macmillan Co., 1963.

Hindle, Brooke, ed. *America's Wooden Age: Aspects of Its Early Technology.* Tarrytown, N.Y.: Sleepy Hollow Restorations, 1975.

Hornaday, William T. *Our Vanishing Wild Life: Its Extermination and Preservation.* New York: Charles Scribner's Sons, 1913.

————. *Wild Life Conservation in Theory and Practice: Lectures Delivered before the Forestry School of Yale University 1914.* New Haven: Yale University Press, 1914.

Howat, John K., et al. *The Hudson River and Its Painters.* New York: Viking Press, 1972.

Hughes, Thomas P. *Networks of Power: Electrification in Western Society, 1880–1930.* Baltimore: Johns Hopkins University Press, 1983.

Hull, William J., and Robert W. Hull. *The Origin and Development of the Waterways Policy of the United States.* Washington, D.C.: National Waterways Conference, 1967.

Hunter, Louis C. *A History of Industrial Power in the United States, 1780–1930, Volume One: Water Power in the Century of the Steam Engine.* Charlottesville: University of Virginia Press for the Eleutherian Mills-Hagley Foundation, 1979.

————. *Steamboats on the Western Rivers: An Economic and Technological History.* New York: Octagon Books, 1969.

Hurst, James Willard. *Law and the Conditions of Freedom in the Nineteenth Century United States.* Madison: University of Wisconsin Press, 1956.

Iowa: A Guide to the Hawkeye State. Compiled and written by the Federal Writers' Project of the Works Progress Administration for the State of Iowa. New York: Viking Press, 1938.

Ise, John. *National Park Policy: A Critical History.* Baltimore: Johns Hopkins Press for Resources for the Future, 1961.

Johnson, Emory R. *Ocean and Inland Water Transportation.* New York: D. Appleton & Co., 1906.

Jones, Holway R. *John Muir and the Sierra Club: The Battle for Yosemite.* San Francisco: Sierra Club, 1965.

Lears, T. J. Jackson. *No Place of Grace: Antimodernism and the Transformation of American Culture, 1880–1920.* New York: Pantheon Books, 1981.

Lendt, David L. *Ding: The Life of Jay Norwood Darling.* Ames: Iowa State University Press, 1979.

Leopold, Aldo. *A Sand County Almanac: And Sketches Here and There.* New York: Oxford University Press, 1949.

Lewis, Sinclair. *Babbitt.* New York: Harcourt Brace & Co., 1922.

———. *Main Street.* New York: Harcourt Brace & Co., 1920.

Long, Stephen H. *Voyage in a Six-Oared Skiff to the Falls of Saint Anthony in 1817.* Reprinted in the *Collections of the Minnesota Historical Society* 2 (1860–1867):7–88.

Maass, Arthur. *Muddy Waters: The Army Engineers and the Nation's Rivers.* 1951. Reprint. New York: Da Capo Press, 1974.

McMaster, S. W. *Sixty Years on the Upper Mississippi: My Life and Experiences.* Rock Island, Ill.: n.p., 1893.

Marsh, George Perkins. *The Earth as Modified by Human Action: A New Edition of Man and Nature.* 1864. Reprint. New York: Scribner, Armstrong & Co., 1974.

———. *Man and Nature.* Edited by David Lowenthal. 1864. Reprint. Cambridge, Mass.: The Belknap Press of Harvard University Press, 1965.

Mason, Philip P., ed. *Schoolcraft's Expedition to Lake Itasca: The Discovery of the Source of the Mississippi.* East Lansing: Michigan State University Press, 1958.

Mathews, John Lathrop. *Remaking the Mississippi.* Boston and New York: Houghton Mifflin Co., 1909.

Melosi, Martin V., ed. *Pollution and Reform in American Cities, 1870–1930.* Austin: University of Texas Press, 1980.

Merrick, George Byron. *Old Times on the Upper Mississippi: The Recollections of a Steamboat Pilot from 1854 to 1863.* Cleveland: Arthur H. Clark Co., 1909.

Merrick, George B., and William R. Tibbals. *Genesis of Steamboating on Western Rivers: With a Register of Officers on the Upper Mississippi, 1823–70.* Madison: State Historical Society of Wisconsin, 1912.

Merritt, Raymond H. *Creativity, Conflict & Controversy: A History of the St. Paul District U.S. Army Corps of Engineers.* Washington, D.C.: GPO, 1979.

———. *The Corps, the Environment, and the Upper Mississippi River Basin.* Washington, D.C.: GPO, 1984.

Minneapolis Board of Trade. *History and Growth of Minneapolis, Minnesota.* Minneapolis: Johnson, Smith & Harrison, 1884.

Moulton, Harold G. *Waterways Versus Railways.* Boston and New York: Houghton Mifflin Co., 1912.

Muir, John. *The Yosemite.* New York: Century Co., 1912.

Nash, Roderick. *Wilderness and the American Mind.* New Haven: Yale University Press, 1967.

Noble, David F. *America By Design: Science, Technology, and the Rise of Corporate Capitalism.* New York: Oxford University Press, 1977.

Pearson, T. Gilbert. *Adventures in Bird Protection*. New York: D. Appleton-Century Co., 1937.

Petersen, William J., ed. *Mississippi River Panorama: The Henry Lewis Great National Work*. Iowa City: Clio Press, 1979.

Petulla, Joseph M. *American Environmental History: The Exploitation and Conservation of Natural Resources*. San Francisco: Boyd & Fraser Publishing Co., 1977.

Pike, Zebulon Montgomery. *An Account of Expeditions to the Sources of the Mississippi . . . during the Years 1805, 1806, and 1807*. Philadelphia: C. & A. Conrad & Co., 1810.

Pinchot, Gifford. *The Fight for Conservation*. 1910. Reprint. Seattle: University of Washington Press, 1967.

Quick, Herbert. *American Inland Waterways: Their Relation to Railway Transportation and to the National Welfare; Their Creation, Restoration, and Maintenance*. New York: G. P. Putnam's Sons, 1909.

Quick, Herbert, and Edward Quick. *Mississippi Steamboatin': A History of Steamboating on the Mississippi and Its Tributaries*. New York: Henry Holt & Co., 1926.

Rasmussen, Jerry L., ed. *Proceedings of the UMRCC Symposium; on Upper Mississippi River Bivalve Mollusks*. Rock Island, Ill.: Upper Mississippi River Conservation Committee, 1980.

Russell, Charles Edward. *A-Rafting on the Mississip'*. New York: Century Co., 1928.

Schoolcraft, Henry Rowe. *Narrative of an Expedition Through the Upper Mississippi to Itasca Lake, the Actual Source of This River; Embracing an Exploratory Trip Through the St. Croix and Burntwood (or Broule) Rivers: in 1832*. New York: Harper & Brothers, 1834.

Swain, Donald C. *Federal Conservation Policy, 1921-1933*. Berkeley: University of California Press, 1963.

Tousley, Albert S. *Where Goes the River: A Canoe Trip from the Source of the Mississippi River to the Gulf of Mexico, Twenty-five Hundred Miles, in Which Its Physical Features, History, Legends, and People Are Portrayed with Word and Picture*. Iowa City: Tepee Press, 1928.

Twain, Mark. *Life on the Mississippi*. New York: Signet Classics, 1961.

Tweet, Roald. *A History of the Rock Island District Corps of Engineers*. Rock Island, Ill.: U.S. Army Engineer District, Rock Island, 1975.

Twining, Charles E. *Downriver: Orrin H. Ingram and the Empire Lumber Company*. Madison: State Historical Society of Wisconsin, 1975.

Upper Mississippi River Improvement Association, *Proceedings of the Upper Mississippi River Improvement Association*. 1904, 1908, 1909, 1911, 1913.

Van Hise, Charles. *The Conservation of Natural Resources in the United States*. New York: Macmillan Co., 1910.

Worster, Donald. *Nature's Economy*. San Francisco: Sierra Club Books, 1977.

Articles

Bakke, A. L. "Report of the Winneshiek Drainage Project." *Outdoor America* 1 (July 1923): 619.

Barr, G. Walter. "Harnessing the Mississippi to Electric Generators: The Power Achievement of the Century." *Review of Reviews American Monthly* 45 (April 1912): 443–48.

———. "A Water Power of World-Wide Effects." *Bulletin of the Pan American Union* 35 (November 1912): 939–49.

———. "Interesting Details about the Keokuk Dam." *Iowa Factories* (June 1913): 26–31.

———. "Water Power for the Million." *Independent* 74 (26 June 1913): 1427–29.

———. "The Commercial Value of the Keokuk Dam to Iowa and the Mississippi Valley." *Proceedings of the Twenty-sixth Annual Meeting, Iowa Engineering Society*, 18–20 February 1914, pp. 67–71.

Barterre, Wallville G. "The World's Greatest Water-Power Development." *American City* 9 (August 1913): 144–46.

"Block-Lighting Plant Absorbed in St. Louis." *Electrical World* 61 (31 May 1913): 1172.

Buchheister, Carl W., and Frank Graham, Jr. "From the Swamps and Back: A Concise and Candid History of the Audubon Movement." *Audubon* 75 (January 1973): 6–45.

"Building the Hydroelectric Plant of the Mississippi River Power Company: One of the Largest Works Now Being Conducted by Force Account by American Engineers." *Engineering Record* 64 (5 August 1911): 148–53.

Burnham, John B. "Our Game." *Outdoor America* 3 (November 1924): 27–30.

"Celebrating the Inauguration of Keokuk Water-Power Plant." *Electrical World* 62 (30 August 1913): 412–13.

Clark, Chester M. "Electric Power from the Mississippi River." *Annual Report of the Board of Regents of the Smithsonian Institution* (1910): 199–210.

Clements, Kendrick A. "Herbert Hoover and Conservation, 1921–33." *The American Historical Review* 89 (February 1984): 67–88.

Coker, Robert. "The Utilization and Preservation of Fresh-Water Mussels." *Transactions of the American Fisheries Society* 45 (December 1916): 39–49.

Cooper, Hugh L. "The Water Power Development of the Mississippi River Power Company, at Keokuk Iowa." *Journal of the Western Society of Engineers* 17 (March 1912): 213–26.

Cowdrey, Albert E. "Pioneering Environmental Law: The Army Corps of Engineers and the Refuse Act." *Pacific Historical Review* 44 (August 1975): 331–49.

Culler, C. F. "Fish Rescue Operations." *Transactions of the American Fisheries Society* 50 (20–22 September 1920): 247–50.

———. "Depletion of the Aquatic Resources of the Upper Mississippi River and Suggested Remedial Measures." *Transactions of the American Fisheries Society* 60 (27–29 August 1930): 279–83.

Davis, Robert H. "The Rape of the River." *Outdoor America* 1 (August 1922): 18–19.

DeMass, Orrin A. "The Carefree Trail." *Outdoor America* 1 (August 1922): 3.

"Destroying a National Asset." *Outlook* 135 (5 September 1923): 5.

Dilg, Will. "The Cork-Bodied Black-Bass Bug." *Outlook* 128 (25 May 1921): 162–64.

———. "It's Up to You Mr. Sportsman." *Outdoor America* 1 (August 1922): 20.

———. "A Message to Outdoor Americans." *Outdoor America* 1 (August 1922): 14–15, 32.

———. "The Drainage Crime of a Century." *Outdoor America* 1 (July 1923): cover, 570, 600–601, 623.

———. "Forty Minutes with President Coolidge." *Outdoor America* 2 (May 1924): 51.

———. "Victory!" *Outdoor America* 2 (July 1924): 38–39.

———. "It Is Impossible to Please Everybody." *Outdoor America* 4 (September 1925): 20–26.

"Electrical Drainage Pumping." *Electrical World* 64 (8 August 1914): 262–63.

"Electricity Versus Steam in Drainage Pumping." *Electrical World* 64 (8 August 1914): 275–77.

Ellis, M. M. "The Artificial Propagation of Freshwater Mussels." *Transactions of the American Fisheries Society* 59 (September 9–11, 1929): 217–233.

———. "Erosion Silt as a Factor in Aquatic Environments." *Ecology* 17 (1936): 29–42.

"Extension of Central-Station Service in St. Louis." *Electrical World* 61 (24 May 1913): 1094.

Flader, Susan L. "Scientific Resource Management: An Historical Perspective." *Transactions of the Forty-first North American Wildlife and Natural Resources Conference* (22 March 1976).

"From Romer Grey: Veritably a Chip off the Old Block." *Outdoor America* 1 (August 1922): 16.

"A Great Hydroelectric Development." *Engineering Record* 64 (5 August 1911): 145.

"The Greatest Thing in All Iowa History." *Iowa Factories* (January 1912): 16–19, 38, 40, 42, 44.

Green, Will P. "Hugh Lincoln Cooper: The Man Who Built the Keokuk Dam Across the Mississippi." *Scientific American* 109 (8 November 1913): 366.

"The Half-Breed Tract." *The Iowa Journal of History and Politics* 13 (April 1915): 151–64.

Hardin, Garrett. "The Tragedy of the Commons." In *Exploring New Ethics for Survival: The Voyage of the Spaceship Beagle*. Baltimore: Pelican Books, 1973.

Hartman, George B. "The Iowa Sawmill Industry." *The Iowa Journal of History and Politics* 40 (January 1942): 52–93.

Hawes, Harry. "Conserving the Outdoors for Health and Profit." Speech before the House, reprinted in *Outdoor America* 2 (March 1924): 36–37, 52.

Hawley, Ellis W. "Herbert Hoover, the Commerce Secretariat, and the Vision of an 'Associative State,' 1921–1928." *The Journal of American History* 61 (June 1974): 116–40.

Hays, Samuel P. "The Environmental Movement." *Journal of Forest History* 25 (October 1981): 219–21.

Heiss, Merton. "Will Dilg and the Early Days." *Outdoor America* 2 (January 1937): 4–5.

"Help Save the Winneshiek Bottoms." *Outdoor America* 1 (August 1923): 25.

Henshall, James A. "Pollution." *Outdoor America* 1 (August 1922): 10.

Higgins, Elmer. "Legislation Proposed in the 74th Congress for the Abatement of Water Pollution." *Progressive Fish Culturist* (July 1936): 5–10.

"Historical Review of the Keokuk Hydroelectric Development." *Electrical World* 62 (6 September 1913): 462–64.

Hoover, Herbert. "In Praise of Izaak Walton." *Atlantic* 139 (June 1927): 813–19.

Hornaday, William T. "The Upper Mississippi Wildlife Refuge: Will H. Dilg's Monument." *Minnesota Waltonian* (April 1932): 3, 15.

Hough, Donald. "A National Preserve for the Mississippi Valley." *Outdoor America* 1 (August 1923): cover, 29.

Hough, Emerson. "Time to Call a Halt." *Outdoor America* 1 (August 1922): cover.

Howard, Arthur D. "Experiments in Propagation of Fresh-Water Mussels of the Quadrula Group." In *U.S. Bureau of Fisheries Annual Report with Appendixes, 1912/13*, pp. 1–52. Washington, D.C.: GPO, 1913.

Hughes, Thomas P. "The Electrification of America: The System Builders." *Technology and Culture* 20 (January 1979): 124–61.

Hutchinson, Don W. "The Story of a Dream Come True." *Iowa Magazine* (October 1917): 5–8, 42–48.

Ives, Marguerite. "The Out-Door Woman." *Outdoor America* 1 (August 1922): 17, 34.

———. "An Appeal to the Outdoor Women for a Great New National Preserve." *Outdoor America* 2 (October 1923): 96–97.

James, William. "The Moral Equivalent of War." In *Essays on Faith and Morals*, pp. 311–28. New York: Longman's, Green and Co., 1949.

Kemper, E. C. "The Crusade." *Outdoor America* 1 (August 1922): 16.

"Keokuk Hydroelectric Development." *Electrical World* 55 (10 February 1910): 337–38.

"Keokuk Water-Power Development." *Electrical World* 58 (28 October 1911): 1043–44.

Kirkland, Harry. "The Great Mississippi Dam." *World's Work* 25 (January 1913): 337–46.

Larner, Chester H. "The 10,000-Horsepower Turbines at Keokuk: Description of the Design, Manufacture and Transportation of the Largest Water-Wheels Ever Built." *Engineering Record* 67 (15 March 1913): 294–97.

"Lazwell Drainage-Pumping Plant." *Power* 37 (17 June 1913): 846–48.

Lefevre, George, and Winterton C. Curtis. "Reproduction and Parasitism in the Unionidae." *Journal of Experimental Zoology* 9 (September 1910): 79–115.

"Lock and Drydock at Keokuk." *Engineering Record* 68 (26 July 1913): 88–92.

"Lonergan Bill Strikes at Pollution." *Outdoor America* 1 (March 1936): 6–7.

McDermid, H. B. "The Turbine Runners of the Mississippi River Power Co. at Keokuk, Iowa." *Engineering Review* 70 (21 August 1913): 242–43.

McGee, WJ. "Water as a Resource." *Annals of the American Academy of Political and Social Science* 33 (May 1909): 521–34.

———. "Our Great River: What It Is and May Be Made for Commerce, Agriculture, And Sanitation—The Largest Inland Project of Our Time." *World's Work* (February 1907): 8576–84.

"A Message from Mrs. Frances E. Whitley." *Outdoor America* 2 (February 1924): 353.

Minton, Warren M. "The Mississippi River Dam at Keokuk, Iowa." *Harvard Engineering Journal* 10 (January 1912): 180–91.

"The Mississippi Goes to Work for a Corporation." *Collier's* 51 (19 July 1913): 14.

"The Mississippi Lock at Keokuk." *Engineering News* 70 (13 November 1913): 964–72.

"Mississippi River Dam." *Journal of History* 11 (January 1918): 64–69.

"Mississippi River Energy for St. Louis." *Electrical World* 55 (19 May 1910): 1287–89.

Mississippi River Power Company. "Electric Power from the Mississippi River." *Bulletin Numbers 1–9* (March 1911-March 1913).

"The Mississippi River Wild Life and Fish Refuge." Statement of Professor B. Shimek before the House Committee on Agriculture, reprinted in *Outdoor America* 2 (April 1924): 33, 47–48.

"Mitering Lock Gate at Keokuk Presents Novel Features." *Engineering Record* 72 (18 September 1915): 344–49.

Moorhead, F. G. "The Industrial Awakening of the Upper Mississippi." *World To-Day* 20 (April 1911): 472–76.

Muir, John. "The Tuolumne Yosemite in Danger." *Outlook* (2 November 1907): 486–89.

"A National Emergency." Editorial. *Outdoor America* 1 (March 1936): 3.

"National Legislation on Stream Pollution." *Sewage Works Journal* 8 (November 1936): 1025–26.

"A National Plan for Water Purification: Pollution Parley Seeks United Action." *Outdoor America* 2 (January 1935): 8–10.

Oberholser, Harry C. "The Winneshiek Bottoms Drainage Project." *Iowa Conservation* 7 (August 1923): 9–10.

Pammel, Dr. L. H. "Speaking of Drainage!" *Outdoor America* 2 (January 1924): 294.

Phillips, Lionel F. "My Own Little River (In Memoriam)." *Outdoor America* 1 (August 1922): 9, 31.

"Power from the Mississippi River." *Power* 38 (5 August 1913): 184–90.

"Power-House for Entire Mississippi." *Cassier's Monthly* 44 (September 1913): 147–54.

Pratt, Joseph. "The Corps of Engineers and the Oil Pollution Act of 1924." Unpublished paper prepared for the U.S. Army Corps of Engineers.

"Production and Sale of Electricity in St. Louis." *Electrical World* 55 (19 May 1910): 1257–87.

Rasmussen, Dr. A. T. "The Passing of the Winneshiek." *Outdoor America* 1 (August 1923): 32–33, 54.

Reid, Kenneth A. "Reports of Special Committees: Pollution Study." *Transactions of the American Fisheries Society* 76 (11, 12, 13 September 1946): 425–32.

———. "A Report on the Pollution Front." *Outdoor America* 12 (July–August 1947): 7.

———. "Water—The Orphan Step-Child of Conservation." *American Nature Association Quarterly Bulletin* (January 1939): 3–34.

———. "We Believe in Clean Streams, But—." *Outdoor America* 1 (June 1936): 6–8.

Rogers, H. S. "Damming the World's Greatest River." *Scientific American Supplement* 74 (10 August 1912): 87–91.

"St. Louis to Take Large Amount of Hydroelectric Energy from Keokuk Development." *Electrical World* 55 (3 March 1910): 505.

"St. Paul Anxious to Solve Disposal Problem, Mayor Asserts." *Minnesota Waltonian* 2 (November 1930): 3.

"Saving Swamp Life." *The Saturday Evening Post* 196 (3 May 1924): 32.

Schneberger, Edward. "Reports of Special Committees: Committee on Pollution Study." *Transactions of the American Fisheries Society* 79 (14, 15, 16 September 1949): 278–82.

Schneider, Henry A. "Upper Mississippi River National Wildlife and Fish Refuge." *Naturalist* 32 (Spring 1981): 7–11.

Schroepfer, George J. "Minneapolis-Saint Paul Sewage Disposal Project." *Sewage Works Journal* 8 (January 1936): 85–93.

———. "Pollution and Recovery of the Mississippi River at and below Minneapolis and St. Paul." *Sewage Works Journal* 3 (October 1931): 693–712.

Shira, A. F. "The Necessity of State Legislation in the Conservation of Fresh-Water Mussels." *Transactions of the American Fisheries Society* 49 (December 1919): 38–41.

Smith, Hugh M. "The Pearl-Button Industry of the Mississippi River." *Scientific American* 81 (5 August 1899): cover, 86–87.

"The Story Behind the Upper Mississippi Refuge." *Outdoor America* 18 (July–August 1953): 18.

Stratton-Porter, Gene. "A Protest from Gene Stratton-Porter." *Outdoor America* 2 (October 1923): 67.

Summer, John D. "An Analysis of Mississippi River Traffic: 1918–1930." Reprinted from the *Journal of Land & Public Utility Economics* (November 1931 and February 1932): 355–66, 11–23.

Tarr, Joel A., et al. "Water and Wastes: A Retrospective Assessment of Wastewater Technology in the United States, 1800–1932." *Technology and Culture* 25 (April 1984): 226–63.

Townsend, C. H. "The Conservation of Our Rivers and Lakes." *Transactions of the American Fisheries Society* 40 (1911): 101–13.

"The Turbines of the Mississippi River Power Co. at Keokuk, Ia." *Engineering News* 70 (21 August 1913): 340–42.

"Twin Cities Dedicate Sewage Treatment Plant." *Outdoor America* 3 (July–August 1938): 12.

"Twin-City Sewage Situation Demands Immediate Action." *Minnesota Waltonian* 2 (November 1930): 1, 3.

"Two Hundred Thousand Horse Power." *Cassier's Magazine* 44 (July 1913): 23–31.

"Two Million Women in Defense of the League's Proposed National Preserve." *Outdoor America* 2 (November 1923): 160–61, 177.

"Unified Public Utilities in Central Illinois." *Electrical World* 61 (31 May 1913): 1146–56.

"The Upper Mississippi Wild Life and Game Refuge." *Science* 66 (26 August 1927): 188.

"Waltonians Ask State Action on Mississippi Contamination." *Minnesota Waltonian* 2 (February 1931).

Warren, Menton M. "The Mississippi River Dam at Keokuk, Iowa." *Harvard Engineering Journal* 10 (January 1912): 180–91.

"Water Power Development on the Mississippi River at Keokuk, Iowa." *Engineering News* 66 (28 September 1911): 355–64.

"The Water Wheels at Keokuk." *Engineering Record* 66 (16 November 1912): 536–38.

"What Our Members Are Saying and Doing About the Winneshiek." *Outdoor America* 1 (August 1923): 38–39.

Wicks, Judson L. "Clean the Mississippi." *Minnesota Waltonian* (May 1933): 2, 13.

———. "Pollution of the Upper Mississippi River." *Transactions of the American Fisheries Society* 60 (27–29 August 1930): 286–96.

———. "Pollution Problem of the Upper Mississippi River." *Minnesota Waltonian* 2 (February 1931): 4, 10–11.

———. "Purity of Public Waters Is Vital." *Minnesota Waltonian* 1 (December 1929).

"The Wild Life Reservation on the Mississippi." *Science* 62 (25 September 1925): 280–81.

Wilson, Ben Hur. "The Des Moines Rapids Canal." *Palimpsest* 5 (April 1924): 117–32.

Woolley, Edward Mott. "Buttons: A Romance of American Industry." *McClure's* (February 1914): 113–20.

"The World's Largest Water-Power Plant." *Electrical World* 61 (31 May 1913): 1157–68.

Index

Adams, Henry: on progress and coal, 43

Adamson, William C., chairman House Committee on Interstate and Foreign Commerce, 71, 72, 73

Alton, Illinois: purchase of Keokuk electricity, 31

American Button Manufacturers Association: M. M. Ellis as research fellow, 77

American Fisheries Society, 105

American Game Protective Association: membership, 119; support for Upper Mississippi River Wildlife and Fish Refuge, 137, 139; "shooting grounds" legislation, 139–41

Atlas Portland Cement Company: purchase of Keokuk electricity, 31

Babbit, George: cultural milieu of league, 121–22

Bakke, Dr. A. L., 132, 144, 147

Barkley, Sen. Alben W., 158

Barr, G. Walter, 51

Bartholdt, Rep. Richard, 69

Bell, Frank T., 183–84

Bennett, John C., 17, 18

Birge, C. P., 22, 22n

Blane, Sen. John J., 173–74

Boepple, John, 84–85, 188

Brown, Gen. Lytle, 176

Burnham, John B.: conflict with Will Dilg, 139. See also American Game Protective Association

Cairo, Illinois, 183

Canton, Missouri, 80, 96

Carson, Rachel, 117

Central Illinois Public Service Company: purchase of Keokuk electricity, 31, 44, 45, 46; consolidation of Illinois utilities, 46; electrification of drainage projects, 46, 47

Central Mississippi Valley Electric Properties: ownership of "Power Zone" utilities, 45

Coker, Robert E.: investigations of Lake Cooper in 1913, 74–75, 191; in 1929, 76; consequences of progress, 76, 79; on exploitation of mussels, 88; on destruction of mussel beds, 89; state regulation of mussel fishery, 101

Cole, Thomas: Hudson School, 129

Commercial clubs: collapse of white-pine industry, 36–37, 39; Upper Mississippi River Improvement Association, 37, 38; Keokuk hydroelectric project, 37, 38–39; 1912 convention of "Power Zone" clubs, 38–39

Conference of State Sanitary Engineers, 161

Conservation: as use, 40, 43, 66–67; multiple-purpose concept, 60–67 passim, 156; origins of Progressive conservation movement, 61; Theodore Roosevelt's program, 61–62, 65; failures of Progressive conservation movement, 66; and proponents of Keokuk dam, 66–67; debate over H.R. 16053, 71–73; as management of useful species, 73–74; and Hetch Hetchy, 142; changing meaning of, 191, 192, 193; in 1920s, 191–92, 192n

Cooley, Lyman E., 22–23, 23n

Coolidge, Calvin, 135, 136, 149

Cooper, Hugh L.: hired as chief engineer, 25, 188; experience and reputation, 25–26; Wilson dam, 26; Dnieperstroy hydroelectric project, 26; recipient Order of the Red Star, 26; search for financial backing, 26; sale of electricity in St. Louis, 26–27, 44; exercised option on Keokuk and Hamilton Water Power Company's stock and franchise, 27; public relations talks, 32; admired by local people, 59; a self-made man, 59; and "golden rule," 59

"Crowfoot": short-term benefits of,

90; unanticipated consequences of, 90–91. *See also* Ellis, M. M.; Lake Pepin; Mussels, freshwater; Smith, Hugh; U.S. Bureau of Fisheries

Curtis, Samuel R.: report on Des Moines rapids, 17–18

Curtis, Winterton: mussel propagation research, 100; propagation technique, 103; on pollution, 106

Davis, Robert H.: 125–26

DeMass, Orrin, 126

Dern, Geroge H., 157. *See also* Dern-Lonergan Conference

Dern-Lonergan Conference (1934), 157

Des Moines rapids, 188; and Zebulon Pike, 4; Robert E. Lee's survey of, 14–15; Missouri General Assembly seeks annexation, 16–17; and Mormons, 17, 18; and Navigation and Hydraulic Company of the Mississippi Rapids, 17–18; and white-pine industry, 21–22; Corps of Engineers report on development of, 23–24; mussel fishery in, 75

Dickinson, Judge Jacob M., 133–34

Dilg, Will, 117–22 *passim*, 180; editorship of *Outdoor America*, 122–24 *passim*; female vote, 122; conservation and religion, 127; as field organizer, 130; conceives of refuge, 131; and Winneshiek, 131–32, 133, 144; personality and leadership, 136–39; on women and refuge struggle, 137–38; public relations for refuge, 144–45; campaign for refuge, 148–49

Drainage of wetlands: electrification of, 46–48; unanticipated consequences of, 47–48; failures of, 132; antidrainage sentiment, 132–33; estimates of, 133n. *See also* Winneshiek Bottoms

Dreiser, Theodore, 123

Durand, Asher: Hudson School, 129

Ebert, J. A. S., 74–75

Einstein, A. C., 57

Ellis, M. M.: experience and reputation, 77; 1931 investigation of Lake Cooper, 77–79, 77n, 107, 173; Field Station for Interior Fisheries Investigations, 77, 109–10, 112, 160; pollution surveys, 77, 109–10, 160; silt and pollution, 78, 107–8, 173; ecological perspective, 79, 190–91; consequences of progress, 79; on "crowfoot," 92; mussel propagation research, 104; on decline of mussels, 104, 107–8; development of nutrient solution for propagation, 104; significance of propagation method, 104–5; attitudes toward pollution, 110; social and biological costs of pollution, 110; reductionist method, 112; on DDT, 160; nine-foot channel, 173; St. Louis garbage disposal, 183–84, 183n

Empire Lumber Company, 36

Energy: transition from solar energy to fossil fuel, 42–44

Evarts, Hal G., 123

Federal Water Power Act of 1920, 61, 66, 156

Field Station for Interior Fisheries Investigations. *See* Ellis, M. M.; University of Missouri–Columbia; U.S. Bureau of Fisheries

Four-and-a-half-foot channel, 166

Garland, Hamlin, 123

General Dam Act, 71, 71n

General Federation of Women's Clubs, 137, 139

Green Bay drainage district, 48, 48n; failure of, 76

Grey, Romer, 126

Grey, Zane, 122, 123

Hall, Maj. Charles L., 169–70

Hannibal, Missouri: steamboat excursions to Keokuk, 34–35; commercial club, 36–37; progress and economic growth, 38–39; buy-local movement, 58; pollution, 165. *See also* Commercial clubs; White-pine industry

Hastings, Minnesota, 4

Hastings, Minnesota, lock and dam: and pollution, 167, 173, 178, 180

Hawes, Rep. Harry: on saving the outdoors, 116; introduced refuge act, 133; on Will Dilg, 136; refuge and religion, 145

Heiss, Merton S., 130

Henshall, James, 123, 125
Hetch Hetchy Valley: conflict over, 142–43, 189. *See also* Upper Mississippi River Wildlife and Fish Refuge
Hoover, Herbert, 123, 149, 155, 171, 192
Hornaday, William T., 123; on Will Dilg, 121
Hough, Donald, 144–45, 146
Hough, Emerson, 123, 124–25; reputation, 125
H.R. 16053, a bill to amend the General Dam Act, 71–73
Hunt, W. H., state senator, 173
Hurley, Patrick J., secretary of war, 177

Igoe, Rep. William, 69
Ingle, J. P., 58
Inland Waterways Commission, 64
Inland Waterways Corporation, 167, 168
Insull, Samuel, 44, 48. *See also* Middle West Utilities Company
Izaak Walton League, Minnesota Division: pollution of upper Mississippi, 106
Izaak Walton League of America, 188, 189, 190; founding of, 114, 117–18; growth of, 114, 115, 119, 135–36; cultural milieu, 115, 121–22; saving the outdoors for boys, 116, 126, 146; basis of appeal, 117; founders, 119; and Christianity, 127; recruitment, 130; role in passage of refuge act, 135; and American Game Protective Association, 139–41 *passim*; use of expert testimony, 147–48; on national pollution control legislation, 157, 158–59, 161, 181; and nine-foot channel, 171–73; and Twin Cities sewage treatment, 180, 181, 182; St. Louis garbage disposal, 185; conservation, 192; membership decline, 193. *See also* Upper Mississippi River Wildlife and Fish Refuge
Ives, Marguerite: wife of Will Dilg, 123; seeks female support for refuge, 123

James, William, 114–15

Kelly, William V., 120
Kemper, E. C., 124, 127
Keokuk, Iowa: social costs of hydroelectric project, 52–55; "official Keokuk," 54, 55; conflicting perceptions of city's problems, 54–55; attracted few factories, 56; street railway strike, 58; ambivalence over Stone & Webster, 58–59; river pollution, 165. *See also* "Power Zone"
Keokuk and Hamilton Water Power Company, 188; founding, 22; and Niagara Falls, New York, hydroelectric project, 22; provisions of franchise, 24; sources of financial backing, 27; and collapse of white-pine industry, 37; franchise criticized, 56–57
Keokuk hydroelectric project: dedication, 12–13; description, 12–13; improved navigation, 13; generation of electricity, 13, 13n; dam, 29; powerhouse, 29; Francis-type turbines, 29, 31, 32n; navigation lock and drydock, 31; high-tension lines, 31; foreign experts visit, 31; publicity, 32, 33, 51–52; tourist attraction, 33; short-term economic growth, 33–35; and steamboat excursion trade, 34–35; long-term expectations of economic growth, 36–39; and collapse of white-pine industry, 37–39; relationship between people and river, 39, 40, 41; progress, 39–40, 51–52; conservation movement, 40; pride and patriotism, 41; emphasis on size, 41–42; novelty of electricity, 42; as local "birthright," 44, 48–49; structure of electric industry, 44–46; utility consolidation, 44–46, 48–49; drainage of wetlands, 47–48; as national conservation issue, 60–61, 65, 66, 67–73; and debate over H.R. 16053, 72–73; changes in attitudes since completion of, 116–17, 149–50, 169; significance of, 187–91 *passim*. *See also* "Power Zone"
Keokuk Industrial Association: public relations, 31–32, 51; manufacturing district, 36; workers' resentment of, 54, 55; promotion of city, 55; opposition to, 56
King, Sen. William, 140, 141

Laclede Gas and Light Company, 27, 27 n
Ladner, Grover C., 157
Lake Cooper: named, 12; description, 12–13; Bureau of Fisheries investigations of, 74–75, 76, 77–79; habitat changes in, 74, 76, 78–79; fish harvest in, 75, 75 n; siltation of, 78; pollution of, 78–79; and nine-foot channel, 173. *See also* Coker, Robert E.; Ellis, M. M.; Uhler, F. M.; U.S. Bureau of Biological Survey
Lake Pepin: and Zebulon Pike, 4; fish harvest from, 75 n; mussel harvest from, 86; use of "crowfoot" in, 90; apparent success of regulation and propagation, 102
Lakes-to-the-Gulf Deep Waterway Association, 62, 166
League of Atlantic Seaboard Municipalities, 154
Lee, Robert E.: and improvement of the Mississippi, 14; survey of Des Moines rapids, 14–15; myth of Des Moines rapids improvement, 15–16
Lefevre, George: mussel propagation research, 100; propagation technique, 103
Lenroot, Rep. Irvine, 72
Leopold, Aldo, 1, 123
Lonergan, Sen. Augustine, 156–57, 158. *See also* Dern-Lonergan Conference
Long, Stephen, 3; appearance and quality of river water, 4–5, 187; resources of the Mississippi valley, 5, 187

McCormick, Sen. Medill, 133, 144
McDevitt, Frank J., 184
McGee, W J: theorist of conservation movement, 62, 63, 64; experience and reputation, 62; involvement with river development enthusiasts, 62; multiple-purpose potential of Mississippi, 63; and Inland Waterways Commission, 64; attitudes shared with fisheries scientists, 111
McGregor, Iowa, School of Wildlife, 170
Mackenzie, Brig. Gen. Alexander, 64
Mckinley Tariff, 84, 188
Magee, Dr. M. D'Arcy, 157

Marsh, George Perkins, 129–30
Marsh, R. O., 36
Meigs, Maj. Montgomery: army engineer in charge of river at Keokuk, 66; on pollution, 165
Middle West Utilities Company: subsidiaries, 44, 46; growth of, 46, 48. *See also* Insull, Samuel
Minneapolis, Minnesota: population, 7, 7 n, 163; sewers, 163. *See also* Twin Cities
Minnesota Board of Health, 151, 164, 178
Mississippi River Power Distributing Company, 26–27, 57
Mississippi River Power Company: replaced Keokuk and Hamilton Water Power Company, 27, 29; sale of Keokuk electricity, 31, 57; public relations, 31, 32, 33, 51; contracts for sale of Keokuk electricity, 45; drainage of wetlands, 47–48
Missouri River, 154
Muir, John, 127; and Hetch Hetchy, 142
Mundt, Rep. Karl E., 161
Murdock, Rep. Victor, 68, 73
Muscatine, Iowa: first pearl-button factory in, 80; pearl-button manufacturing, 86; economic significance of button industry, 95–96
Mussels, artificial propagation of, 81; research on, 100, 101, 104; commercial-scale, 100; centers of propagation, 100; found favor with bureau and industry, 100; as a means of controlling nature, 100, 103, 104, 105; combined with rescue of fish, 103; scale of bureau's activity, 104; and nine-foot channel, 108; failure of, 108–9. *See also* Curtis, Winterton; Ellis, M. M.; Lefevre, George; Pearl-button industry
Mussels, freshwater: uses of by Indians, 80; species used by industry, 80, 83; pearls, 81–83, 99, 99 n; centers of mussel fishery, 86; "common property" resource, 88–89; laws regulating harvest of, 89; apparent abundance of, 89; technological developments contributing to destruction of, 88–94; "crowfoot," 90–92; reproductive cycle, 103; and habitat

change, 107–8. *See also* Pearl-
button industry
Mussel camps, 87–88
Mussel gatherers, 86–89 *passim*,
97–98, 97n, 98n

National Association of Audubon So-
cieties: membership, 119, 119n
National Association of Button Manu-
facturers, 91
National Coast Anti-Pollution League,
154, 155
National Industrial Recovery Act,
156, 157
National Resources Committee, 158,
159
National Rivers and Harbors Congress, 66
Nelson, Dr. E. W.: on drainage, 47;
and "shooting grounds" legislation,
139–40
Newlands, Sen. Francis, 64–65
Newport, Minnesota, 167
Nine-foot channel: and pollution,
169–77 *passim*; controversy over,
169–77
Nolan, Rep. W. I., 176
North American Company: St. Louis
subsidiaries, 44, 45, 57; market for
Keokuk electricity, 44, 45, 46;
growth of, 45; purchase of "Power
Zone" utilities, 48; selling Keokuk
electricity to itself, 57; accused of
monopolizing the benefits of Keokuk project, 67, 189

Oil Pollution Act of 1924, 155
Outdoor America: readership, 122;
appeal to women, 123; contributors,
123–27 *passim*; first issue, 123–29;
common themes, 124–29 *passim*;
advertisers, 128; chapter news, 128

Pearl-button industry: life cycle of,
80–81, 94; emergence of, 84; process of shelling, 86–87; technology
of production, 92, 94; double automatic machine, 92, 94; button output, 94, 94n, 95, 96; regional
economic importance, 94–95, 97,
99; "saw works," 95; local economic
significance, 95–96; factory workers, 96–97, 97n; stimulated scientific research, 112–13

Pearl hunters: pattern of exploitation,
82–83; expectations and practices
of, 83
Pearls, freshwater. *See* Mussels,
freshwater
Pearson, T. Gilbert, 139; on Will Dilg,
136; on refuge campaign, 149. *See
also* National Association of Audubon Societies
People's League (St. Louis): origins of,
67; requests congressional investigation of Keokuk project, 67–68
Pepper, Rep. Irvin, 65–66
Pike, Zebulon, 4
Pinchot, Gifford: social significance of
conservation movement, 64; attitudes shared with fisheries scientists, 111; and Hetch Hetchy, 142
Poindexter, Sen. Miles, 68, 69
Pollution: sewer systems, 78; and silt,
78, 79, 107–8; impact on fishery,
105–13 *passim*; evolving problem
in United States, 151–52; opposition to oil pollution, 154–55
"Power Zone": designation of, 36;
competition for factories in, 36; rising expectations in, 52–55, 189;
discontent in, 52–56, 188; failure to
attract factories, 55–56; protests
over price of Keokuk electricity,
56–57; protests over erosion of
decision-making authority, 57–59;
river users protest, 59–60
Progressive Party Club of St. Louis, 68
Public Works Administration, 156;
grant for Twin Cities, 180; grants for
water purification, 180, 185

Quincy, Illinois: purchase of Keokuk
electricity, 31

Rainey, Rep. Henry T.: opposed
Keokuk-type waterpower bills, 66;
as conservationist, 70; responds to
Keokuk controversy, 70
Reid, Kenneth A.: on Water Pollution
Act of 1948, 162
Rivers and Harbors Act of 1899, 153,
155, 176, 177, 184
Roosevelt, Franklin, 180, 192; na-
tional pollution control legisla-
tion, 160
Roosevelt, Theodore, 192; strenuous
life, 115, 124. *See also* Conservation

St. Croix River, 4, 19, 173, 187
St. Louis: population, 43–44, 164; protests over price of Keokuk electricity, 57; pollution, 153, 165; garbage disposal in Mississippi, 165, 177, 182–86, 182n; Department of Streets and Sewers, 182, 183, 185
St. Paul, Minnesota: steamboat traffic, 5; ice prevented navigation at, 6; population, 7, 7n, 163. *See also* Twin Cities
Scott, George C.: financial support of league, 119; refuge campaign, 149
Shimek, B., 148
Sierra Club, 139; membership, 119; and Hetch Hetchy, 142, 143
Six-foot channel, 37, 166
Smith, Hugh: 1898 investigation of mussel fishery and button industry, 81; on wasteful practices of mussel gatherers, 89; on "crowfoot," 90; purchase of uncut shells, 95, 95n; on mussel gatherers, 97; destruction of mussel fishery, 99; statutory controls, 99; on pollution, 105, 112, on highest use of river resources, 111
South St. Paul, Minnesota, 167, 176
Spence, Rep. Brent, 161, 162
Steamboats: Pre–Civil War, 5; limits on, 6; pilots, 6; decline of, 6–7
Stimson, Henry L., 66
Stone & Webster, 188; financed Keokuk hydroelectric project, 27, 44, 45; workforce, 33–34; manufacturing district, 36; growth of, 45; control of "Power Zone" utilities, 45; protest against, 116, 189
Stone & Webster Engineering Corporation: supervised construction, 27; design and construction of high-tension lines, 31, 32n
Stone & Webster Management Association, 29; subsidiaries, 45

Thoreau, Henry David, 129
Townsend, Dr. C. H., 105
Twin Cities: pollution from, 106–7, 153, 163–64, 167; pollution controversy, 173, 175–77 *passim*, 178–82, 185–86; sanitary district, 179–80; Metropolitan Drainage Commission, 179, 181
Twin Cities Lock and Dam: and pollution, 167, 176–77, 178, 185

Uhler, F. M., 173
Underwood, Rep. Oscar, 72
Union Electric Light and Power Company: purchase of Keokuk electricity, 27, 44; purchase of isolated power stations, 45–46
United Railways Company: purchase of Keokuk electricity, 27, 44
University of Missouri–Columbia: Field Station for Interior Fisheries Investigations, 77, 109, 189, 193
University of Missouri, School of Medicine, 77
Upper Mississippi Barge Line Company, 167, 168
Upper Mississippi River: habitat change in, 7–8, 78, 106–11 *passim*; interest group conflict, 8, 151, 152, 190–91; changes in attitudes toward, 10–11, 189–92 *passim*; fish harvest from, 75n; pollution of, 78, 79, 106–8, 110, 151, 153, 175–77 *passim*; siltation of, 78, 79, 107–8; as interdependent system, 79, 113; mussel harvest from, 80, 81n, 85–86; as common property resource, 153, 191; growing sentiment for pollution control, 162–63; ice harvest, 165–66; unanticipated consequences, 188–89
Upper Mississippi River Improvement Association: collapse of white-pine industry, 37; six-foot channel, 37; river terminals, 37–38
Upper Mississippi River Wildlife and Fish Refuge, 114, 115, 130, 188; hearings, 133, 138–39; legislation, 133–34; administration of, 134; act amended, 134; purchase of, 135; factors contributing to success, 136–41 *passim*; supporters, 137–39; and Hetch Hetchy, 143–49 *passim*; social value of undeveloped land, 144–46; and religion, 146; and nine-foot channel, 170
U.S. Army Corps of Engineers: unfavorable ruling on lakes-to-the-gulf deep waterway, 64; opposed to multiple purpose, 65, 156; conference on nine-foot channel, 77; at conference on interior waters, 106; authority under Rivers and Harbors Act, 153; authority under Oil Pollution Act of 1924, 155; strict construction of Rivers and Harbors Act

of 1899, 155, 155n, 176–77, 184; national pollution control legislation, 159–60; dredging garbage from upper river, 164; constituency building, 167–69; controversy over nine-foot channel, 169–75 *passim*; controversy over pollution below Twin Cities, 175–77; disposal of St. Louis garbage in Mississippi, 182–85 *passim*

U.S. Bureau of Biological Survey: 1931 investigation of Lake Cooper, 77; support for "shooting grounds" bill, 139–40, 141; nine-foot channel, 171, 173, 175

U.S. Bureau of Fisheries: Field Station for Interior Fisheries Investigations, 77, 109; constituent relationship with button industry, 91, 91n, 109; "crowfoot" dilemma, 91–92; surveys of mussel fishery, 99; artificial propagation of mussels, 100–105 *passim*; campaign for state regulation of mussel fishery, 101–2; closure provisions, 102; rescue of fish from overflow lands, 103, 104n; habitat degradation, 105–6; 1921 conference on interior waters, 106, 190; habitat degradation in upper Mississippi, 106–11 *passim*; pollution of upper Mississippi, 106–8, 110; changing attitudes of fisheries scientists, 108–9, 111–13; urges repeal of mussel protection laws, 108; seeks new constituency, 109; biological productivity of water, 109, 113, 189; water pollution as a new concern of, 109; and national pollution control legislation, 110–11; reductionist method, 112; water pollution investigations, 159; nine-foot channel, 171, 173, 175; pollution investigation below Twin Cities, 179; and

Twin Cities sewage treatment, 180, 181–82; disposal of St. Louis garbage in Mississippi, 183–84; conservation, 192

U.S. Department of Commerce, 159

U.S. Fish and Wildlife Service, 160, 161; water quality below Twin Cities, 180; budget cut, 193

U.S. Fish Commission, 81, 99, 100

U.S. Geological Survey, 164

U.S. Public Health Service, 156–63 *passim*; pollution investigation below Twin Cities, 179

Walton, Izaak, 117–18

Ward, Henry Baldwin, 171

Warren, Frank M., 171

Water Pollution Act of 1948, 153, 162

Welling, Lt. Col. Wildurr, 176–77

White pine: uses of, 19–20; rafts, 20, 21; markets for, 20–21

White-pine industry, 187; development of, 19–20; Ingram, Kennedy and Company, 20; Empire Lumber Company, 20; depression of 1893, 20–21; in Hannibal, Missouri, 20, 36, 39; and development of Des Moines rapids, 21–22; boom and bust, 36–37; search for alternatives to, 36–39

Whitley, Mrs. Francis E., 137, 139, 146. *See also* General Federation of Women's Clubs

Wicks, Judson L., 181

Wiebe, A. H., 106, 187

Winneshiek Bottoms: proposed drainage of, 131; and nine-foot channel, 171. *See also* Bakke, Dr. A. L.; Dilg, Will

Wisconsin and Minnesota legislatures, joint interim committee of, 106, 178–79